# A Martyr's Crown
## Joyce Coronel

Holy Angels Press, Arizona, USA
A Martyr's Crown
Joyce Coronel

Copyright 2013 by Joyce Coronel

No part of this publication may be reproduced,
stored in a retrieval system or transmitted in any form
or by any means, electronic, mechanical, photocopying,
recording or otherwise without written permission of the publisher.

For information regarding permission, contact Joyce Coronel

Cover and production by Mick Welsh - Slick Graffix
Cover photo by Bob Mullen - www.catholicphotographer.com

First Edition
10 9 8 7 6 5 4 3 2 1

ISBN 978-0615731384
Published by Holy Angels Press, Arizona, USA
For reorders, www.joycecoronel.com

Acknowledgements

I am deeply grateful for the support, advice and encouragement of Monsignor Felix Shabi, Corbishop of the Chaldean Catholic Vicariate of Arizona. Sincere thanks to all my Chaldean brothers and sisters in the faith who welcomed me and shared their stories. Heartfelt thanks to Bishop Thomas J. Olmsted, Father John Auther, SJ and Father Jim Kelleher, SOLT, for their insights and guidance. To my beloved parents: I know we will see each other again one day soon. Thank you for teaching me how to love. And to my dear family and friends, thank you for helping the dream become a reality.

*All the watchers in the heights laud the glory of the just,*
*placing crowns upon their heads, and shout together,*
*"Halleluiah!"*
-- Sunday Morning Prayer,
from The Book of Before and After

**A Martyr's Crown**

# Chapter 1
Mosul, Iraq
Tuesday, September 15, 2009

Light from the east was just beginning to seep through the cream-colored bedroom curtains when the first pain struck, jolting her from sleep. "Fadi, *aziza*, wake up," Hanne pleaded, her voice sounding a note of alarm. "It is time."

Fadi's eyes blinked open instantly. His outstretched hand, which normally fell protectively across Hanne's pillow as they slept, caressed her cheek, brushing tendrils of dark hair from her eyes. "Our baby...Hanne, darling, are you certain?"

Even as he posed the question, she could feel the pain rising again, twisting like a knife, foretelling the birth of their child. She sat up then, nodding vigorously, unable to speak. Fadi sprang from the bed and helped Hanne to her feet.

Dawn had broken, and the powerful rays of the sun burst forth, illuminating the mostly deserted streets of Mosul. Another contraction hit just as Fadi rounded a bend in the road. Hanne tried to summon her courage, tried to breathe through it, but the pangs of labor took her breath away.

"Hurry, Fadi!" she begged as she bent forward, holding her belly, hard as a rock beneath her trembling hands.

"We'll be there soon, *azizta*," Fadi said as calmly as he could, reaching across the seat to take her hand and kiss it. "Do not worry." He began to pray a Hail Mary then, imploring the Blessed Virgin to wrap her mantle of grace about Hanne and their unborn child.

*"Shlama, illakh Maryam, mleetha na'ami...."*

Hanne leaned her head back and closed her eyes, listening to Fadi pray the familiar, soothing words. Surely the Blessed Mother and her Son understood the fear that gripped her soul.

Fadi kept his eyes on the road, on the lookout for trouble. Mosul was still a city in the throes of war, where bands of insurgents roamed the streets and the explosions of car bombs shattered their days and nights, instilling dread. "Please, Lord," he prayed silently, biting his lip, "Help us get to the hospital safely." Glancing in the rearview mirror, he saw a stray dog sniffing his way through a pile of rubble. "Just a few more minutes, Hanne," Fadi said, straining to keep the note of worry from his voice.

He double parked and managed to walk her to the front door of the hospital. A nurse took one look at Hanne, heavy with child and doubled over in pain, and ordered her onto a gurney.

When at last their child was born, the cries echoed through the delivery room, the newborn's eyes shut tightly against the blinding bright lights overhead. "Congratulations," the doctor announced through his pale blue surgical mask, "You have a daughter." Hanne watched as he expertly snipped the umbilical cord, marveling at the wonder of this child brought forth, the fruit of their love, their precious Noor.

The instant she held the baby in her arms, Hanne felt her heart flood with deep joy. She traced the sign of the cross on Noor's forehead and held her to her breast tenderly, in awe of this fragile life entrusted to her by *Marya Alaha*, the Lord God. Looking up at Fadi, she felt as though she had crossed the threshold of heaven. The beauty—the sheer grandeur of the moment—filled her heart with a love she'd never known before. Neither of them dared to speak a word, overcome by the holiness of the moment, knowing they had crossed mysteriously into a sacred realm.

"Now your fate will forever be bound to that of another," Hanne's mother observed sagely as she beheld Noor two days later, stroking her delicate cheek with crooked, swollen fingers. "Whatever befalls this child will also befall you, dear Hanne. Every joy and every sorrow," Mariam explained solemnly. "This is what it means to have a mother's heart."

The moment in which a woman became a mother, Hanne decided, changed her life forever. Mariam was right. Her poor mother, her *Yemmi,* had surely known her share of heartaches through the years as a widow with five children, living in the midst of war and persecution. She remembered seeing Mariam sitting in a chair by the front door, day after day, her eyes closed as she fingered the smooth black rosary beads. How her heart must have bled, thinking of her sons, forced to join Saddam's army. Hanne saw it through a mother's eyes now, the worry and fear, the uncertainty of it all.

She wondered then at her mother's courage, not knowing if the child of her womb was alive or, heaven forbid, lay dying. Hers was a courage built on unwavering faith, of that Hanne was sure.

Back at their apartment, rocking Noor to sleep in the evenings, Hanne sang the lullabies that Mariam once sang in the little stone house with the orange tree, its fragrant blossoms perfuming the air that drifted in through the living room window.

"Sleep, my child and peace surround thee," Hanne crooned as Noor settled in the crook of her arm. And so the days passed, one to the next, a rhythm of feeding and sleeping and changing.

"Motherhood becomes you, my dear," Fadi remarked one morning as he watched Hanne bathing little Noor, who cooed and splashed, delighted by the cascading water.

"And you, my dearest, are a wonderful papa, to be sure," Hanne laughed. "Isn't our Noor the most beautiful child in the world? Look, Fadi—see how she loves the water?" Fadi bent to kiss the baby's chubby feet. "You are daddy's angel, aren't you my sweet?"

"Baptism," Mariam clucked late one Sunday afternoon when they visited her. "The child needs baptizing. These are dangerous times, Hanne. One never knows. Come now—why the delay?"

"Father Ameer has already set the date, *Yemmi*. Noor will be baptized December 6."

"December 6," Mariam repeated. "I will prepare the gown."

In her mind's eye, Hanne could see Mariam setting aside the lovely white gown after her youngest sister Nora's baptism all those years ago. As she folded the garment carefully and placed it in the cedar chest that stood at the foot of her bed, Mariam smiled at Hanne knowingly.

"Someday, Hanne dear," she said, "you will make a splendid mother and your own child will wear this baptismal gown, *inshalla*—God willing." Hanne, who was only 10 years old at the time, thought then what a miracle it was that God Himself had come into the world in just this way, as an infant, completely dependent on His mother's care.

When the day came for Noor's baptism, the family gathered at the church, Mar Addai, scene of every wedding, funeral and baptism—all those moments of joy and sorrow and faith the family had known through the years. Hanne held Noor close, wondering at this precious child in her arms, her firstborn. She was surely the fulfillment of every hope and dream.

For as long as she could remember, Hanne had wanted to be a mother. As the eldest daughter in her family, she had plenty of training, helping raise her younger siblings. "Hanne, *azizta*," Mariam would say, "how patient you are with the little ones! God bless you, my child. May the Lord God grant you many children of your own one day."

Two years had passed since the wedding. Hanne would hold that day in her heart forever, a golden Saturday in late fall, when the sun cast diamonds on the shimmering water of the Tigris. Fadi

## A Martyr's Crown

was a loving husband, the kind of man who went out of his way to show her that he cherished her.

On the one-month anniversary of their nuptials, he presented her with a single red rose, plucked from her mother's garden, to be sure, but it was the love behind the gesture that melted her heart. She was loved completely, just as she was, by a man who had promised to hold fast to her unto death.

"Beyond the moon and the stars," Fadi whispered to her one night, "my love for you is greater than that, and deeper. I will never leave you, Hanne, darling."

With those words, he touched her most terrible wound, the loss of her father, with healing love. She was never alone; *Marya Alaha* was there at every moment, but this gentle husband He had sent her was tangible proof of love unseen, a love she could hold in her arms.

When she first discovered she was with child the following spring, she could hardly wait to tell him the news. The tiny life growing within her, she knew, was a blessing from God. They lay awake in bed at night, dreaming up names and wondering if their child was a boy or a girl.

"It's a boy, I'm sure of it," Hanne told Fadi early on, resting her head on his chest, comforted by the steady beat of his heart. "*Yemmi* thinks so, too. He will be smart, just like his father."

"And his mother," Fadi said, holding her close. Such bliss!

Hanne began to read everything she could about pregnancy and childbirth. "It says here on this website that it's completely normal to have some nausea early on," she told Fadi one night, "but so far, I haven't had any."

"Thank God for that," Fadi said.

Nine weeks later when the pregnancy ended in miscarriage, Hanne was devastated. "Do not despair, *azizta*," Fadi told her tenderly, "we'll have other children. You're young."

*Other children—but not this little one*, Hanne thought sadly.

She sank then into what seemed like a black, bottomless hole of depression. She tried to busy herself cooking, taking care of their apartment while Fadi went to work, but the days stretched on and on into nothingness. Her heart was full of worry for him when he was away and she sighed in relief when she heard his footsteps approach, sometimes late into the night, outside their door.

"You're safe," she would exclaim, embracing him as he came through the door. "Thank God, you're home."

"Pray for me, *azizta*," is all he would say when she asked what he did. She knew it was dangerous, whatever it was, but he never would speak of it, not to her. There were days Hanne sensed sorrow in him, and she felt that perhaps something terrible had happened. She dared not ask him. They knocked on doors, Hanne knew that much, and sometimes there were people waiting inside who meant to do them harm. Months went by; Hanne wondered if their city would ever know peace, if she would ever bear another child.

"Patience," Mariam told her. "Trust in God, my child. He is faithful."

And He was. Miraculously, it seemed, they had conceived this gorgeous child, this gift from heaven. Noor was a healthy newborn, with rosy cheeks and delicate hands that closed tightly around Hanne's index finger. They had chosen the most fitting name for her—she was the light, the *Noor* of their eyes.

"Such a proud day, Hanne dear," Mariam beamed that morning on the way to church. "How I wish your father, God rest his soul, were here to see it."

Hanne leaned back in the pew and listened to the prayers of the Mass, joining in with the chants, mesmerized by the beauty and grace of the moment, wishing she could remain immersed in this ocean of peace forever. Mariam, so proud to be a grandmother at last, prayed beside them there in the first pew, surrounded by her other children.

## A Martyr's Crown

All around her in the church, Hanne could see old friends and neighbors. Frail Mrs. Sawa with her black veil, mother of the pastor, sat up front, too, listening intently to her son's preaching. The church wasn't as crowded as it was in Hanne's youth. The war and the grinding misery and violence in its wake had driven many to flee the country, though some, like Hanne's aunt and Mrs. Sawa, vowed they would never leave.

Noor stirred briefly in her sleep, stretching and yawning, the way newborns often do. As Father Ameer chanted prayers over the bread, the congregation knelt in quiet reverence. Hanne, still seated in the hard wooden pew with Noor in her arms, silently thanked God for the gift of love, the gift of life.

"He broke and gave it to His disciples, saying: take, all of you, and eat of it: this is My body, which is broken for you, for the forgiveness of sins," Father Ameer sang in his rich, full voice. Hanne closed her eyes, focusing on the words, entranced by the beauty of the divine mysteries. The congregation was silent, caught up in the presence of God.

What happened next would reverberate around the world, its agonizing details forever etched in Hanne's mind down through the years.

שׁ שׁ שׁ שׁ שׁ שׁ שׁ

# Chapter 2
Phoenix, USA
Friday, December 4, 2009

Sarah Castillo was late for work. Again.

"C'mon boys! You're going to be late for school!" she called up the stairs. *As if they care,* she thought to herself.

"Where's my backpack?" 13-year-old Ben asked on his way through the kitchen. "I can't find it anywhere," he said with a frown. "Maybe I left it at Sam's house again."

"Dude, chill," Thomas said, closing the refrigerator. "It's sitting by the back door." Calmly spreading cream cheese on a bagel, 15-year-old Thomas perceived no emergency. He dreaded his first hour class anyway. Algebra. Pointless pursuit of "x."

"Mom, where's my jersey?" Zach called from upstairs.

"It's probably still hanging in the laundry room," Sarah called up the staircase again, somewhat exasperated. She could spend the weekend doing laundry, but no one ever seemed to be particularly motivated to retrieve it from the laundry room. Here they were, with less than three weeks until Christmas, and she had a million things to do. She wasn't about to add clean-clothes delivery to the list.

Finally, the three teenage boys made their way to the garage, stepping over a jumbled stack of boxes of old clothing and sports equipment. "I've got to go through that stuff," Sarah said, making

# A Martyr's Crown

a mental note to herself. More chores for an already packed weekend.

They all piled into the white Toyota van. Sarah glanced in the rearview mirror as she turned the key in the ignition.

"Seat belts on everyone?" she checked.

The kids nodded their heads silently. Mom was always worrying about safety, reminding them to buckle their seatbelts. As if they needed reminding. As if they could ever forget what happened to their brother.

Nothing was going to happen on the way to school.

Sarah, however, knew better. She knew that teenage boys thought they were indestructible. She also knew this was a dangerous illusion, that life could turn on a dime, that a perfectly normal day could be shattered at any moment by a phone call, an unwelcome knock at the door.

Ever since that call in the middle of the night two years ago, she'd wondered. What if they'd been more careful? More importantly, what if Javier, her husband, had been more careful? Things would never be the same for any of them. *Never,* she thought to herself as she backed out of the cluttered garage.

By the time she arrived at the office downtown, most of her co-workers were already bent over their computers, typing furiously. Some of them held the phone on their shoulder as they listened, fingers flying over the keyboard.

Sarah quickly sat down at her desk, stacked with clippings, folders and scribbled-upon note pads. Pens—Bic ballpoints with blue ink, her favorite—were jammed into a coffee cup next to the picture of Javier and the boys at Christmas three years ago. *Before*, she murmured to herself solemnly. Life was seen through this inexorable lens of grief now: before Patrick was taken from them—and after. The agony of "after" had swallowed the present. And as far as Sarah could tell, it seemed to have swallowed the future, too.

Sipping peppermint tea and silencing her cell phone, Sarah was able to squeeze in a couple of phone interviews before cranking out the story she knew Rick would want by that afternoon. By the time she headed toward the parking garage, it was nearly 4:30 p.m., too late for the carpool lane. It was Friday, and everyone was in a rush to get home for the weekend.

Javier, she knew, would have a long list of handy-man projects that would ensure his unavailability all weekend, successfully keeping the wall of ice between them intact. There was the oil change for the van, *"It's been over six months!"* and the out-of-whack garbage disposal in the kitchen, *"Who dropped a chicken bone down this thing again?"* and the drywall repairs in the upstairs bathroom. *"Dad, the shower's leaking again!"* The man's "honey-do" list was unbelievable.

And then it hit her: maybe that was why he never got around to having the airbag inspected and reset on the car he fixed up for Patrick. The green SRS light on the dashboard lit up just two weeks before the accident. The thought of that—with all the attending what ifs—would haunt Javier and Sarah for the rest of their lives.

Sunday morning dawned cold and clear, and Sarah's eyes fluttered open in the dark stillness of their bedroom. Javier was curled up on his side under the blankets, still deeply asleep. Pulling on her blue fleece bathrobe and tying it about her, she padded down the stairs for a cup of coffee.

Standing there before the opened cabinet, she beheld her trusted favorites: a canister of oatmeal, a box of raisins. For the first six months after Patrick died, it was all she could eat. *"Comfort food,"* her sister assured her. *"Trust me, Sarah. Your appetite for other foods will come back eventually."*

And she was right. The shock and trauma of those first months was excruciating, but that had faded into the omnipresent black cloud that since then enfolded her. Oatmeal, with a good dose of

## A Martyr's Crown

brown sugar and raisins, was still the thing to eat for breakfast. Oatmeal, the same soft mixture she'd spooned into her firstborn all those years ago, delighted at his chubby fists, his toothless grin, his cooing.

Folding up the *Sun-Times* an hour later, she glanced at the clock. Too late for the 9:30 a.m. Mass; maybe they should just skip church altogether today. Sarah knew Javier wouldn't mind. It was the "before and after" thing again. God was always there in the before. But where was He now? Silence and emptiness—it was all she could feel.

Pushing aside the stack of newspaper with a sigh, she took a sip of her lukewarm coffee and considered her options. "I think I'll just let everyone sleep in, Reilly," she said to their calico cat, perched on an overstuffed chair by the window, grooming herself. "We're all tired from a long week."

What the *Sun-Times* didn't reveal, what Sarah couldn't have known sitting there in her comfortable suburban home, trying to rationalize her alienation from God, was that 8,000 miles away in the city of Mosul, a storm of hatred had unleashed hell's fury. And in the eye of that storm stood a woman —a mother like her—whose future Divine Providence had ordained should be intertwined with her own.

Across town, in the chapel at Mar Ephrem Church in North Phoenix, Father George Rama had just finished chanting his morning prayers when he heard the unmistakable, still, small voice:

*"Rescue her, for My sheep has wandered astray."*

"Who, Lord? Rescue whom?" Father Rama asked, gazing at the crucifix.

But there was only silence.

# Chapter 3
Mosul
Sunday, December 6, 2009

Ahmed carefully placed the razor on the bathroom counter. His body was shaved clean. It was time to dress and gather the other men.

"Strike boldly," he told them. "You must strike the enemy without fear."

They drove in silence.

Arriving at the target, he parked the car behind the building where no one would see. Opening the trunk, he handed each man a weapon.

"Come, Ali," he said to the teenager. "Put on the vest."

Trembling, Ali submitted.

"The most beautiful virgins of paradise will be yours this day," he told the boy as he threaded his thin arms through the vest. "It is a day of glory for Allah—for all of us."

Tightening the straps, Ahmed looked intently at the boy. He reached into his pocket for the pills.

"No pity," he told him, "No pity for the infidels—only justice. Here," he said to the boy. "These will give you courage."

Ali swallowed the pills obediently.

The six hooded figures strode toward the door.

שׁ שׁ שׁ שׁ שׁ שׁ שׁ

# A Martyr's Crown

It was the screaming that Hanne would always remember, the way the sounds rose from deep within her own throat. Just as Father Ameer raised the Host for them to adore, the doors of the church crashed open.

Six hooded men clad entirely in black, their faces concealed by dark scarves, charged into the sanctuary toting weapons, screaming "*Allahu Akbar!*—God is great!"

One of the men raised his AK-47, aimed at Father Ameer, and began firing. The young priest was instantly thrown backwards, falling to the floor with a sickening thud. Two deacons standing beside the altar were caught in the spray of gunfire and collapsed, one on top of the other. Hanne looked on in horror, terrified at the sight, at the swiftness of the violence.

Noor, startled from her sleep, began to shriek. Hanne clutched the baby tightly, willing the terrorists to leave them alone, frozen by fear, her mind spinning. *We've got to get out of here! But how? We're trapped!*

Beside them in the pew, Fadi jumped to his feet, furious, eyes flashing, sizing up the situation. He turned and looked at Hanne, hunched over baby Noor, terrified. No way was he going to let these cowards hurt his family.

One of the attackers, a burly man in his twenties, planted his feet at the end of their pew, blocking their exit. All around the church, people were screaming, running, frantically trying to escape.

No one saw a young boy, quick-thinking 11-year-old Jacob Samoud, dart out the back door and slip away amid the confusion. Somehow, he knew he had to find help. The police station was only a few blocks away.

One of the terrorists—the skinny one with the cold hate in his eyes, the one who shot Father Ameer and the deacons—fired his weapon into the air. Chunks of plaster fell from the ceiling and landed on the floor, scattering. "Silence!" he thundered. "Shut up, all of you!"

Shaking, Hanne pressed trembling lips against Noor's face, trying in vain to soothe her. Fadi gritted his teeth. *How dare these men invade their church! How dare they!*

"Make that brat shut up!" one of the terrorists growled at Fadi. The poor child was terrified, her face turning deeper and deeper shades of red, screaming wildly in a way Hanne had never heard before.

"We're holding you for ransom," the apparent leader bellowed as he stepped over the bodies of the deacons. "Let's see what your infidel families pay to reclaim you." He spat on the floor and smirked at the terrified congregation.

The more Hanne and Fadi tried to calm Noor, the louder the baby howled. She kept dropping the pacifier from her mouth, her high-pitched newborn cries still echoing through the church. "Hush, little one," Fadi begged. Hanne's heart was pounding, thumping in her chest as though it might explode. *How could this be happening?*

"Make that kid shut up or I will," snarled one of the attackers as he made his way toward Fadi and Hanne. Beside them, they could hear Mariam whispering the Hail Mary, over and over. "*Shlama, illakh Maryam...*"

Fadi reacted quickly, knowing there was only one thing he could do. He pushed Hanne, arms wrapped about Noor, onto the floor and clenching his teeth, covered both of them with his body. Still Noor's muffled cries rang out.

Two of the terrorists stomped over and tried to pull Fadi to his feet. He wouldn't budge.

"*Shlama, illakh Maryam...*" Hanne could scarcely breathe, but she could hear Mariam still praying above them.

And then it happened.

One of the fanatics grabbed Fadi's arms and flipped him over. The other raised his gun. Fadi fought back ferociously and in that instant, a single bullet pierced his side. Hanne looked up, aghast, and it was then that they yanked Noor from her arms. Another shot

## A Martyr's Crown

rang out and just like that, the crying stopped. Noor lay on the floor, lifeless.

"No!" Hanne screamed, "Please God, *no!*"

Blood was oozing from Fadi's side and pouring from Noor's chest, her gown instantly soaked. Hanne was sobbing, pulling at her hair. Throughout the church, people began panicking, screaming. Mariam crouched down on the floor beside them, gasping for air, her eyes squeezed shut, as if to negate the reality of the destruction around her.

"*Mart Mariam, yemma de Alaha*," Mariam prayed, Holy Mary, Mother of God…"

Hanne scooped up Noor's broken body, tears streaming down her cheeks, not wanting to believe what had happened. "My baby! You killed my baby! How could you!" she screamed. "And Fadi! No!"

Hanne, still cradling Noor, collapsed on Fadi's back, sobbing.

One of the terrorists grabbed her by the hair and yanked her to her feet, dragging her toward the sacristy.

"All of you, get up," he shouted. "Up!" The other men began shoving the terrified parishioners toward the room behind the sanctuary.

Before they could be herded into the sacristy, however, the side doors of the church swung open as police burst into the sanctuary. Seeing them enter, one of the terrorists—a young man, a teenager, perhaps—pushed a button and detonated his suicide vest.

More screaming and wailing erupted; everywhere, there was confusion, panic. In less than five minutes, their once beautiful church had become a scene of destruction and death.

The officers charged toward the terrorists, firing their weapons, taking out two of the attackers nearly simultaneously. A third terrorist, the one who was dragging Hanne away, reached for his gun.

Realizing what was about to happen, another officer raised his weapon, aiming squarely at the man who now had Hanne in a chokehold. Firing expertly, the bullet found the terrorist's forehead. A barrage of gunfire from other officers sliced through the remaining two fanatics.

Hanne fell to the floor, coughing, gasping. The air was thick with dust and smoke. All around her there was confusion, chaos, crying. *Dear God, where is Fadi? What just happened?*

At that moment, Fadi's eyes began to flutter. He felt a searing pain in his side, the warmth of sticky blood as it trickled through his shirt and onto the icy cold floor. The heavenly messenger who had whispered to him that his time on earth was not yet finished, unfurled his wings, rose and departed.

"Someone," Fadi said weakly, "Someone, help me, please."

# Chapter 4
Phoenix
Monday, December 7, 2009

Sarah gently brushed the dry leaves and tiny pebbles off the gravestone, then carefully placed an arrangement of bright yellow sunflowers in the vase attached to the marker. "I miss you, Patrick," she said, blinking back tears. "We all do."

Though in her heart she felt far from God, she bowed her head and said an Our Father and Hail Mary, the way her parents taught her to do, the way she always said them growing up.

Finishing, she stood and walked slowly through the cemetery, being careful not to tread on any of the markers. The routine was the same every Monday. She climbed into the white Toyota van afterward, the one with the "Mom's taxi" bumper sticker on the back and a chip in the windshield, wiped the tears from her face and blew her nose. It was time to get to the office.

Glancing in the rearview mirror, Sarah ran her fingers through her shoulder-length, light-brown hair. Her green eyes were a little puffy from crying, but she planned on spending most of the day at work holed up in her cubicle anyway.

A couple of years ago, before the accident that changed their lives, she often listened to music during the commute. Nowadays, it was simply stillness and peace she sought. She drove on in silence, past the red brick walls of the cemetery, oblivious to the changing leaves on the majestic oak trees at the entrance. Life was gray, an utterly colorless stream of the passing of time since Patrick left them.

Once at the office, an aging, high-rise building in downtown Phoenix, Sarah stashed her lunchbox in the refrigerator that occupied the corner of the break room. She didn't care for fast food and generally made an effort to bring something healthy to work for her midday meal.

She thought back to when Patrick used to drive over to the hamburger place near their house in the car he and Javier fixed up. How that kid loved a burger and fries! What she wouldn't give to have him sailing through their front door again, his arms laden with bags of the stuff.

Arriving at her cube, she stowed her purse in the cabinet, rolled back the gray padded chair in front of her computer monitor and sat down to examine the messy stack of mail accumulating on her desk. Many of her readers—at least the ones who wrote her letters—were either elderly or inmates at the state penitentiary.

"I'm serving 20 to life," one prisoner scrawled in a three-page, rambling letter about the 12-step program he'd joined behind bars. "I liked your article about the people who visit prisoners here. You should come out here yourself sometime." Sarah shuddered and set the letter aside, wondering what he'd done to land in prison, possibly for life.

"You're not going to write back to those guys, are you?" Javier always asked her when she showed him these letters. "Not likely," she would say to reassure him. "I can barely keep up with the birthday cards for relatives at this point."

Mostly, the handwritten cards and letters were from older people who thanked her for her work or, as was more often the case, pitched story ideas for the human interest and religion stories Sarah wrote. A few invited her to their place of worship to cover events.

"I hope you'll come to our Christmas pageant at United

## A Martyr's Crown

Methodist Church of Mesa on Dec. 17," one obviously elderly woman penned in shaky handwriting. "We're beginning with a spaghetti dinner for the homeless." People always thought they could rope in a reporter with free food.

The letter continued: "Members of our church will be part of a live Nativity scene with one of our young mothers dressed as Mary, holding her infant Son. We'll have a real donkey and a few sheep, too."

Sarah instantly flashed back to the Christmas she dressed her three older sons as the Magi and wrapped up fourth son, newborn Ben, in swaddling clothes for their annual picture. With Patrick gone, now there were but two Wise Men left. And Ben was in the eighth grade. Sarah put the invitation aside for consideration later. Might be a good photo op.

Another reader, this one from Temple Shalom, hoped Sarah would be on hand the following week when a visiting rabbi from Jerusalem would address the congregation before they unveiled a new menorah.

Jerusalem. That was the place Javier had always wanted to go. "To see where Jesus was crucified and raised from the dead," he would say to her. "That would be something, wouldn't it, Sarah? To walk down the *Via Dolorosa*?" With a lump in her throat, Sarah realized Javier never mentioned wanting to go there anymore, not since their world came crashing down.

She turned her attention to reviewing the news coming in off the wire service. A 6-year-old girl was still missing in Michigan. A governor on the East Coast was caught up in a scandal that threatened to topple his administration. Sarah scanned the headlines, looking for something that piqued her interest.

Then, she spotted it, near the bottom of the webpage: a short piece about an attack the day before on a Catholic church in Mosul. There wasn't a great amount of detail in the story other than the fact that a priest, two deacons and some three dozen members of the congregation were killed by a band of terrorists.

Sarah sat up straight in her chair. Maybe, just maybe, there was something here to write about, even though Iraq was some 8,000 miles away. She decided to check out the Vatican website—no doubt they had made some kind of statement about the massacre.

Though she'd been raised Catholic—and an Irish Catholic one at that—Sarah hadn't given much thought to her faith since graduating from St. Dominic High School nearly three decades ago. Her teachers at the small, now defunct Catholic high school in central Phoenix had all seemed so sure of their faith. Sarah, on the other hand, wasn't sure of anything anymore. The Castillo family attended church most Sundays, of course—Sarah felt they should—but her heart really wasn't in it anymore. She knew Javier harbored the same sad emptiness inside, the same lurking doubts.

She clicked on the Vatican website and saw the headline at the top of the page. The pope strongly condemned the brutal attack on Mar Addai Chaldean Church and asked for prayers for peace in the Middle East.

Chaldean Catholic Church? Where had she seen that before? Sarah leaned back in her chair and closed her eyes, trying to recall. A couple years ago, she'd been out reporting on a story—something about a church that was building a school in Africa, wasn't it? Traveling the busy thoroughfare that snaked through north Phoenix, an unusual sign off to the right with bold, black letters caught her eye: "Mar Ephrem Chaldean Catholic Church."

At the time, Sarah remembered wondering what it meant. During 12 years of parochial school, no one ever said a word about Chaldean Catholics, although one of Sarah's classmates went to some kind of Byzantine Catholic Church.

Staring at the computer screen, Sarah was startled to hear the chime of the instant messenger system. It was Rick, her editor, summoning her to his office.

✌✌✌✌✌✌✌

Hanne stood there, slumped against the wall, her head throbbing

## A Martyr's Crown

at the incessant beeping of the monitors, the endless clatter and clamor of the hospital in downtown Mosul. A woman in the next room was crying out in pain, pleading for help. Fadi, meanwhile, still hadn't regained consciousness after emergency surgery. Hanne was exhausted, having stood by his side all night there in the intensive care unit. The conversation her brother had with the doctor just before the operation hadn't given her much hope.

"Is he going to make it?" Raad asked the surgeon anxiously as they prepared Fadi for the operating table.

"There's no telling with these kinds of injuries," the doctor said grimly. "He's lost a considerable amount of blood. We'll do everything we can."

The next thing she knew, they were wheeling him through the double doors to the operating room, leaving her standing there, praying with all her heart that Fadi would pull through.

All night long, she'd kept vigil at his side, not daring to close her eyes for even a second. The sun rose—she could feel its warmth through the window—but the room remained hushed and dark and cold. Hanne's knees suddenly buckled. Somehow, she had fallen asleep while standing beside his bed. Nahida, thank God, was there to catch her.

"You need to go home to rest a while," Nahida said, her eyes wide with concern. "It's morning now. You'll collapse if you don't!"

But Hanne shook her head; she would have none of it. Her husband had been nearly killed. How could she leave him here? As she stared at Fadi's swollen and bruised face, evidence of where he'd slammed into the granite floor, all she could think of was Noor, her precious child, gone from her arms.

"Dear God in heaven, Nahida, I can't leave him! I can't!" Hanne wailed.

Finally, Saeed prevailed.

"I promise, Hanne. We'll come back after you've had a chance to go home and rest a bit," he said putting his arm about her and escorting her from the room. "It would be good for *Yemmi* to see you too, don't you think? Our poor mother is worried sick about you."

She was too tired to protest any longer. Though she tried to raise her voice, tried to explain that she was afraid to leave Fadi's side, Saeed insisted. She leaned on him then, sobbing, as they made their way past the nurses' station and toward the elevator. Would Fadi still be alive when she returned?

ש ש ש ש ש ש ש

A Martyr's Crown

# Chapter 5
Phoenix
Monday, December 7, 2009

At six feet four inches tall, Rick Stallings cast an imposing shadow. Back in high school, he was quarterback of the school's football team, the Highland Park Tigers, leading them to a state championship.

Twenty-five years later, Rick had worked his way up to editor of *The Arizona Sun-Times Newspaper*, with one of the largest circulations in the Southwest, second only to the *Los Angeles Times*. He was a bit heavier than back in his college days—a few too many adult beverages and not enough exercise, he thought to himself wryly whenever he caught a glimpse of his protruding belly in a mirror—but he was still in fairly good shape.

Rick's hairline was only just now beginning to recede, a fact he managed to conceal from most people unless he sat down, granting them a generous view of his balding scalp.

Clicking through emails, Rick thought about his intrepid religion reporter and features writer. She was a hard worker, that Sarah Castillo, and he half suspected that keeping busy at work helped her cope with what he assumed was an enormous burden of grief. How did people survive losing a child?

A knock at the door interrupted his train of thought.

"You wanted to see me?" Sarah asked, standing in the doorway, looking nervous.

"Yeah, come on in," Rick said, motioning to the blue upholstered chair opposite his desk.

Sarah sat down and took a deep breath, hoping it was good news.

"You've been working hard, Sarah," Rick said, "and I know it hasn't been easy. We really appreciate how you're generating reader interest with your stories."

Sarah's heart began to beat a little faster. Rick smiled broadly. "The article you wrote about the young man who was badly burned in a house fire—people are still mentioning it to me."

Relaxing a bit, Sarah managed a smile. She'd received lots of letters after the story ran a few months ago. The community had rallied around the victim, donating money to help with medical bills and sending get-well cards, promising to pray for his recovery.

Rick swiveled in his chair and picked up something from the credenza behind his desk. He handed her a small plaque.

"You won second place in the Southwest Newspapers Association contest for a human interest story. Congratulations, Sarah."

Sarah took the plaque in her hands and beamed. "Second Place, Sarah Castillo, 2009," it proclaimed. There it was, engraved in elegant script: recognition from her peers for all the hours behind the keyboard.

"Your work is outstanding, Sarah, really," Rick said. "We're lucky to have you. I know it's been a while since you've had a raise. You can expect one in your next paycheck."

Sarah blushed. She'd dreamed about moments like this and today, on an ordinary Monday, it was actually happening.

"Now, down to business," Rick said, turning his attention to his computer screen. "Did you see the story off the wire about the attack on the church in Iraq yesterday?"

"Yeah, I was just looking at that actually," Sarah said. "I'm

## A Martyr's Crown

thinking there might be a local connection. We've got a lot of Iraqi refugees living in the Valley."

"I know. I figured you would see an angle," Rick said.

"The story didn't have much detail," Sarah said slowly, "but one thing definitely caught my eye."

"Oh?" Rick queried. "And what was that?"

"The report says the attack happened at Mar Addai Chaldean Catholic Church," Sarah said. "I remember seeing a sign for a Chaldean Catholic church in north Phoenix a while back when I was out on another story. I'm thinking maybe I can contact someone there for comment."

"If they speak English," Rick replied. "You don't speak Arabic too, do you?" he asked teasingly.

Rick knew Sarah had a love for languages and had learned Spanish, her husband's native tongue, as well as a smattering of French and Italian.

"I'll make a call," Sarah said as she stood up. "I have a feeling there's someone at that church who will want to talk about this." She was intrigued by the possibility of a unique story to write. This was no Christmas bazaar or women's conference: this piece had that international flavor Sarah loved.

"I'll let you know if I find something worthwhile," she said to Rick as she turned to walk back to her desk. *Shouldn't be too difficult. Just needs a few good quotes.*

"Try to put a face on some of the victims," Rick told her as she headed out the door. "Find out who they were."

Back at her computer, Sarah searched for "Mar Ephrem Chaldean Catholic Church in Phoenix" and came up with a website. Dialing the phone number listed on the church's homepage, she held her breath, hoping the person who answered the phone spoke English.

On the second ring, someone picked up.

"Mar Ephrem Church."

25

"Hello. This is Sarah Castillo. I'm a reporter from *The Arizona Sun-Times Newspaper*," she said to the voice on the other end of the line. "I was wondering if I could talk to someone there about the attack on the Chaldean church in Mosul yesterday."

"What is it you need to know?" the man asked warily.

"I saw your church one time and thought you might know something about the attack yesterday in Mosul. Was anyone from your parish related to the victims?"

"Is anyone related?" the man asked incredulously. "Of course we have people related! As a matter of fact, we're having a prayer vigil and candlelight procession tomorrow night if you'd like to come."

The man was obviously fluent in English and Sarah could see the makings of an interesting story.

"What's your name, sir?" she asked the man.

"I am Father George Rama, the pastor of Mar Ephrem," he answered authoritatively. Sarah noticed he had a moderate Middle Eastern accent but seemed to have no trouble expressing himself in English. "So you will come to our vigil?" Father Rama pressed.

"Uh, yeah," Sarah said. "Sure. I'll be there. What time does it start?"

"Mass to pray for the victims is at 6 p.m. and the procession is afterward, at 7," Father Rama said. "You are welcome to join us for the Mass, too, if you like."

Sarah bit her lip and quickly tried to think up an excuse. The candlelight vigil would be a good photo op and she'd be able to get quotes. But Mass?

"Um, I don't think that's going to be possible," Sarah hedged.

"OK," Father Rama said. "But you will be here for our vigil?"

"Yes, I will," Sarah said. "And I hope we can talk afterwards. I'll need to get some information from you."

"That would be fine," Father Rama said. "See you tomorrow."

Sarah hung up the phone and scribbled the address for Mar

## A Martyr's Crown

Ephrem on a thick yellow legal pad. The church was about a 30-minute drive from her house. With any luck, she'd be able to jot down a few quotes and get out of there in a hurry.

If by some miraculous, momentary lifting of the veil that shrouds the future, a sage were to tell her that the meeting with Father Rama would prove to be a turning point in her life, Sarah would have laughed it off as some preposterous notion.

At 46, she was sure there were no more turning points in life. Her son was gone. Her 22-year marriage was on the rocks. The only bright spot was her work, and these days, newspaper reporters had a career trajectory that matched that of carriage drivers. What could some foreign priest tell her that she hadn't already heard before?

She tried not to think seriously about anything, about what life meant, and what its purpose was. In the two years since Patrick died, she did her utmost to live life on the surface, to avoid feeling things too deeply, anything that would reopen the wound, wrenching the pain from the recesses of her heart.

"Turn that off, please," she said rather sharply to Thomas that morning on the way to school. They were playing that song on the radio for the millionth time, that one with the wistful lyrics that advised listeners "how to save a life." As if you could. As if you could stop someone who was on a path to self-destruction. She couldn't stand to hear the slightest tenderness in music, any sort of sentimental themes in music or books.

"No thanks," she told Diane, her co-worker, when she'd offered to loan her a best-seller, a love story about a woman who winds up with breast cancer. "I've got stacks of books at home I haven't read yet."

She no longer tended the flower garden that once flourished in a stunning array of color and beauty in their backyard. Weeds had begun to grow in their place and she ignored them, refused to care. The world no longer held beauty for her.

## Joyce Coronel

She avoided her friends—who didn't and simply couldn't understand what she was going through— and threw herself into her work, cranking out story after story, thankful for the distraction, but retaining nothing of what she'd written.

This interview with the priest was just an interview, a way to make a living, one more means of escape from the emptiness of her life after losing Patrick and now, she feared, losing Javier, one drop at a time.

ψψψψψψψ

Father Rama placed the phone back in the receiver and closed his eyes. Though he was sitting at his desk in Phoenix, arranging an interview with an American journalist, his heart was in Mosul. They hadn't seen each other in six years, but Father Ameer had been his closest friend in the seminary. The two of them kept in touch after their ordination, calling and emailing each other as often as their duties allowed. Now his brother priest had received a martyr's crown.

His office had suddenly grown dark. Gazing out the window, he saw storm clouds sweeping across the sky, threatening rain. Rising from his chair with a heavy sigh, Father Rama made his way toward the chapel for his holy hour of adoration. It was there, kneeling before the Blessed Sacrament, that he drew his strength.

"How can we stand in the place of Christ if we do not know Him intimately ourselves, if we do not bask in His presence each day, allowing ourselves to know Him and be known by Him?" Those were the words Father Ameer challenged him with shortly after their ordination. "Until you understand that soaking up His presence is what separates our priesthood from social work, George, you'll never have time for it." That stark proclamation was burned into his memory. Ever since that day, Father Rama had made a daily holy hour his top priority.

## A Martyr's Crown

As the war and violence around him escalated, he knelt there, surrendering his heart each morning. In place of fear and distress, God had placed an unshakable, boundless peace in his soul, a peace he carried with him when he was sent to America, at least until today. The news of Ameer's death had shattered it.

His brother had called him with the devastating announcement.

"I'm so sorry to have to tell you this," he said as he told Father Rama of the massacre. "I didn't want you to hear of it on the news."

The minute he learned of the loss of his closest friend, he was back in that hellish warehouse, reliving the horror of what he endured when they'd captured him. It was never far from his mind, really, the agony inflicted by the fanatics. Four years later, he slept a mere three or four hours a night before awakening from tortuous nightmares, often crying out, bathed in sweat and sometimes tears.

He remembered the day as though it were yesterday. It was a Thursday, of that he was certain. He'd just come from anointing a young man in the hospital and was on his way home to prepare the homily for Sunday's Mass. Three gunmen overpowered him on the street, shoving him into the back of their Chevy Trailblazer and speeding away.

They pushed him to the floor of the car and held a gun to his head, gloating about how they'd captured another infidel. Later, they took turns beating him, spitting in his face all the while and smashing his teeth, his nose and his jaw with ferocious blows of a hammer and swift kicks.

After nine days of their brutality, they'd dumped him on an empty street, a few blocks from his church. An elderly woman heard the commotion, and peering out her window, saw him there lying there on the crumbling sidewalk, bleeding, hands bound behind his back. His leg, bent at an odd angle, had been broken days before. Father Rama would never forget the agony of hitting the pavement when they pushed him from the moving car, of feeling as though his body would explode with the pain.

Here in America, he was thousands of miles away from the war-torn city, but Mosul was never forgotten, not even for a moment. He walked with a pronounced, painful limp, a constant reminder of the torture he'd suffered. The fiery pain in his back was unceasing and Father Michael had to help him put on his socks and shoes, as if he were an old man with rotting teeth, unable to care for himself. When would it end, this persecution for the faith, this savagery?

Father Rama felt tears filling his eyes.

He wearily sank to his knees there before the ornate, golden monstrance in the chapel and gazed at the Host, feeling as though his heart had been crushed anew by sorrow.

*My God, why? Why do You allow this suffering of our people? How could you let them kill Ameer? Tell me: why should I believe in a God who seems not to care? Where are You?*

Father Rama knelt there as the tears rolled down his cheeks, overcome by his grief for Ameer and wondering if this God he'd devoted his life to even existed. After a long while, he sat down in the pew and stared up at the crucifix. The words of the Psalmist came back to him, the words he prayed each morning from his breviary: "I will be with him in distress, I will strengthen him and honor him; with length of life I will content him."

*Tell me, why should I believe these words anymore? My God, have you forgotten me?*

Father Rama could hear the roll of distant thunder, the promise of rain. The chapel grew darker and darker as he sat in the gloom, alone with his troubling thoughts, haunted by the vision of Ameer, raising the Host, chanting the words, only to be cut down by hatred. Was it all an illusion, this faith of theirs?

He listened as rain began to fall, gently at first and steadily growing to a downpour, flashes of lightning illuminating the window above him momentarily. He thought then of his childhood in Mosul and of his mother, who used to sing to him the songs

## A Martyr's Crown

of their people, songs of peace, when the thunder and lightning frightened him in the night. Exhausted by grief, Father Rama closed his eyes and breathed in the coolness of the chapel amidst shadows.

*He was drenched. The rain was pouring down as he stood there in the mud, staring up at the Master, the cruel blows of the hammer having pinned Him there in agony. He looked and there was blood on his hands, blood streaming down from the wounds of the One who hung there between heaven and earth, in a great and terrible silence.*

*And then he heard it.*

*"Eloi, Eloi, lama sabachthani? My God, my God, why have You abandoned me?"*

*For a lingering moment, their eyes met. And he knew. He knew that the Master himself felt utterly abandoned by the Father.*

*In his heart, he listened to the whisper, to words of love that conquered the night.*

*"Trust in Me. No servant is greater than his master. If the world hated Me, it will also hate you. Know this: I will never, ever leave you."*

He awakened then and looked up. The ceiling was leaking yet again. Father Rama pulled himself to his feet and headed toward the rectory in the pouring rain. He would send Father Michael to set up a bucket.

ש ש ש ש ש ש ש

# Chapter 6
Mosul
Monday, December 7, 2009

It was late morning and the immense reality of their situation was beginning to sink in. Heavy winds buffeted the walls of the Garmo home, shaking the fronds of the date palm tree just outside the kitchen door.

Mariam Garmo turned from the window and pressed her hands to her temples. She had a raging headache that seemed as though it would crush her skull. Twenty-four hours had passed since the horrific scene inside Mar Addai Church and she'd been awake ever since. In a matter of moments, what should have been a glorious, joyful day of celebration became a nightmare from which she'd yet to awaken.

Mariam closed her eyes and tried to block out the images that flooded her mind: Fadi, collapsed and bleeding on the floor with tiny Noor, obviously dead, lying beside him; Hanne being dragged by her hair by those monsters who at this very moment she was sure were being lauded as martyrs for Allah; the bodies of the other victims strewn about Mar Addai Church—the place she'd worshipped with her family for decades. How could she ever forget seeing such things?

From the living room, she could hear Nora and Nahida talking in hushed tones to their sister Hanne. Her sons, Raad and Saeed, were watching the news, waiting to see which terror group would claim credit for yesterday's brutal attack.

Mariam took the pot of tea she had prepared and placed it on a tray with some cups. Carrying it into the living room, she stumbled and nearly fell just as she made it to the dining room table to set it down. She was weary, utterly spent.

"*Yemmi*, why didn't you ask us to help you?" Nora exclaimed as she and Nahida sprang to their feet.

"Here, *Yemmi,* you sit down and rest. I'll get the tea," Nahida said, taking the tray from her. Gratefully, Mariam sank into the couch beside Hanne, patting her eldest daughter's hand silently.

Nahida poured them each a cup of steaming tea. She carefully carried the delicate china teacups to her mother and Hanne. "Here, a little tea will be good for you," she said.

Hanne shook her head no, but Nahida insisted. "You need a little something in your stomach," she said gently.

Hanne hadn't spoken much since returning to the house from the hospital that morning with Saeed and Nahida. Mostly, she'd been crying, rocking herself back and forth on the couch, or staring blankly at the wall. Her eyes were puffy and red and she spoke in one- or two-word sentences. Later today she would return with her brothers and sisters to visit Fadi in the hospital.

Forcing herself to take a sip of tea, Hanne thought about what the emergency room doctor said to her and Saeed last night after the surgery.

"Your husband has suffered grave injuries, Mrs. Garmo," Dr. Haddad told them. "He's lost quite a bit of blood. He's already had one transfusion and he'll probably need another."

Hanne nearly fainted when the doctor explained what the shooting had done to poor Fadi. He said it was a miracle he survived, that the bullet caused quite a bit of damage but somehow missed striking any major organs. Hanne was sure he was whitewashing some of the details, trying to spare her more grief.

Poor baby Noor, Hanne knew, never had a chance. The second bullet fired by the terrorist extinguished her life immediately. Hanne still had the taste of blood in her mouth from scooping up her baby's broken body, so utterly silent, from the cold, pitiless floor, and holding her close, refusing to let go, willing her back to life. But it was not to be. They'd given her a shot of something at the hospital and finally taken Noor away.

"Fadi is young and from what you say, he was in good health before the attack," Dr. Haddad said when they spoke after the surgery. "That helps, but I won't lie to you. He's going to have a tough recovery—and a lot of pain."

"So you're saying he is going to survive this then, doctor? Is that what you're saying?" Saeed prodded.

"Probably. But he's going to need to stay here in the hospital for a while. A week at least. We'll be giving him antibiotics and pain medication through his IV."

Hanne leaned against Saeed, overwhelmed by the doctor's description, realizing now that there was no way at all that Fadi would be able to attend Noor's funeral. *How on earth can I face this without him?*

Even then as they stood there in the dimly lit hospital corridor just outside the emergency room, police were sifting through the chaos at Mar Addai, trying to identify the bodies of the victims. In the midst of the ongoing war and in a country that did not generally embalm its dead, funerals needed to be held as soon as possible.

The first of the neighbors and relatives began stopping by the Garmo residence Sunday night as word spread of the vicious attack. By Monday, it was a veritable parade of mourners. The ancient Mrs. Hakim, a frail Muslim widow who lived next door and had been friends of the Garmos for years, came by with her daughter to offer condolences. The two women, each wearing a black *hijab*, brought a dish of beef stew with rice to share with the family.

# A Martyr's Crown

"We are so sorry for your loss," the younger woman said sincerely, hands over her heart in a gesture of sympathy. "We do not condone this violence against Christians."

"Of course not," Mariam said softly. "We know you are not like that."

Hanne sat on the couch, haggard, numbly watching the growing presence of visitors to their home. No one was really sure what to say to her—no words seemed adequate. It was as though they were speaking a foreign language, Hanne thought to herself. She heard the sounds but failed to grasp their meaning.

The thought of facing her daughter's tiny white casket the next day was almost too much to bear. Thinking of it, Hanne bent forward and began to sob. Suddenly, she rushed from the room. Her sisters jumped from their chairs and followed her.

Hanne dashed to the bathroom around the corner and knelt in front of the toilet, retching. Nora and Nahida got down on the floor beside her, placing their hands on her back and exchanging glances. Their poor sister! How could they comfort her? What could they do?

Hanne sat back on her heels, and stared blankly ahead, sweating profusely, panting for air. Nahida helped her to her feet and over to the sink.

"Here, Hanne, wash your face," Nora said gently.

"Let me brush your hair," Nahida said. Hanne looked at her sisters, bewildered. "We'll help you change your clothes." Dark stains of dried blood streaked across the front of Hanne's pale blue dress, evidence of where she had held her daughter's lifeless form to her heart. Tears streamed down her cheeks. "My baby," she whispered, leaning on her sisters. "Noor. My God, why?"

"Shhhh, Hanne, shhhh," Nora said, wrapping her arms around Hanne. "We will be right here beside you. We love you, dear sister. We'll get through this together, God help us."

Nahida nodded sympathetically. "You can count on us, Hanne,

## Joyce Coronel

I promise. We'll go with you to the hospital to visit Fadi. We won't leave your side."

Hanne steadied herself, then bent over the sink, brushed her teeth and splashed cool water on her face. Nahida handed her a towel. Both sisters stood next to her, looking at her with deep concern, unsure of what more they could say or do. Hanne knew she would be lost without them, that their love would somehow carry her through the rest of this hellish day and the ones that would surely follow.

Looking in the mirror, she barely recognized herself. There were heavy dark circles under her blood-shot, puffy eyes and her nose was red and swollen from all the tears she'd shed since yesterday. She felt exhausted, and with each beat of her heart, her head throbbed.

Nahida picked up the hairbrush from the bathroom counter and carefully began to brush her sister's long, dark tresses. Since their childhood, Hanne had always had lovely hair that fell to her waist in ebony waves. Nora leaned against the door, wishing there was something they could do to comfort Hanne, knowing it was impossible. Finishing, Nahida set the brush down and embraced Hanne silently.

"Fadi," Hanne said hoarsely. "I must go to him."

They walked her to the bedroom they shared growing up in the little stone house with the orange tree, the room with the gray-tiled floor that Nora and Nahida still occupied. There in front of the window was the tall, battered table with the embroidered cloth that held a hand-painted statue of the Virgin Mary, the same one that stood in the room since Hanne's First Communion day. A collection of rosaries of varying hues was piled in front of it. Nahida bent and picked up a set of pink plastic beads and gently placed them in the palm of her sister's hand.

"The rosary," she said, "You don't have to say the prayers, Hanne—just hold onto the beads and let the Blessed Virgin hold

# A Martyr's Crown

you. Remember? That's what we did after Daddy—" she choked on the words, thinking of the day *Yemmi* woke them and said that it was time.

Hanne clasped the beads to her lips, remembering her father and the way their family would surround his bed and pray together each evening at dusk. In three months, they'd said dozens of rosaries for him, but the cancer proved relentless.

"He is with God," their mother said the day he left them. Hanne remembered kissing his cheek, still warm, and wishing with all her heart that he could stay with them. What was it the priest told them later? Eye has not seen, nor has ear ever heard, the consolations that await those who love Him? Her father loved, and was loved deeply. And Noor—well, she was pure innocence, love incarnate.

She couldn't bear to think of what they'd done to her beautiful baby, the child she'd longed for all her life. Nahida was right: she couldn't pray, but holding onto the beads was something. She still believed that, in spite of everything, there was in fact a God. There had to be. And one day, somehow, she would hold Noor again. She would see her father. They all would.

There was a chill in the air that day in Mosul, and they all donned sweaters and wrapped scarves about their necks. Raad was already on his feet, jingling the car keys, nervously peering out the window. Saeed stood by the front door frowning, lost in thought, wishing he could get his hands on the men who had orchestrated the massacre. They were out there, somewhere, gloating about what they'd done, celebrating death. He was sure of it. It sickened him and he felt a cold, hard rage building within his chest.

Mariam took one look at him and made the sign of the cross.

"Saeed, you must not. You cannot," she said to him firmly, just as Hanne entered the room, pale and trembling. Mariam glared at Saeed and his expression immediately softened. His sister looked frail standing there, as if the slightest breath of air would knock her down.

"Give Fadi our love," Mariam told Hanne softly as she kissed her goodbye. "Tell him we're praying for him." She tried her best to steady her voice against the rising emotion. She wanted to visit the hospital too, but realized she could barely walk. Her feet were swollen and her back was aching after what seemed like the longest day of her life.

"Mariam, come sit down now with us," one of the cousins urged. "We'll keep an eye on her, girls, don't you worry."

Raad tried to take the shortest route possible to Mosul University Medical Center, but there was heavy traffic, even now at midday. Nora rolled the window down for a little air. The long line of cars in front of them suddenly stopped. Horns were blaring—a taxi had ploughed into the side of another car and both vehicles were blocking the way. Hanne could see two men had jumped out and were shouting at each other, waving their arms and cursing, eyes wild with anger.

"Dear God, I hope they don't pull out guns," Saeed said under his breath. He'd seen violence erupt over less. It didn't take much really, not in war-torn Mosul.

Hanne tried to be patient as she stared out the window at the mess. A dented car, a broken door—some such trifle that could be repaired or replaced. Human beings—her precious Noor, to be precise—could not. Life was forever changed, just like that. And what about Fadi? Oh why couldn't they get past this snarled traffic so she could run to his side? He needed her, she felt it in her bones. What if he awoke and didn't see her? Hanne felt panic beginning to rise, felt her heart starting to pound. She squeezed the rosary beads, tried taking a few deep breaths.

"Do not worry, Hanne," Raad said calmly when he caught a glimpse of her in the rearview mirror. "We will get there a different way."

Quickly, he made a u-turn to escape the snarled traffic and headed down a narrow side street. When Mosul University Medical Center finally came into view some 15 minutes later, they were

## A Martyr's Crown

all relieved to get out of the car and begin walking. Hanne folded her arms across her chest to brace herself against the gusts of cold wind that blew her hair in her face. Just as they reached the main entrance, it began to rain.

Inside the hospital, they shook off the cold and made their way to the bank of elevators. Punching the button for level 4, Saeed stood back and looked at his sister. How he wished one of them could have saved Noor, spared her this horror. He hoped seeing Fadi would bolster Hanne's spirits a bit.

He thought of their wedding day and how radiant Hanne looked then. It was as though a century had elapsed since then and not merely two years. He wondered if his sister would ever know such joy again. How could anyone find happiness again after what she'd suffered?

Fadi was like a brother to them now. They all saw the way he looked at Hanne, the way his face lit up when she entered the room, as if no one and nothing else existed. His first reaction yesterday was to protect her and Noor, even if it cost him his life.

The elevator chimed and they stepped out into the hallway. At the far end of the corridor, they could see a couple of middle-aged nurses, clad in their blue scrubs, engaged in deep discussion with a doctor.

"I'm warning you, she's far too sick to be discharged," one of the nurses was saying.

"We need the beds. She'll be fine by tomorrow. Trust me," the doctor replied.

The nurses looked unconvinced.

An elderly man wearing a hospital gown and pushing an IV pole was being helped along by a relative. Hanne was immediately struck by the heaviness of the air around them, the smell of sweat, of disinfectant and the cries of suffering she heard coming from the rooms that lined the hall.

Fadi's room was on their right. They filed through the door

silently, not sure what to expect. Though he was sleeping, his eyes fluttered slightly as Hanne bent down to kiss his forehead. Somehow, even sedated, he was aware of her presence. He was on oxygen and still had an IV needle taped to the back of his hand that lay atop the white sheet.

"Oh, Fadi," Hanne said, covering her mouth with her hand and stifling a sob. For all of them, it was a shock to see Fadi—Fadi who was so full of life and joy and vigor—lying in a hospital bed, entirely helpless. Saeed put his arm around Hanne; he knew she must be remembering those final moments inside the church when all hell broke loose—they all were.

The five of them stood there in silence, watching Fadi's chest rise and fall, rise and fall. A few minutes later, a nurse, a twenty-something woman with dark hair pulled back in a loose braid, came in to check on her patient.

"Hello there," she said to them glancing about the room. "You must be the family. Now, which one of you is Hanne?" she asked, turning to the three Garmo sisters.

"I am," Hanne said wanly.

"Your husband is a lucky man," the nurse said softly. "Many patients with these kinds of injuries don't survive. It's going to take a while for him to recover from this."

Hanne nodded her head, trying to grasp what the nurse said. Everything seemed so confusing. "Has he woken up yet?"

"We're keeping him medicated as the pain is so severe, but he does wake up now and then. He keeps asking for you," the nurse explained kindly. "It's good you're here to reassure him." Checking the IV pump and making a note in Fadi's chart, she turned to leave. "Let me know if you need anything," she added. "The doctor was already here, but he will be back again tomorrow."

Hanne took Fadi's hand in her own and gently squeezed it. Her husband had always been the one to hold her hand, to reassure her

## A Martyr's Crown

in moments of doubt or trial. Now it was her turn. His palm felt warm and soft and she thought she felt him squeeze back, ever so slightly. She bent down and kissed his hand, then whispered in his ear, tears falling down her cheeks and spilling on him, on the bed.

"Fadi, *aziza*, I am here," Hanne breathed. "I love you, darling. Please wake up. Please," Hanne begged.

Nora and Nahida stood beside her, watching Fadi to see if he might stir, but there was no discernible response, nothing. Hanne stood up, biting her lower lip. *How long would he be like this?* How she ached to hear his voice again, to see his eyes. But the only sound in the room was the steady beep, beep, beep of the monitors.

Raad and Saeed stood by the window and spoke to each other quietly. There was nowhere for visitors to sit, and the two men leaned against the wall, weary.

Hanne's sisters worried that she might faint. Her face was deathly pale and her hands trembled as she stood there staring down at Fadi.

"I'll go see if I can find some folding chairs for us," Nora ventured.

"And I'll go with her," Nahida said. "We'll be back soon, Hanne, dear. Do you want us to bring you something to drink?"

Hanne shook her head no. How could she swallow anything? She could barely speak, could scarcely fathom the reality of this moment.

Gripping the metal guard that ran alongside the hospital bed, she looked down at Fadi and gently pushed the hair back from his swollen face. He had the beginnings of a beard growing, something she knew he wouldn't have liked. But such things didn't matter now.

They could never have imagined what happened yesterday, even in the midst of the violence and war that shook their country. To be Iraqi—and more precisely, to be Chaldean—was to face death, to face danger every day. It was the stern reality of their world. But they never expected that on the day they sought to baptize their child, this world they inhabited would come crashing down around them.

It was Father Ameer who had frequently reminded them how precious life was, that life and love are the great gifts of God, meant to draw us closer to Him. "Greater love has no one than this, that he lay down his life for his friends." Father Ameer had lived that to the last drop of his blood, right in front of them. As long as she lived, Hanne would never forget the look in his eyes when the doors of the church crashed open. He was chanting the prayers, raising the Host. In a heartbeat, he was lying in a pool of blood on the floor before the altar. But in that fraction of a second between raising the Host and the explosion of gunfire, he surely knew what was coming.

And it was an unfathomable peace, a look of surrender—not fear—that she saw in his eyes. After so many death threats, Father Ameer knew they would come for him eventually. No servant is greater than his master, and so to give his life for the faith was to follow in the footsteps of Christ.

Watching Fadi laying there unconscious before her, hooked up to an inexplicable tangle of tubes and wires, his face bruised from where he'd collapsed on the floor of the church, Hanne hardly recognized him. He still had the breath of life in him, having somehow survived the shooting, but it was Hanne who felt as if she herself were dying. She almost wished for it.

The bleak afternoon at Fadi's side passed slowly, punctuated by the comings and goings of the benignant nurse. As evening drew near, she gently informed them that visiting hours were over. "You need your rest, too," she told Hanne kindly. "Your husband will need you when he is released. You'll have to help him a lot until he's stronger."

Hanne nodded weakly. She felt hardly able to care for herself.

### A Martyr's Crown

The simple acts of speaking, of walking were monumental challenges and in her mind, seemed pointless. How would she manage taking care of Fadi?

Before they left, they joined hands around Fadi's bed and prayed an Our Father together. *"Baban dyli bishmayya..."* As they finished, he opened his eyes for just a moment, just long enough for her to see. "My Hanne," he said through parched lips before he drifted back to sleep.

# Chapter 7
Phoenix
Tuesday, December 8, 2009

Sarah had just finished writing up the story she owed Rick about the free medical clinic on Phoenix's south side. After a barrage of voice mails and emails, Dr. Emily Shallal, the physician she'd been hounding all week, finally returned her calls. Once the two of them spoke, Sarah understood why it took so long for them to connect.

"I'm sorry for the delay in getting back to you," Dr. Shallal explained apologetically when she called. "We've had so many patients this week, the most ever. Why don't you come by around 4 o'clock today? We'll be winding down by then."

Sarah found the clinic in an aging strip mall in one of the city's more decrepit neighborhoods. Parking, she noticed a homeless man picking through the garbage in the dumpster behind the nearby thrift store, tossing aluminum cans into a billowing plastic bag. Presenting her business card to a bubbly receptionist who sat answering phones, she was ushered back to the examination area to observe Dr. Shallal at work.

An attractive, slender woman with shoulder-length chestnut hair and dark, expressive eyes, Dr. Shallal was dressed in a spotless white jacket, a stethoscope dangling about her neck. She moved gracefully among her patients, pausing before drawing back the

## A Martyr's Crown

curtain that separated each one from the others, then smiling gently at each, peppering them with questions and listening carefully to their complaints.

An elderly woman with no teeth and a long, bedraggled gray braid running down her back was suffering from severe headaches. A heavy-set man dressed in tattered jeans, his arms and neck covered with tattoos, told her he was sure he had strep throat. Sarah could see the place was jammed with broken-down people who weren't sick enough for the emergency room, but didn't have the money to pay for a doctor's care.

"We see the face of Christ in the people we serve here," Dr. Shallal told her when the last patient left. "That old woman with the long braid and no teeth? She was a young girl at Auschwitz. She still has nightmares about the place, about what they did to her there. And the guy with the tattoos? He grew up in foster care and group homes. He's a drug addict. These are the forgotten ones—the people no one wants to look at."

She led Sarah through a short, narrow hallway to a cramped, airless office. Clearing a wobbling pile of thick charts from a molded plastic chair, she gestured for her to sit down.

"I hope you'll forgive the mess—it's been a little chaotic around here this week."

"Oh, please. This isn't bad at all. You should see my desk," Sarah said, hoping to set the doctor at ease. She sat down and took out her pen and notebook. "So what was it that made you want to open this place?"

"Several years ago I lost my husband. It made me re-think things."

"Oh—I'm very sorry to hear that," Sarah said softly, somewhat taken off guard. "That had to be incredibly difficult."

"It was. Ron and I—we loved each other so much," Dr. Shallal said with a sigh, picking up a framed photo of them in happier times and handing it to Sarah.

"It seemed we had it all: the big home, the fabulous vacations, a couple of sports cars. But after he died, I did some serious thinking about my life and what it meant. Why was I here? What was the point of it all? It's like there was this big hole in my life without him. A friend of mine said something wise to me one day about a year after Ron died. She said, 'I wonder what you'll find to fill that huge hole in your heart. Maybe you'll discover a new purpose in life.' That got me thinking."

Sarah shifted in her seat, suddenly uncomfortable. Dr. Shallal was opening a door to a place in the soul Sarah had been running from for two years. *A new purpose in life? How could anyone think that after losing a loved one? How could there be a new purpose in life when your heart had been smashed to a thousand bits?* She felt flames of anger beginning to build in the pit of her stomach, but at the same time, there was something inside holding her back, telling her to listen, really listen, not just with her mind, but with her heart.

"I found my way back to God—that's a whole other story—but ultimately, I decided I wanted to make the most of the rest of my life—that I wanted it to really mean something. My friends helped me dream up this idea of a clinic to care for the poor."

"What about your big house and the sports cars?" Sarah asked, hoping to shift the conversation toward the more practical elements.

"I sold everything, simplified my life. Ron and I—we never had any children. Anyway, I moved to a smaller home. There's a peace now that I didn't have before."

Sarah sat in front of her computer monitor the next afternoon, chewing on her pen absentmindedly and thinking about what Dr. Shallal said. She'd left her sitting there in her dingy, cluttered office after the interview, surrounded by stacks of paperwork and half-empty coffee cups. There was something different about this woman.

# A Martyr's Crown

*How did she get past the pain? What was she drawing on to find the strength?* Sarah shuffled through her notes and did one last review of the story before hitting "send." As she tidied up her desk and gathered her things to head home, her cell phone rang. Glancing at the display, she saw "Mom" beside the smiling profile picture. The matriarch of the Murphy clan had been endowed with an amazing sense of timing.

Ever since Sarah's father died, she'd been trying to keep a closer eye on her mom. They talked to each other almost every day, usually when Sarah was in the car on her way somewhere. *Seems like I'm always on my way somewhere*, Sarah thought to herself. Whoever came up with the moniker "taxi mom" was a genius.

"Hi, honey," Kathleen Murphy said brightly when Sarah answered the phone. "Is this a bad time?"

"Of course not. Your timing's perfect like always, Mom," Sarah said as she pulled the strap of her purse over her shoulder and locked up her desk. "I'm just walking out the door." It was 4 p.m., so she'd have just enough time to get home and make dinner before heading out again to the vigil at Mar Ephrem.

"I thought you said something about leaving work early today," Kathleen said. "Where is it you're going tonight? Some kind of Middle Eastern thing? Why aren't you going to Mass for the Feast of the Immaculate Conception?"

Sarah cringed. Twelve years of Catholic education and she still forgot holy days. She headed toward the elevator, feeling guilty.

"Well, as a matter of fact, I'm going out to north Phoenix for a prayer vigil at a Chaldean Catholic Church tonight," Sarah said as she pushed the down button. "Remember I told you about the attack on the church in Iraq on Sunday? Some of the victims have relatives who belong to the church here in Phoenix. I'm supposed to cover the candlelight vigil."

"Don't they have any happier stories you could be working on?" Sarah's mom prodded. "Or a different reporter they could send? I thought you were writing up Christmas pageants and that sort of thing this time of year."

Sarah suppressed a sigh. She knew her mother meant well and was only trying to protect her. Isn't that what mothers did? Walking toward the van, she decided to sidestep the discussion altogether by changing subjects. That usually worked. For some reason, it suddenly dawned on her that her mom often used the same strategy. *How clever of her,* Sarah thought to herself with a sly smile.

"Remember, I'm making Christmas cookies this weekend," Sarah said breezily as she stepped into the van. "You know, the chocolate cut-out kind that you always made when we were kids. So are you still coming over to help out?"

"Of course I'm coming," Kathleen said. "My cookie cutters are already on the front seat of the car along with some magazines for you."

Sarah grinned. Her mom was getting more forgetful lately and one of her coping strategies was to place needed items in the car ahead of time. Come to think of it, that wasn't a bad idea.

"The reason I'm calling is to ask you something else though," Kathleen said tentatively. "Why don't we all go to 5:30 Mass at St. Clare's after we finish baking? I want to take the whole family out for dinner afterward."

*She's only trying to help,* Sarah thought to herself, trying not to resent the gesture. Kathleen Murphy, a devout Catholic, was an extremely perceptive woman and she sensed that her daughter's faith had diminished since Patrick's death. She herself drew great comfort from going to church, especially after her husband of 53 years passed away suddenly following a colossal heart attack.

The death of Sarah's father hit her particularly hard. She and her dad had always been very close; losing him just one year after the devastating blow of Patrick's death seemed too much to bear. The coming holidays would only sharpen the pain of loss.

## A Martyr's Crown

Sarah remembered how stoic, how dignified her dad was at Patrick's funeral. She pictured him standing there beside them in the pew, looking suddenly so much older, as Patrick's dark walnut casket was carried forward by his brothers and teammates.

Her mom was talking about restaurants now and Sarah tried to refocus on the conversation at hand.

"That's really nice of you, Mom," Sarah said, swallowing the lump in her throat. "Are you sure you wouldn't want to just come back to the house for dinner afterward? I could fix something quick," she hastened to add. "How about stir fry?"

"Nonsense, Sarah," Kathleen said. "We'll both be exhausted from all the baking by then. Let's go out to eat. How about that new sports grill with the big screen TVs. What's it called? Jimmy's?" She was off in another direction now, talking about restaurants, about the boys' upcoming games, about the weather. Sarah listened, trying to keep up with the banter. She was back to Saturday night now.

"Alright—that sounds good, Mom, thanks," Sarah said as she pulled into the parking lot of the grocery store. "We'll talk about the details tomorrow. I'm on my way into the grocery store now."

Inside the suburban supermarket, "Jingle Bell Rock," was playing—again, Sarah noted, as she selected a loaf of fresh bread and a large jar of spaghetti sauce. As long as they didn't play any sad songs, she was OK with Christmas music. She remembered last December, when she'd actually walked out of this same store when "I'll Be Home for Christmas" came on, abandoning her cart right there in the cereal aisle, next to the bran flakes. She had to sit in her car for a while until the sobs subsided and she could drive.

Finally home, Sarah found Ben sprawled on the well worn, floral print couch, reading. Reilly was curled up on his feet, sound asleep.

"Hey, Benny," Sarah said as she bent down to kiss him. "How was your day?"

"Good, but I'm hungry. What's for dinner?"

"Spaghetti. Your favorite," Sarah said as she set the groceries down on the counter.

Ten minutes later, she heard the garage door go up and the back door close. Thomas came through the house, limping and scowling.

"I rolled my ankle at practice," he said with a sour face, setting down his gym bag and sinking into the recliner.

"I'll get you an ice pack, honey," Sarah said, placing the wooden spoon down and reaching into the freezer. With a houseful of boys, she always kept a bag of frozen peas on hand for moments like this. Years ago, she'd learned it was a great way to ice an injury. *There was that time Patrick fell going up to block a shot and hit his back pretty hard,"* Sarah remembered. He was out of commission for about 10 days after that and was heartbroken when he had to miss an important tournament in Las Vegas.

Sarah looked at the bag of frozen peas, thinking of Patrick. She could hear Javier and Zach walking toward the kitchen, debating something.

"All I'm saying is that you've got to put in the time for a class like that, Zach," Javier was saying patiently. "You can't cram it all into the night before the final. We'll take a look at that book after dinner."

Zach had a physics final the next morning and Sarah knew he was dreading it. While she was out covering the prayer vigil, Javier would be home, bent over the dining room table with Zach, cramming for the test. Physics was definitely not her forte. Thank God it was one of Javier's specialties.

"How was your day?" Javier asked Sarah, innocently enough.

"Hmmm. I guess you didn't see my text," Sarah said, making no attempt to hide her disappointment. She dumped the pasta into the large pot of boiling water on the stove.

"I've told you how busy I am at work, Sarah," Javier answered evenly. "I didn't hear a text come in. I didn't even look at my email today. It's been crazy." And it was true. Javier had been working long hours for months. It was so noisy down in the lab where the testing took place on the airplane parts he designed that he often missed calls and texts.

"Yeah, I know," Sarah said with a sigh, still suspecting that Javier kept himself occupied at work the way she did—to avoid the issues they had at home with each other, to try to block out the pain of all they'd lost. "We'll talk about it later," she said, a bit sharply as she chopped tomatoes for the salad. Somehow the raise and the award she'd won didn't seem like such great news after all.

Javier shook his head and turned to Zach and Thomas, who were already checking out the contents of the refrigerator.

"Why don't you guys go put your stuff away and take a shower," Javier said. "We'll call you for dinner." The boys exchanged glances and closed the fridge.

"OK, so what's your news?" Javier asked patiently. "C'mon, Sarah. Out with it. Tell me." He looked at her with those tender brown eyes, the same ones she'd fallen in love with back in college.

"Well, I got a raise, for one thing," Sarah said as she stirred the sauce. "That should help out. We've got Zach's California tournament to pay for."

"Congrats, Sarah—that's great," Javier said, grinning. Sarah couldn't help but smile.

"And, I got a second-place award for that story I wrote about the young man injured in that house fire," Sarah said.

"Hey, that's fantastic!" Javier said, and he meant it. "It's about time they recognized all your hard work, *muchacha*. And I'm sorry I didn't answer your text. Really." He took out his phone and glanced at the text, frowning slightly. "So you're going out again tonight?" he asked Sarah coolly.

"Not *going out*," Sarah said, trying not to sound defensive as she stirred a can of mushrooms into the sauce. "Working. It's a prayer vigil at a church in north Phoenix."

"So you're going to a prayer vigil on a Monday night," Javier said slowly. "Why do you have to go? Can't you just interview them over the phone? It seems like you're always gone, Sarah. It's like you don't want to be around," Javier said with a sigh. "You're always finding some reason to get out of here."

"Well, it's not like we talk when I'm here!" Sarah said hotly. "You're either on the computer or taking a nap!" Sarah took the large pot of water from the stove and emptied the pasta into the colander in the sink, clouds of steam rising.

Javier took a can of soda from the refrigerator and opened it. "Thing is, we're drifting apart, Sarah. That's the truth. I miss you when you're not here," he said softly. "I miss the way things used to be."

Sarah felt angry and sad all at once. She swallowed hard and took a deep breath.

"I have to go to this event tonight, Javier," she said firmly, brushing the bangs out of her eyes. "It's a big story and I told the priest I'd be there."

"Priest?" Javier said as he took a swig of his coke. "Where's this vigil?"

"It's at a Chaldean Catholic church," Sarah replied. "They're immigrants from Iraq, people fleeing the war."

"Never heard of Caldinos. And what's the vigil for? Why tonight?" Javier pressed.

"*Chaldeans*," Sarah corrected him. "A bunch of people— some of their relatives—were killed in an attack on a church in Iraq on Sunday. I told Rick I would find a local angle on the story. And you know what? I really want to go, Javier. This isn't the typical story I get to do," Sarah said. "I should be home around 8:30."

Javier folded his arms across his chest and nodded. "OK, fine, whatever. Just go then. I guess I'll be helping Zach with physics." Feeling angry and defeated, he headed toward the living room to turn on the television and check the news.

There was Ben, still lying on the couch, reading quietly, pretending not to have overheard anything. He and Sarah had both forgotten he was there, probably hanging on every word of their argument. A wave of guilt washed over him then. They had an unspoken agreement to never fight in front of the kids.

"Oh, hey, Ben," Javier stammered. "I didn't realize you were in here. Go tell Thomas and Zach it's time for dinner, OK?"

Sarah was standing in the doorway, wooden spoon still in her hand, frozen. As Ben climbed the stairs, she walked back to the kitchen, ashamed that her youngest had heard their quarrel. Javier came up behind Sarah, encircling her waist with his arms. "Sorry," he whispered in her ear.

"Thanks," Sarah said softly. "I won't be out late."

ש ש ש ש ש ש ש

Hanne gazed at herself in the oval-shaped mirror that hung in the hallway by the front door, startled by what she saw. Her eyes were still swollen and red; her hair, even after Nahida's careful attention, looked dreadful. In moments, they would leave for the funeral at the cathedral. Somehow, she would have to get through it without Fadi. She would steel herself, will her heart to be strong, to not fail under the weight of grief. She was Chaldean; the blood of martyrs pulsed through her veins, flooded her heart. She thought then of Father Ameer's words.

"Courage, my brothers and sisters," he told them just two weeks ago. "We must ask the Lord for the courage to embrace our cross."

She took a deep breath. By the grace of God, she would summon the strength to get through this hideous day.

Joyce Coronel

# Chapter 8
Mosul
Tuesday, December 8, 2009

Bishop Stefan Abbo sat at his desk in the chancery of the Diocese of Mosul, pondering what he would say later that afternoon at a funeral for the 39 people murdered. In his more than 30 years as a priest, he had given many funeral homilies, but never one that represented such profound tragedy. Not only would they lay to rest a beloved priest and two deacons, there were also dozens of parishioners who had been killed inside Mar Addai Church, too. One of his priests reported that there was even a newborn baby killed. What could he say to the victims' families in the face of such catastrophe? It was the feast of the Immaculate Conception, but there would be no feasting, not a shred of joy to be found in this day. He breathed a heavy sigh then, weary to his bones with the sorrow, the enormity of what lay ahead.

He thought back many years ago to when he was pastor of Mar Addai and 7-year-old Ameer Sawa wanted to become an altar server. His mother, a pious woman often seen praying the rosary before Mass, presented her youngest son to him one Sunday as he stood outside on the steps greeting parishioners.

Young Ameer was a quick learner who from the first day showed his love for the Mass, its rhythms, prayers and chants. *"Qasha,"* he said one day, "Father, may I assist at *Qurbana*—at Mass again

# A Martyr's Crown

tomorrow? Please?"

"Don't you have school in the morning, Ameer?"

"We have a holiday tomorrow. Please—I want to serve."

Who could deny such a request? No one was surprised when he entered the seminary right out of high school.

Ameer was an excellent student, but he was also full of fun, the kind of young man who had a knack for making people laugh. The rector told him of Ameer's spot-on imitation of a cantankerous old woman who frequently criticized the young ladies of his home parish.

"No respect, Father," Ameer squawked, affecting a falsetto voice and shaking an invisible cane above his head. "They've no respect for their elders! And those outlandish clothes they wear! Pants? In church? Why, in my day…" His fellow seminarians roared with laughter. But they also noticed how Ameer spent extra time in the chapel, went out of his way to help the ones who were struggling with their studies. Bishop Abbo knew then he had great leadership potential.

"Two of our new seminarians say that Father Ameer helped them discover their vocation to the priesthood," the rector told Bishop Abbo. "He has a way of reaching into people's souls with his good counsel."

Undoubtedly, Father Ameer's emphasis on adoration of the Blessed Sacrament, the countless hours he spent in the confessional and his zeal for the rosary had rekindled the faith of many. But it was his fearlessness in the face of continued death threats that inspired Bishop Abbo.

"Close this place, or we will destroy it!" a mob of fanatics shouted at Father Ameer when they saw him leaving the church one day. "We won't have you infidels infecting our land anymore!"

Father Ameer ignored them.

Finally, they'd done it: they'd killed him, spilled his blood right there on the altar during the consecration, all in an effort to shut him up. What they didn't realize was that the blood of the martyred Father Ameer Sawa would now cry out in testimony against them. His death would not succeed in scaring people away from the faith—it would instead draw them even closer to Christ. No one could silence such testimony; no gun, no grenade could ever extinguish a love so deep.

Bishop Abbo rose and crossed the room to the window that overlooked Mosul. His beloved city was under siege by these maniacs. He would never give into them. He would not relent. The Church would stand as it always had, a beacon pointing out the way of salvation, the path of peace in a troubled land.

ש ש ש ש ש ש ש

Raad drove Hanne and her sisters and their mother to the cathedral for the funeral that afternoon, a 10-minute journey during which no one uttered a single word. There was nothing to be said; they simply had to get through the day.

As they approached the aging cathedral, Hanne could see hundreds of mourners, all dressed in black, gathered in front of the church around a myriad of caskets. They were weeping and wailing, collapsing in each others' arms, many carrying flowers or pictures of their loved ones. Hanne leaned her head against the windowpane and clutched the bouquet of white roses for Noor she'd gathered from her mother's garden that morning.

It was time to face the unthinkable—Noor's coffin. She felt sick to her stomach envisioning the sight. Impossibly, the sun shone overhead, but the December air was decidedly chilly. Stepping from the car, Hanne shivered and wrapped her scarf more tightly about her neck, blinking back tears. *How could this be happening?* It didn't seem real.

## A Martyr's Crown

It was 12:30 p.m., the time she usually sang lullabies—the same melodies her mother had sung all those years ago—and rocked Noor to sleep, carefully laying her in the crib for an afternoon nap. *She should be home right now, resting with her baby, not here at her funeral!* The thought of that, the realization that such an ordinary daily routine would never be repeated, sickened her. Hanne felt the crush of grief closing in on her heart, choking her. Suddenly dizzy, she clutched Saeed's arm. They stopped walking for a moment. Saeed looked down at her with worry.

"Do you need to sit down, *azizta*?"

Hanne shook her head. She felt as though her legs were locked, as though she couldn't move. They stood there for a moment, brother and sister, arm in arm, the wind whistling about them. Finally, Hanne took a deep breath and stepped forward cautiously, still clinging to Saeed.

As they rounded the corner and walked toward the cathedral, the crush of mourners gathered on the steps came into view. Caskets, more than three dozen, crowded the landing. Then she saw it: a tiny white coffin. Even though she knew it was coming, the sight of it took Hanne's breath away. Her knees buckled. Saeed caught her before she fell to the ground.

"Dear God in heaven!" Nahida cried. "Hanne!"

She put her arm around Hanne's shoulders and they all stood there for a moment, staring in disbelief at the sight of Noor's casket, tears pouring down their cheeks. Mariam, suddenly looking frail and spent, leaned on Raad's shoulder and wept. Hanne couldn't understand the words being spoken by those around her; it was a swirl of faces, a cacophony of wailing.

Slowly, a procession began to form. Bishop Abbo, flanked by an entourage of priests and deacons, blessed each coffin with holy water as the families hoisted them on their shoulders and carried them into the church. Saeed and Raad carried Noor's casket between them.

## Joyce Coronel

The bishop stood before the packed cathedral and looked out over the sea of faithful and the staggering array of caskets that lined the center aisle of his church. He pressed his hands together and steadied himself. Now was the time to show courage, to demonstrate the enduring ideals of the faith.

"My dearly beloved brothers and sisters in Christ," he began, "At a time like this, we might rightfully ask ourselves, where is God? And how could He allow such a thing to pass?

"I admired Father Ameer just as you did, having watched him serve the Mass as a very young boy. His love for God and for the Church was remarkable, even at an early age. You saw this same love and faith in him.

"I believe that Father Ameer is watching us from heaven today. He wears a martyr's crown, like so many of our saints, and like our loved ones whom we grieve today. I believe that if he could speak here today, he would tell you all that love is stronger than death, that faith is greater than fear, that the cross of Christ will *always* reign victoriously over sin and hatred and oppression.

"Father Ameer would tell you to take courage and know that God is near to the brokenhearted, that He hears the cry of the poor. God knows what it is to suffer, since He Himself suffered an agonizing death for love of us.

"Our loved ones whom we bury today have not died in vain. Among those we mourn today are mothers and fathers, sons and daughters, brothers and sisters, and yes, even a precious newborn baby."

Muffled sobs echoed throughout the cathedral. Nora and Nahida, sitting on either side of Hanne, simultaneously squeezed her hands at the mention of little Noor.

Finally, mercifully, the funeral came to an end. Outside the doors of the cathedral, the skies were overcast and gray, threatening rain. One could smell the drops forming in the clouds above, as though God Himself would shed tears at so sorrowful

## A Martyr's Crown

a sight. Police vehicles, lights flashing, guarded the throng of mourners as they made their way through the city streets and toward the cemetery.

As they lowered Noor's coffin into the ground, Hanne felt first her legs, then her whole body beginning to shake uncontrollably. Her sisters stood beside her, their arms about her waist, fearing she might faint. She stood there, frozen, looking down into the hole, at the dark expanse of it. How could they leave Noor here?

It was then that Bishop Abbo began to pray. Hanne closed her eyes, listening to the words, knowing it was true what he said, that Noor was with God now, resting in His arms, though with all her heart, Hanne wished she could hold her baby in her own arms instead. When the prayers ended, the bishop walked among the graves, sprinkling holy water.

Hanne broke down then and fell to her knees, wanting to fling herself into this terrible opening in the earth, to be buried there with her daughter. How could she possibly go on? And why? What sort of life could be lived after this moment?

Nahida and Nora knelt there beside her in the soft, brown dirt as the rain fell. Finally, after the sobs subsided, Nora spoke up.

"Let's go home, Hanne," she said softly. "It's time to go home now, *azizta*."

Hanne nodded her head and they helped her to her feet.

"I have to see Fadi," she said, blowing her nose. "I must."

"There will be visitors expecting us back at the house, wanting to offer condolences," Mariam said.

Hanne sighed, knowing her mother was right.

"I'll take you to him later, Hanne, I promise," Saeed whispered. "Don't worry."

## Chapter 9
Phoenix
Tuesday, December 8, 2009

As she drove to the candlelight vigil, Sarah tried not to think about the nasty little quarrel she'd had with Javier. Over the years, she'd learned how to compartmentalize, how to stay focused and bury her feelings or at least set them aside. Really, it was a matter of being a competent professional, she told herself. And it certainly was easier to think about the newspaper and meeting the next deadline than it was her marriage problems. Compared to the stresses of family life, journalism could be downright relaxing.

She thought of the day she first went back to work outside the home, the year Benny started kindergarten.

"And here's your cubicle," Rick told her the first day at the *Sun-Times* as he gave her a tour of the place. "I hope it's alright—I'm not sure what you're used to."

"Oh, no, this is perfect," Sarah replied, examining the empty shelves, admiring the computer work station. After years of changing diapers, managing toddlers' meltdowns and surviving all-nighters with sick babies, the newsroom was a veritable sea of tranquility. "Is it always this quiet in here?"

Rick raised an eyebrow. "You call this quiet?"

Sarah grinned. "Compared to a house full of kids, yes. Thanks for the tour." Her working-mom career was launched.

## A Martyr's Crown

The first thing she noticed when she pulled open one of the heavy double doors that led into Mar Ephrem's sanctuary was that every single person in the congregation was dressed in black. Their voices were raised in a mournful, haunting hymn, and though she listened carefully, Sarah didn't understand any of the words. It certainly wasn't English and it didn't sound like Arabic either.

There were no seats left, so Sarah stood in the very back, next to a woman holding a sleepy little boy who looked to be about 3 years old. With his tousled, dark brown curls and green eyes, he reminded Sarah of Patrick at that age. She closed her eyes, willing herself not to think of him, the feel of his sweet skin and the smell of it after the bath she gave him each evening. She listened then to the choir and congregation singing a melody that reached down into her soul. *What was it about that music?* Though she couldn't comprehend what they were voicing, Sarah sensed that the songs were heartfelt and she felt strangely soothed by the sound of a language she'd never heard before.

As the hymn ended, she checked her watch discreetly: 7:15 p.m. and a few people were still in line for Communion. The church was packed, with people standing all along both side walls and clustered in a large group at the back. Some of the women in the congregation—and not just the elderly ones—were wearing veils, similar to the kind she'd seen her mom wear in old Murphy family photo albums.

When it was over, a murmuring began as people stood, gathered their belongings, and turned to process out of the church. One of the priests picked up a large processional crucifix, trailed by the deacons and at least six young altar servers dressed in white albs. The two eldest children solemnly carried tall white candles in brass candleholders.

Sarah stood back, taking in the scene. She noticed that the taller priest walked with a pronounced limp and bore a deep and jagged scar on his left cheek. *I wonder if he was in some kind of accident.*

*A car wreck maybe? He walks as though he is in great pain.*

Many of the people who waited patiently to join the procession carried pictures of loved ones. Some were dabbing at tears; others sang and held out their hands to receive candles from a couple of volunteers who stood by the double doors.

There was a chill in the air and Sarah buttoned up her pink sweater, silently reproaching herself for not wearing something black that might seem less obtrusive. She pulled the camera from her purse and began taking pictures of the people walking in procession.

"Excuse me, sir, but do you speak English?"

The older gentleman shook his head and turned away.

*This might be tougher than I thought.*

Then, out of the corner of her eye, she noticed a well-dressed woman with a long, black lace veil who looked to be in her sixties, walking beside a younger woman. *Her adult daughter maybe?* The older woman was holding a picture of a cherubic newborn baby girl dressed in a purple and white dress, festooned with tiny bows and rows of lace.

"Excuse me," Sarah asked the younger woman, falling into step beside her, "but do you speak English?"

"Yes," the woman said with a heavy accent. "I do."

"My name is Sarah Castillo and I'm a reporter with *The Arizona Sun Times Newspaper*. Is this your mother?" Sarah asked, nodding at the older woman.

"Yes, but she doesn't speak English," the younger woman replied. Sarah noticed both women's eyes were puffy and red.

"What's your mother's name?"

"Samira Namin."

"And who is the baby in the picture?" Sarah asked.

A look of anguish passed over the younger woman's face. "That's a picture of Noor, my cousin," the woman replied, her voice shaking. "She was shot and killed in the attack yesterday."

## A Martyr's Crown

"What? A baby? They shot a *baby*?" Sarah looked at the woman in horrified disbelief, suddenly feeling light-headed, as though she might faint.

"Her father tried to save her," the younger woman ventured haltingly, brushing away tears. "He was wounded, too. But Hanne—the baby's mother—survived. My mom talked with the family this morning."

Sarah stopped walking, stunned by what the woman said. She suddenly felt as though someone had punched her in the gut. The wire-service account she read regarding the attack said about three dozen people were killed, but it didn't mention a word about a newborn baby girl dying. Not a single word.

The procession continued past her in the dark, people singing and weeping. Sarah stood there numbly, feeling sick to her stomach, everything around her spinning faster and faster. She tried to watch the people going by, but she felt so lightheaded, that for a moment she thought she might faint. She tried to steady herself, sucking in her breath, remembering the reason she was there—to get a story.

*Got to get the story and get home.*

It wasn't as though tragedy was something new to her. She'd reported on plenty of them over the years, and the details tended to fade with time. Children with cancer, survivors of ethnic cleansings, burn victims—it went with the job.

"Just call me Little Miss Tragedy," she told another reporter after what seemed like one too many of these stories. "Maybe I ought to switch to sports."

"Not a chance, Sarah. You own this stuff. Nobody can make readers cry like you."

"Gee, thanks. I'll remember that the next time I read your account of the planning and zoning commission meeting."

"Anytime."

She took another deep breath and looked intently at the pictures the people were carrying as they passed. Every image bore a person's name. The victims were no longer a vague number—they were individuals, human beings with families who loved them, who were devastated by their deaths.

Sarah saw portraits of smiling young men, posing for the camera in happier times. A few of the victims looked to be businessmen, while others were middle-aged ladies, dressed in their Sunday finery. There was even a photo of a set of twin teenage girls wearing matching, sapphire-blue formal gowns, dark hair piled high on their heads. Sarah noticed that the clergy were carrying pictures of the murdered priest and deacons.

The procession was making a turn now and she could see the mourners' flickering candles, dripping wax. Every so often a blast of cold air would extinguish a candle and each time, someone would patiently hold a lighter over the wick to reignite the flame, refusing to let the darkness overcome the fragile ray of faith and hope.

Watching them, Sarah felt, angry, shaken. *Who could shoot a baby? Attack a church full of innocent people? Gun down a priest? What kind of evil was responsible for such cruelty?*

She could still glimpse the outline of the old woman with the veil, the one who had lost her great niece. And in that singular moment, Sarah was no longer simply a journalist, blithely scribbling notes and checking the batteries on her recorder. She was a mother—a mother who knew what it was to lose a child, who knew the gut-wrenching grief that shatters the soul when a parent buries a child.

She thought of the baby's mother. What was her name? Hanne? A woman not much different than she was, Sarah suspected. It was one thing to lose your child in a terrible accident, as Sarah had. It was quite another to have your baby killed in front of you by jihadists.

When the singing ended, the people continued to walk, but now

## A Martyr's Crown

they were fingering rosary beads. Sarah listened to the prayers being recited in the mysterious language and realized the rhythm and cadence sounded much like the rosary in English.

Finally, the vigil came to an end. As people began to say goodnight to each other and walk to their cars, she spotted the two priests making their way toward her.

The taller of them, the one who limped so badly it made Sarah wince, spoke up first, extending his hand. "Are you the reporter who called yesterday?"

"Yes, I am," Sarah replied. "And you must be Father Rama. Thank you for inviting me this evening. I know it's late, but do you still have time for a few questions?"

"Yes, that is fine," Father Rama said gravely. "Let us go to talk in my office. Father Michael, he will lock up the church," he said as he nodded to the other priest.

Sarah handed him her *Sun-Times* business card. He glanced at it briefly, and then tucked it in the pocket of his jacket. Night had fallen and there was a sliver of a moon overhead, barely illuminating his profile. Even in the darkness, Sarah could see the deep scar that cut across the priest's face. She wondered what could have befallen him. Even the war veterans she'd interviewed over the years didn't look like this.

Father Rama unlocked the door of the office and flipped on the lights. An enormous, dark wooden desk covered with stacks of papers and brightly colored folders dominated the far corner of the room. Behind the massive desk were large, framed images of the Virgin Mary and the Sacred Heart of Jesus. A desktop computer was off to the side on a smaller, separate table.

They sat down on opposite sides of the desk and Sarah took out her notebook and recorder. She would gather a few details, some strong quotes, and a little local color to fill out the story, and then she could get home, away from the anxiety and sorrow she felt welling up inside.

"Let me begin by asking how long you've been pastor here," she said to Father Rama, pen poised. He looked to be in his late thirties.

"Well, I came to the United States three years ago," Father Rama said slowly, "and I have been the pastor here for two years."

"I see," Sarah said as she began scribbling notes. "Is it alright if I record our conversation? I want to be sure and get accurate quotes from you."

The priest nodded his head. "Yes. What is it you wish to know of my people?"

"Well, you said some of your parishioners are related to the victims in the attack on the church in Mosul last Sunday," Sarah said. "I met an older lady tonight who was carrying a picture of her great niece—a baby girl who died." Sarah's voice cracked a bit. She paused a moment to regain her composure.

Father Rama waited, surprised by the reporter's show of emotion. *That's unusual for a journalist,* he thought to himself. *If I'm not mistaken, those were tears in her eyes.*

"I mean, can you give me any more details on the attack, anything your parishioners may have told you?" Sarah asked, clearing her throat, hoping she wasn't making a bad impression.

Father Rama thought for a moment, searching for the right words. "Yes. Well. It is not the first time our people have been attacked in this way. We have the blood of martyrs running in our veins."

Sarah was scribbling furiously. "The blood of martyrs?" she repeated. No one had ever given her a quote like that before.

"Our people have suffered century after century for their faith in Jesus Christ," Father Rama said. "This massacre is just the latest example. We have been persecuted for 2,000 years."

Father Rama stood up and crossed the room. On the wall behind where Sarah sat was a framed map of ancient Mesopotamia. He pointed to the image and began describing early Chaldean civilization. Sarah listened, but furtively looked at the clock over

# A Martyr's Crown

his shoulder. It was getting late and she didn't see the connection between the history lesson and the article she needed to write.

"OK, well, let's get back to the attack on the church on Sunday now," she said, biting her lip, trying to guide them back to the present. "That woman I met at the vigil tonight—the one who told me about the baby killed in the attack," Sarah began. She paused for a moment to steady her voice again. "I...well, I've heard a lot over the years as a reporter, but that has to be the worst ever. Honestly, I've never heard of anything so awful." And as the words formed, she found herself shedding tears, thinking of the people trapped inside the church, of the beautiful baby, torn from her mother's arms. She put her hand to her face, embarrassed.

Father Rama sat down, leaned forward and handed Sarah a tissue. He waited a moment for her to gather herself.

"I'm sorry," she ventured. "This has never happened to me with a story before. I'm just....horrified."

"These fanatics," Father Rama scoffed, "they have no conscience, no mercy. This is nothing to them."

At that, they both fell silent for a moment. Sarah blew her nose, trying to be as lady-like as possible and feeling as though she was not succeeding in the least. She stuffed the crumpled-up tissue in her purse and tried again to fire off some questions, anything to get the interview back on track.

"Were there any attacks on churches while you were still in Iraq?"

"As I say, we have experienced many centuries of persecution. I myself was captured by the terrorists once. They especially hate priests." Father Rama sighed. He never discussed his ordeal with anyone, beyond just a brief explanation about what had happened. "They kidnapped me a few years ago. I was gone nine days. This scar on my face, the way I walk—they did that to me," Father Rama said looking away.

Sarah felt a chill run through her body; she wasn't sure what to say next. She'd never met a victim of torture before and Father Rama talked about it as if it were the most ordinary of occurrences, as though images like the ones forming in Sarah's mind were normal. She could feel another emotion rising up inside, too, and this time it was anger—outrage at the injustice of it, that human beings inflicted such cruelties on each other.

"That's terrible," Sarah stammered. "I'm so sorry." Even as she spoke them, the words struck her as so trite, so utterly unworthy. What could one say to a man who'd been mercilessly beaten for his faith? She felt a profound respect at this priest's courage, at the dignity of his bearing.

She glanced at her watch and noticed it was past nine. Javier would be more than a little steamed. There was still a long drive home ahead of her and she had a few more questions for Father Rama. It didn't seem appropriate to rush the interview, not after he'd just told her about what he'd suffered for his faith. She'd have to try to move him back toward the attack last Sunday.

"So tell me now, Father, did a lot of your parishioners know the victims in the attack? Are they related to them maybe?" Sarah asked.

"Some, they are related, yes," Father Rama said. "Others, they know the victims or they studied with them in school. The people—they loved the priest who was killed. He was in the seminary with me—we were close friends."

"I'm very sorry to hear that," Sarah said, hand over her heart. "I'm sure this is a very difficult time for you and your whole community."

"Thank you," Father Rama said softly. He turned away again, overcome thinking of his friend, Father Ameer. *Why, Lord? Why Ameer?* Sarah waited a moment, and then began gently asking him more questions.

"Will any of your parishioners be going back to Iraq to visit, do you think? Or will any of the victims' relatives come here?"

## A Martyr's Crown

"I do not know, but I doubt it," Father Rama said. "This all just happened. I can tell you that once someone is granted asylum here, they are never able to return home."

"Never? Never able to go home again?"

"Never. This is the system. But there are other reasons people do not return. Not everyone here has been granted asylum. For example, the baby who died—her great aunt came as a refugee a couple years ago, but she will not be going back. The funeral was this morning. And she and her husband have two stores to run here. But I hear she has been trying to get her nephew to come to the United States. She thinks perhaps he will work at the university here. He is a language scholar. Who knows what will happen now?"

Listening, Sarah thought about the mother who'd lost her baby. *Hanne. Her name was Hanne.*

Father Rama was saying something about the refugees, how there were more and more of them settling in Arizona. How his parish was growing, and that his people had so many needs.

Sarah listened politely, jotting down a few notes, and then closed up her notebook.

"Thanks so much for your time, Father Rama," Sarah said gathering her things. "You've given me a lot to write about. I wish I had time to hear more, but my husband is waiting for me at home."

"Please. You may call me Father George. The people here, this is how they call me."

Sarah smiled gently. "OK. Father George it is, then. Thanks for your time tonight."

"Maybe you will come to our Christmas party for the refugee children? It will be on Saturday and you could meet some of them. You could bring your husband, too."

Sarah hesitated for a moment. Hearing from the children and their parents would add a lot of depth to the article, bring out the local angle better. It was a story she was sure hadn't been told in Phoenix before.

"Maybe," Sarah said. "If I can, I will." She remembered her mom was coming over to bake Christmas cookies on Saturday afternoon. "What time is the party?"

"We will start at 10 a.m. here at the church hall," Father George said. "I hope you can come. I did not have a chance to tell you about our kids. They have been through so much. And now this news."

"Well, I hope I can come then," Sarah said as she stood up from the chair. She knew her presence on Saturday was probably unlikely but she didn't want to seem rude. "Thanks for the interview." Father George opened the door for her. Cool air came rushing in and Sarah buttoned her sweater again.

"I will walk you to your car."

"Thank you. That's very nice." It was a dark winter night and the empty parking lot seemed a little spooky.

"If you do not mind my question, are you Catholic maybe?" Father George asked casually as they made their way through the darkness.

"Actually, yeah," Sarah said. "I am." She knew that she was Catholic, even now in the midst of all her unsettling doubts. The Catholic religion stayed with you, even when you wandered a bit. Somehow it was always there, just beneath the surface. They were almost at her van now.

"I had a feeling you were. Here, let me give you my blessing." Father George extended both hands over her head and began to pray, first in his language, then in English. Sarah stood there silently, listening.

"May the blessing of the One who blesses all, the peace of the One who gives peace to all, and the protection of our adorable God be with us, among us, and around us, and protect us from the evil one and his hosts, at all times and ages, O Lord of all, Father, Son

## A Martyr's Crown

and Holy Spirit, forever."

Sarah made the sign of the cross as he finished blessing her. She felt a sense of peace come over her then, as though all the anxiety and tension of the evening had melted away.

"Thank you, Father," she said softly, pulling her keys from her purse. "What language is that, by the way?"

"Aramaic. The language of Jesus Christ."

*People still speak that?* Sarah made a mental note. *Aramaic. Wow.*

Father George looked into her eyes then, and his steady gaze seemed to pierce her very soul. She stood there, frozen, exposed, unable to look away. Her mother said something once about a famous priest—Padre Pio was it?—who could read souls. Was Father George somehow reading her soul?

And that's when he saw it, if only for an instant. Sarah had experienced great sorrow—he could see it in her eyes. She had lost hope and was trying to hide from God—as if that were possible. Perhaps this was the lost sheep the Lord meant him to find. He'd searched his flock these last days and his heart told him she was still out there, lost and afraid.

"Thank you for telling the story of my people, Sarah," Father George said slowly as it dawned on him who Sarah was and why she'd contacted him. Surely Divine Providence had guided her way. "No one here seems to know about us. I hope you will come back on Saturday. Something tells me you will."

"I'll try, Father," she said then quietly, "I really will." Even as she said the words, she surprised herself. What would she tell Javier? She could imagine his reaction. Not good. What had she gotten herself into?

♕♕♕♕♕♕♕

Javier waited and fumed. Eight-thirty had come and gone. By nine o'clock he'd had enough. Sarah was playing games with him again, pretending as though her work required her to be gone for the entire evening. She knew he had to be up by 4:30 a.m. to get to the office. He could tell she was avoiding him, that she'd rather be anywhere but here at his side.

It was the way she looked at him. He could see it in her eyes, the disapproval. The disappointment. She blamed him for what happened to Patrick, and nothing he could do would ever fix that.

More and more lately, he wondered why he even stayed. Their marriage had grown cold, each of them stranded on their own island of grief and guilt.

"Good night, boys," Javier said as he turned from the family room and trudged up the stairs. He turned off the light and climbed into bed, pulling the blanket up around his chin. Sleep came within moments.

ש ש ש ש ש ש

Sarah tiptoed into the darkened bedroom, holding her breath and closing the door softly, sure that Javier was already asleep.

Javier sat up in bed immediately. "What time is it?" he asked, clearly annoyed.

"Um, about 10 o'clock," Sarah said innocently. *What, did she have a curfew?*

"I thought you said you'd be home much earlier than that," Javier said, frowning.

"Well, things took a little longer than I expected," Sarah said carefully. "I figured you would be asleep by now."

"I was," Javier said coldly.

Sarah took off her earrings and placed them in the jewelry box Javier had given her their first Christmas together. She felt a

## A Martyr's Crown

pang, recalling the sweetness of those first days of their married life, when their love was yet untarnished by bitterness and disappointment.

"Sorry for waking you up," Sarah said quietly.

Javier sighed. "It's alright. It's just…oh, never mind."

"What?" Sarah said, her voice rising. "Never mind what?"

"You always say you're going to be home at a certain time, but then you never are," Javier answered. "It's like I told you before, you don't seem to want to be around us. It's like you're like off in your own little world!"

"Oh! And you're not?" Sarah practically shouted. "You're either at work or you're zoned out in front of your computer! You don't even listen to me when I talk! What difference does it make if I'm here or not? You barely notice me when I am!" Sarah was mad, but she felt tears stinging her eyes. "You say I'm busy all the time, but who was the one who was too busy to…"

Javier interrupted her. "I don't believe it! You're not going to drag the accident into this again, are you? You really do blame me for what happened to Patrick, don't you?" he said, his voice breaking.

"I didn't mean…," Sarah began to say, but Javier stopped her.

"You don't think *I* think about that stupid air bag every day? You don't think I wish I'd had it fixed?" By now, Javier had tears running down his cheeks. He angrily brushed them away. "I've had it with this. You know what? I'm done. I should go away for a while, go visit my family back home in Puerto Rico. They don't blame me the way you do."

The words hung in the air. Sarah swallowed hard. *Did he really just say that? Is he really thinking about leaving me?*

"But, Javier," Sarah pleaded, putting her arms around him, "You know I didn't mean…"

"Don't," Javier said, pulling away swiftly. He strode to the closet, pulled on his jeans and an old T-shirt, grabbed his shoes and stormed out of the bedroom. Sarah knew it was best to let him cool off. She sat down on the bed, feeling dazed. Pretty soon she heard the garage open and shut: Javier was gone.

"Oh, God," she said softly then, "What have I done? What have I *done?*"

Sarah lay awake in their bed, restless, unable to sleep. She thought about the distance growing between her and Javier. It seemed they were at a breaking point and the thought of what might happen next terrified her. For almost 22 years, they'd stayed together, even through some tough times. But nothing they'd endured—Javier getting laid off a few years back, nearly losing their house, Benny being born prematurely and spending a month in the hospital—none of it prepared them for the immense grief at the loss of a child.

Patrick's death had taken an enormous toll on their marriage. Deep down, Sarah knew it was unfair to blame Javier—the accident wasn't his fault. Patrick shouldn't have been drunk. He should have worn his seatbelt. They'd told him again and again that they didn't approve of him drinking, but like so many teenagers, Patrick did it anyway. They'd grounded him, taken away his cell phone, but he still disobeyed them. No one they asked seemed able to help them control their son. One cop even told them they should lock Patrick out of the house.

"As long as you leave a cot with a sleeping bag and food for him on the patio, you can't be charged with neglect," the officer said. As if they'd do that. As if they'd even consider it!

The night of the accident, Patrick had gone to a friend's house after a basketball game. The other boy lived about a half a mile away. When it was all over, when they pieced everything together, the boy, a teammate, admitted that a couple dozen kids were there for a party—no parents around—and there was plenty of beer flowing.

At some point, later on in the evening, Patrick grabbed his keys.

# A Martyr's Crown

His friends told him he shouldn't drive, but Patrick scoffed.

"I live right around the corner. I'll be fine! No worries, man." *Why didn't they take his keys?*

Just moments later, as he rounded the bend near the neighborhood playground, he lost control of the car, ran over the curb and struck an enormous eucalyptus tree. Instantly, he was thrown through the front windshield of the car.

Neighbors heard the loud impact and came running.

Later, when police called Sarah and Javier, they were dozing on the couch, sleeping through a movie, some silly action thriller they'd rented. The phone rang and Sarah answered it groggily. Who could be calling them at midnight?

"Is this Mrs. Castillo?" an authoritative male voice asked.

Sarah leapt to her feet, alarmed. "Yes, that's me." Javier stood up, eyes wide with concern.

"I'm sorry to tell you this, ma'am, but there's been an accident."

"What!" The receiver fell from her hands and she stood there, reeling.

Javier quickly scooped up the phone.

"Who is this? What's going on?"

"Sir, this is Officer Mike Evans of the Tempe police department. I'm sorry to tell you this, sir, but there's been an accident. You and your wife need to get to the hospital immediately."

They jumped in the car and raced to the trauma center, praying and crying the whole way, but Patrick was already gone. He'd died of a massive head injury.

That was two years ago; in little more than a week they would have their second Christmas without him.

By now, hot tears were running down Sarah's cheeks. All the times they had talked about safety, about the dangers of drinking and driving. *Why did he do it? Why?*

She always came to the same conclusion, every time she thought about that horrible night: *maybe if the airbag had worked*

## Joyce Coronel

*Patrick would still be with them. Why didn't Javier have it fixed?*

And that was what was standing between them. Sarah had so many responsibilities, but managing the cars was not one of them. She barely knew how to open the hood on the van. Javier did everything for them in that regard. Oil changes, brake jobs. He even fixed cars for their nieces and nephews.

In moments of honesty, Sarah knew that Javier wished more than anything—probably even more than she did—that he could go back in time and do things differently.

By now it was 2 a.m. Sleep was out of the question. Sarah slipped down the creaking stairs to get a glass of water. Reilly was sound asleep on the chair by the door, but opened her eyes and yawned when Sarah switched on the light over the table.

Pouring herself a glass of water, Sarah thought about why Javier was mad: she was out much later than she said she would be at that prayer vigil. Maybe, just maybe, there was some good news in there: he missed her. And he really did hate it when she was away.

When they were in college together, they couldn't bear to say goodnight, to have their time together end. "We'll never have to say goodbye again," Javier told her when they got engaged a couple weeks after graduation. "We'll be together forever."

"Forever is a long time," Sarah's mother used to say.

Sarah wondered if forever was about to come to an end.

How she'd wanted to tell Javier about the woman at the prayer vigil who was carrying the picture of the baby girl. Like her, Javier loved babies—that's how they'd ended up having four of their own. Javier would be as horrified as she was by what happened to that poor child.

Sarah picked up Reilly and sat down on the couch, sinking into the cushions. How the old, rickety cat loved having her neck scratched. Sarah gladly obliged and was rewarded with the feline's rhythmic purring.

In her mind, she kept seeing the image of the baby, the one

## A Martyr's Crown

the terrorists murdered. She couldn't fathom that such evil, such cruelty could be inflicted on a tiny, helpless child. *Who were these people? How could they do this? And why? What about all the other innocent people they killed? What did they hope to accomplish with their hatred?*

In the small amount of coverage the attack received, no one mentioned the fact that a baby had been slaughtered. Just the bare facts: three dozen dead, a church in Mosul. Nameless, faceless victims. Turn the page. Next story. It made Sarah want to vomit. She didn't want any part of such soulless reporting. She wanted to tell this story, to shout it to the world: *Look what they're doing! Someone stop this madness!*

She let out a deep sigh then, terribly disturbed by what she'd witnessed that night at Mar Ephrem, afraid to think about how angry Javier was and what he might do. *Would he really leave them?* She knew she'd never be able to sleep now — she was far too wound up for that. The computer beckoned, promising a few hours of distraction. The crafting of stories was always cathartic anyway, particularly in the wee hours when one couldn't sleep. God knew she'd had more than a few sleepless nights since they lost Patrick.

Placing Reilly back on the chair, she refilled her glass of water and plopped down in front of the desktop in the den. She had a little more than four hours before the kids woke up and needed to be taken to school.

Pulling out her camera, she uploaded the pictures taken at the vigil that night. The candlelight illuminated the faces of the mourners as they walked along singing and praying, candles flickering in the wind, carrying pictures of their loved ones. In one shot, she saw Father George walking alongside the other priest, leading the congregation in a hymn. In another, an elderly man with a cane was staring off into the distance in anguish.

Sarah clicked through the images, looking for the woman who'd lost her great niece. Even though she'd been at the vigil, seeing the pictures all at once brought out all the emotions of the evening again—the shock that such horrors had taken place, the anger at those who unleashed such hatred on the innocent, the desire to do something about it—something beyond merely telling a story.

Then she saw it, there on the screen; the older, regal-looking woman with silvery hair, weeping, holding the picture of the precious baby who had been slain. Sarah's hand flew to her mouth to stifle a sob. She sat there, staring at the picture, sickened that anyone could do such violence to a child, to a family. Unto her last breath, she would never forget that little one's face. Biting her lip, she silently offered a prayer for the mother who was undoubtedly crushed by a grief Sarah knew all too well. Mother and child, torn in two. Was there any pain as deep as that in all the universe?

ש ש ש ש ש ש ש

Across town, inside Mar Ephrem's darkened rectory, Father George knelt on the floor before the crucifix that hung over his bed and prayed with all his heart for guidance.

He listened then in silence, listened for the voice of the One who watches over all, who neither slumbers nor sleeps. And he heard it then, clear and strong, the quiet voice that spoke so clearly:

*"If you love Me, feed My sheep."*

ש ש ש ש ש ש ש

### A Martyr's Crown

# Chapter 10
Mosul
Monday, December 14, 2009

Fadi lay in the lumpy, narrow bed on the third floor at Mosul General Hospital and stared out the window, as if in a trance. The 600-bed medical center comprised the training grounds for Mosul University's medical school. Although he was a faculty member at the university, his credentials didn't afford him any particular favors as a patient. He knew they barely tolerated his presence. They begrudgingly appreciated his skill in languages, but he was a Christian, after all.

His nurse — Fadi couldn't recall her name just now — had just come in to inform him that he would be going home tomorrow. He'd spent a miserable week in the hospital, but there were large gaps in his memory. The pain killers they were giving him, the shock of what he'd survived — he still wasn't certain of many details — had landed him in a fog. He knew one thing was true: Noor, his precious daughter, was gone. He hadn't been able to save her. He felt the tears forming at the corners of his eyes as he thought of those final moments inside the church.

Mercifully, the nurse had pulled the IV out of his wrist, apologizing when the tape tugged at his skin as she held a cotton ball over the site.

A soft-spoken woman with thick glasses, she came back a few

minutes later, placed a tray of food on the table straddling his bed and encouraged him to eat. "You need to get your strength back, Mr. Yacoub," she'd said. "You've hardly eaten a thing since they brought you in here."

Fadi nodded his head silently. He had no appetite and the food, a cup of soup and an anemic-looking array of chicken and vegetables, did nothing to entice him.

"Your wife went home to rest and gather some clothing for you. She said she'll be back in the morning with her brothers and sisters to take you home," the nurse continued. "I'll be by to check on you a little later. Use the call button if I can get anything for you," she said as she turned and walked out of the room.

Fadi took a sip of the room-temperature water on the tray, then pushed it away. He fought back tears as he thought of those last moments, crouched on the floor of the church, trying to shield Noor and Hanne. He'd tried his best to save their baby, but it wasn't enough. He hadn't even been able to attend the funeral. How could he live with what happened? He couldn't protect his family. He wished then with all his heart that he had been the one to die.

Here he was, lying here in a hospital bed, with a mass of bandages on his belly, fighting waves of pain that never seemed to go away, even with all the Percocet they'd given him. There was no painkiller that could ever alleviate the grief he felt crushing his heart. They said he could go home tomorrow, but go home to what? To face an empty crib in the room they'd so carefully prepared for Noor? To see her pink blankets and pacifiers piled up on the chair where Hanne used to rock her to sleep? It was too much for any man. His daughter had been ripped from him. He hadn't been able to stop the bullets that pierced her tiny heart. He felt useless.

Hanne, dear Hanne, had visited him often during the week, he was sure, though his memory was spotty. Could it be that just

## A Martyr's Crown

a week ago, they'd been anticipating Noor's baptism? They had counted the days leading up to that Sunday, wanting to share their joy with their loved ones and friends. In a few cruel moments, that dream had been shattered, along with so many others. The daughter Hanne and he had longed for was gone. Gone!

Although the horror inside Mar Addai had taken place only a few days ago, in some ways, it felt longer. He was still having trouble getting his mind around what happened. The pain meds only made it all the more confusing. That, and the grief, he thought to himself sadly as he fell into a fitful sleep.

The insistent chime of an alarm in the next room awakened him sometime later. Light from the window near his bed was streaming through now and Fadi turned his face toward the wall. It was late afternoon, but was it Wednesday or Thursday? He was groggy, but he could hear the doctor next door talking to a patient and his family. Something about more tests being needed, that they would have to wait and see.

He tried to turn over a bit in the bed and groaned as a stabbing pain shot through him. He was sweating and hot and this hospital with its noise and smells and alarms was driving him crazy. The sooner he got out of here, the better, he thought to himself. He was wide awake now, his mind racing, spinning, considering what lay ahead.

Even in the midst of all the pain and the grief, Fadi was sure of one thing: he and Hanne were going to have to leave Iraq. He'd been thinking about it even before the attack on the church. Their battered country held no future for them. They were Christians in a land increasingly hostile toward followers of Christ. The fact that he'd done extensive translations and interpreting work for the U.S. military made their situation even more dangerous.

Many of Hanne and Fadi's friends had already left, seeking refuge in nearby Turkey, some hoping to eventually make it to America. That could take years, Fadi knew. His Aunt Samira and her husband, along with their daughter and son-in-law, left Iraq three years ago and had only recently settled in Arizona.

"The climate's a lot like it is at home, Fadi," Aunt Samira told him in an email just a month ago. "You and Hanne should come here. There's a Chaldean church near where we live—you'd fit right in! And there's a large university here, too!"

"Thank you, Aunt Samira. Maybe we can come visit you there someday. But you know how close Hanne is to her family—she'd never agree to leave Iraq for good."

Convincing Hanne now would be impossible, Fadi was sure of it. He'd need divine intervention. How could he expect her to leave her mother, her sisters, her brothers, when she was hurting so much? His mind ached thinking of the terrible mess they were in.

Somehow he would have to convince her that leaving was the best thing for them, that they could find their way in America, build a new life for themselves and live in safety. They could leave right after Christmas. He could work for his aunt, after he was back on his feet, and maybe someday, for the university.

Outside the window, Fadi heard the cries of the late-afternoon Muslim call to prayer issued by the *muezzin* that rang from the minarets throughout the land five times a day for centuries. *Allahu Akbar! Allahu Akbar!*

Down below in the city and all around the university grounds, Muslims—at least the devout ones—were dropping to their knees, facing Mecca and reciting their prayers. The sun cast long shadows across his bed and onto the stark white wall beside him. He closed his eyes and silently prayed an Our Father. "*Baban delee beshmaya...*"

He reached down deep inside himself then, wishing with all his heart he could go back in time and save Noor somehow, that he could erase what happened and have another chance. Why? Why had God allowed this horror? Even as he posed the question, he knew the answer. Tragedies, injustices; these were the stuff of

## A Martyr's Crown

Chaldean existence, trials to be endured. It was part of who they were as a people. He still believed, even now, even after what happened inside that church.

He fell into a quiet slumber then, imagining himself in the arms of Jesus, dreaming, curiously, of the day Noor was born. He awoke with a start a short time later, and remembered with sorrow where he was.

♛♛♛♛♛♛♛

# Chapter 11
Phoenix
Monday, December 14, 2009

Sarah looked with dismay at the long line of cars ahead of her waiting to merge onto the I-10. It was 4:30 p.m. and the on ramp was jammed with vehicles, every driver seemingly anxious to get home and prepare for next week's "winter holiday," heretofore known as Christmas. Sarah, though she didn't feel as close to God as in earlier years, still bristled at the notion that the celebration of the birth of Jesus Christ needed to be erased from public consciousness. Scott, her Evangelical neighbor, felt much the same way and had a "Jesus is the Reason for the Season" banner hanging out in front of his house.

Sarah thought about Scott and how he always found a way to bring up the topic of salvation, no matter what the conversation was. "*I could use a little salvation right about now*," Sarah thought to herself wryly as she considered the strong possibility that she might be late to Zach's basketball game.

She and Javier were barely speaking to each other, but they'd called a truce for the time being. Javier would wait and go to Puerto Rico after New Year's. Leaving the boys at Christmas seemed heartless. Even though he drove her crazy sometimes, Sarah knew she had married a basically good, kindhearted man. *So why do I keep pushing him away? Why can't we move past the pain?*

## A Martyr's Crown

Finally, she eased her way onto the interstate, inching along for what seemed like an eternity. At least she didn't have the commute every day; working from home two days a week was a definite bonus. She pulled up to the house 30 minutes later, just in time to see Javier raising the hood of his car.

"Oh, hey, you're home," Javier said coolly as she got out and walked toward him. He was still staring at the engine. "How was your day?"

"OK, I guess," Sarah said. "What's up with your car? We've got the game tonight—remember?"

"Of course I remember," Javier said testily, "but I need to charge the battery in this thing again. It's giving me trouble starting," he said as he searched through the junk littering the workbench. "I'll be there in a sec."

Chagrined, Sarah went into the house and set her keys and purse on the scratched oak table next to the back door. Why couldn't Javier trade in that old Honda? They'd had it for years and it seemed he was constantly tinkering with it.

Later, they sat around the table eating dinner quietly. Sarah and Javier didn't say a word to each other. The boys, picking up on the tension, ate their soup quietly, wondering if they'd done something wrong. Afterward, Javier drove them in silence to Zach's basketball game, the last one for a couple weeks. They were set to play at Sierra Mountain, the rival school's campus.

Sarah busied herself checking her email on her smart phone and saw there was a message from Father George.

"I've been praying for you and your family, Sarah. Something tells me you need to hear this message: God loves you and will never leave you. He has the answer to every one of your problems. Forgiveness brings peace."

Sarah reread the message a few times. *What did he see in me that made him want to tell me this? Could he really read souls?* She flipped down the visor and looked in the mirror. Admittedly, there were dark circles under her eyes, but other than that, nothing remarkable that might betray how torn up she felt inside. *Maybe he was one of those incredibly perceptive people who saw through people's facades—kind of like Mom—with that laser-like probe that saw right into your heart and blew past all the carefully constructed "do not enter" signs.*

Javier parked the car and walked ahead of her, beside Benny and Thomas. Sarah was still thinking about Father George's message. Though it seemed a bit unsettling at first, it was also strangely consoling. A priest—a very courageous priest—was praying for her and her family.

As Sarah and Javier and the boys climbed into the crowded bleachers, rock music blaring from the loudspeakers, Zach's team paraded into the gym, arrayed in their blue and gold uniforms. Thomas hobbled over to sit with his teammates.

"Can I go sit on the top bleachers?" Benny pleaded.

"Sure, honey." Sarah knew it was because he wanted to take a look at Patrick's jersey, number 15, retired two years ago and now hanging from the rafters over the top bleachers.

Sarah and Javier looked for where the Washington High families were sitting and spotted Sholeh Kashani, the mother of Andrew, Zach's new teammate.

The two boys had become friends earlier that year when they had an algebra class together and discovered a mutual passion for basketball. Andrew came by the house several times over the last couple months, usually to shoot hoops in the driveway with Zach and Thomas, although lately it had been to do homework together.

"Hi, there," Sholeh said with a smile as she scooted over and made room for Sarah and Javier on the bench. "How are you guys tonight? Think we'll win this one?"

"I sure hope so," Javier said airily, as though everything was normal, as though he and Sarah were just fine. "The boys have been on a winning streak lately but Zach says Sierra Mountain is a

## A Martyr's Crown

tough team."

Down on the floor, the Sierra Mountain cheerleaders were getting the crowd revved up. The refs were standing at the scorers' table, methodically checking the team rosters, when the buzzer sounded.

The opening tip went to the Eagles, and Zach and Andrew ran down the court, looking for a pass. The ball went to Zach, who dribbled, then expertly sank the shot, scoring the first two points of the game.

Sarah and Sholeh clapped and cheered. Javier jumped to his feet, beaming. "Way to go, Zach!" Javier shouted. "Great start, son!"

Sholeh was already busily snapping pictures of the action with her cell phone and posting them to Facebook. Sarah noticed that she was impeccably dressed as usual, even though it was just a high school basketball game. Her long, dark hair was parted on the side and cascaded down the back of her pale blue silk blouse. No matter what she had on, Sholeh always wore a gold crucifix and medal of the Virgin Mary.

She wondered how it was that Sholeh was a Catholic, and an apparently devout one at that. *Didn't Zach say she was from Iran? I thought Iranians were mostly Muslim.*

By halftime, the Washington High Eagles were up, but only by five points, which in the world of basketball, really wasn't very much. Sarah could tell Javier was nervous. *He takes this stuff so seriously. It's just a game!* Both teams headed for their locker rooms and the Sierra cheerleaders took to the court again, this time forming a pyramid.

Sholeh turned to Sarah.

"How do you think Zach did on that physics final today?" she asked Sarah.

"It's not his favorite subject, but he studied hard for the test," Sarah said. "I know Andrew was helping him over the weekend.

Zach said he's really good at math and science."

"Yeah. Those are his favorite subjects," Sholeh said. "He sometimes tutors a few kids from the youth group at St. Clare's."

"Really?" Sarah asked. "You mean like, as a job?"

"There's one mom who pays him because he goes every week, but mostly he just volunteers," Sholeh said. "I bet Zach would love the youth group. Maybe they can go together some time."

"Maybe," Sarah said, but she kind of doubted it. They were a strictly try-to-show-up-for-Mass-on-most-Sundays kind of a family. The Castillos never did anything extra at church, even before the accident that shook their faith. She was sure the boys would have little interest in Andrew's youth group. Among the five Castillos, Benny was the only one who inherited his grandmother's religious sensibilities. He never let them forget to say grace before meals.

"What are you guys doing this weekend?" Sholeh asked. "Christmas shopping done?"

Sarah winced. She hadn't done much shopping and time was running out. At least she'd mailed the Christmas cards.

"I've got to work tomorrow morning," Sarah said, "but my mom is coming over in the afternoon and we're going to bake some Christmas cookies."

"The paper has you working on Saturday mornings, too?" Sholeh asked incredulously. "So close to Christmas? On what?"

"Well, I kind of volunteered," Sarah explained, lowering her voice. She hadn't exactly told Javier about her attendance being voluntary. Good thing he was busy talking with the other team dads.

"I went to this prayer vigil the other night for the victims of that attack on the church in Iraq. The priest invited me to attend their Christmas party for the refugee kids tomorrow so I could get to know some of them and tell a better story."

Sholeh's eyes widened. "Who is this priest?" she asked. "And what does he have to do with the terrorist attack on the church in Iraq?"

"Well, there are actually a lot of Iraqi refugees here in the Valley," Sarah said, thinking back on what Father George had told her. "Some of them are Chaldean Catholics. I called the parish and talked with the priest."

Sholeh was intrigued. "You know I'm Persian—right?"

"Yeah, Zach did mention that," Sarah admitted a little sheepishly. She didn't want it to seem as though they were talking about her behind her back. "How long have you been in the U.S.? Your English is perfect. "

"Thanks," Sholeh said, her cheeks flushing, obviously pleased with the compliment. "I came in 1978 with my parents and my two sisters, right before the Shah was exiled," Sholeh added.

"When was the last time you went back?"

"Oh, about three years ago, just for a couple weeks," Sholeh explained. "I still miss it there. I go to visit my relatives and some of my old friends in Tehran."

"Yeah. Javier misses Puerto Rico sometimes," Sarah said, thinking worriedly about how he said he'd leave the week after New Year's. *Was he really going to leave them?*

"You'll have to tell me all about the refugee children you meet," Sholeh said, moving the conversation back. "I didn't realize we had Iraq war refugees here in Phoenix. And you say they're Catholic?"

"Well, these refugees are," Sarah said. "I'm hoping to take some pictures on Saturday and talk with the children a little bit. They probably don't speak much English, but the priest does."

Sholeh reached into her purse pulled out a black leather wallet. She opened it and casually withdrew several 20-dollar bills.

"I want you to give this to the priest and tell him it's a gift from a woman who was once a Muslim and converted to Catholicism 20 years ago," Sholeh said as she pressed the cash into Sarah's hands. "We're unlikely brothers and sisters in the faith," she added with a sad sort of smile. "Our countries fought a long and bitter war against each other."

"That's very nice of you, Sholeh," Sarah said, a bit taken aback by the spontaneous gesture. "I'm sure Father will appreciate it."

"They must have a lot of needs," Sholeh said. "Refugees always do."

Sarah nodded, still amazed that this woman she hardly knew was willing to give such a generous gift so readily. "I didn't realize you were a convert from Islam. That's kind of rare, isn't it?"

"Definitely," Sholeh admitted. "It's a long story. Maybe I can tell you about it sometime."

"I'd like that," Sarah said. "Might be something good for the newspaper."

"Well, no, I wouldn't want anything in the newspaper," Sholeh said quickly. "I still have relatives in Iran. That kind of story could endanger them."

The game buzzer sounded loudly and Zach and Andrew walked back out on the floor with their teammates.

"Let's go, Eagles!" Javier shouted. He'd purposely been avoiding Sarah during halftime, relieved that she was talking with Sholeh. Now his eyes were focused on the court below, anticipating the rest of the game. He and Sarah had been to their share of interminable YMCA matches at 8 a.m. with 5-year olds. High school competition was far more entertaining.

With any luck, he thought to himself, Zach would be playing next year at the college level, the way Patrick should have. Javier frowned. Patrick was never far from his mind. *That damn air bag. Why didn't I get it fixed?*

שׁ שׁ שׁ שׁ שׁ שׁ

A Martyr's Crown

# Chapter 12
Mosul
Tuesday, December 15, 2009

Raad and Hanne walked down the long corridor of the hospital, toward Fadi's room. He would be leaving there today, going home at last.

The nurse handed Hanne some prescriptions and instructions for taking care of Fadi's wound. "You should send one of your brothers out to get this medicine as soon as you get home," the nurse told her. "I've just given him his pain medication, but he'll need another dose in four hours."

Hanne nodded and numbly stuffed the prescriptions in her purse. Raad helped Fadi out of bed so he could change into the clothing Hanne brought for him.

"I'll go see about getting you a wheelchair," the nurse said. "You'll need one for a few days until you're stronger."

Fadi sat on the edge of the bed, feeling winded. After a week of nothing but lying in the hospital, trying to recover, the effort to get dressed was exhausting.

"You've lost a lot of weight," Hanne said, shocked at Fadi's shrunken mid-section. He winced as she gently touched the bandaged area on his side.

"Oh, *aziza*, I'm sorry. I didn't mean to hurt you." Hanne's eyes filled with tears, but she swallowed hard, trying to maintain her

91

composure. Fadi needed her now.

"No, really, it's OK, Hanne," Fadi said lightly. "It's not so bad, really. Just a little tender. I'll be better in no time. Don't worry about me."

When the nurse returned with the wheelchair, Fadi sat down gingerly, thankful to be finally leaving the confines of the hospital. He wouldn't miss the constant noise and confusion, the way days and nights seemed to melt into each other. He'd been having nightmares, terrifying ones that shattered the drug-induced sleep the pills caused.

Home. As they drove up to the apartment that he and Hanne shared, just blocks from Mariam's house, Fadi saw all the familiar sights, but he was struck by the sense that it all seemed surreal. The last time he'd driven down this street, life was beautiful. *That was before*, he thought to himself sadly.

By the time Raad managed to help him out of the car and into the wheelchair, Fadi felt ready to get back into bed. As Hanne unlocked the door, he braced himself. Back to reality. Noor was gone; there would be no tender embrace of her, no tiny hand reaching for his face when he crossed the threshold.

Nora and Nahida were waiting inside, standing in front of the stove. They'd spent the afternoon making *shorba 'd rizza bil kathatha,* chicken and rice soup, and the flavorful aroma filled the sparsely furnished apartment.

"*Shlama*, hello!" they'd cried in unison when Raad wheeled Fadi through the door. They came over and gave him the customary kiss on both cheeks.

"We've got just the thing for you, Fadi. A good meal. No more of that awful hospital stuff," Nora said kindly.

Hanne took off her sweater and hung it over the back of a chair. Nahida put her arms around her warmly. "Welcome home, dear sister."

"*Bessimta*, thank you," Hanne said. Her sisters had surrounded

## A Martyr's Crown

her with love and support in the days following the attack and Hanne knew she'd be lost without them. They had promised to stay there with her as long as she needed.

"Whatever you're making smells delicious," Raad said, hoping Hanne and Fadi would try to eat a little. They both looked haggard, spent. Hanne gave the prescriptions to Raad. There was a small drug store just around the corner from their apartment and the pharmacist was a childhood friend of Hanne's father, someone they trusted.

"The nurse said Fadi will need these medicines this afternoon," Hanne said. "Can you get them for us please?" She reached into her purse to give him some money.

"Of course I will, *azizta*," Raad said, "but I don't need your money. Don't worry—I'll go now, before it gets late. Save some soup for me though," he said with a smile.

Nora pushed Fadi's wheelchair up to the small kitchen table. "Let me get you a bowl of soup, dear," she said to him kindly. "Here, Hanne, you sit down and eat, too. You must be hungry."

Hanne sat down opposite Fadi. "Thank God you're home," she said wanly. Fadi reached across the table and took her small, smooth hand in his. That simple motion of extending his arm was surprisingly painful. Recovering from all this was going to be rough, of that he was quite sure. But he would do it, *inshallah,* God willing.

Nora and Nahida brought bowls of the hearty soup and a plate stacked with fresh, homemade bread to the table. Although she had no appetite, Hanne didn't want to hurt her sisters' feelings. She'd have to force down a few bites out of love for them. Her hand trembled as she lifted the spoon to her lips. The broth—Mariam's recipe—tasted warm and soothing.

When they'd finished eating, Hanne pushed Fadi's wheelchair the short distance down the tiled hallway to their bedroom. He was a large man by Iraqi standards, nearly six feet tall. Hanne, with her petite frame, never envisioned the day Fadi would be dependent on her for anything.

She maneuvered the chair up to the edge of their bed, and bending down, gently removed his socks and shoes. As she untied his shoelaces, she realized that she'd never had to care for him this way, almost the way a mother would care for her little boy. Fadi needed her; he was counting on her to help him through a painful recovery.

And in that moment she felt a little guilty about some of the thoughts that had been tormenting her. *Why couldn't he save Noor? Why didn't he shield her better?* Fadi, brave and loving father that he was, had risked his life, done everything possible to spare Noor. He'd suffered terrible agony because of what they did to him. It wasn't his fault Noor died. She brushed away tears.

"Ah, Hanne, dear," Fadi said tenderly.

Hanne threw her arms around his neck and sobbed.

"Oh, Fadi," she cried, "thank God you're home. These past few days, it's been horrible without you here!"

"Shhh, I know, I know, *azizta*," Fadi said softly. "I'm so sorry I couldn't be there for the funeral." He was weeping now, too. "I needed to be there with you, but I couldn't. There was no way—they wouldn't let me. I hardly knew what was going on!"

"I know, Fadi," Hanne said, wiping her tears. "It wasn't your fault. None of it was, my love." Hanne pulled the sheet up over Fadi, tucking him in tenderly. The man was exhausted, if only from the trip home from the hospital and the simple meal. She sat there in the wheelchair next to the bed, holding Fadi's hand as he drifted off to sleep.

Hanne stared down at him, lying there peacefully, as if their world had not come crashing down. She was thankful that he was home, that he had survived the shooting, but she agonized over what she knew could never be, that she could hold her baby again.

She tried not to think about those last moments inside the

## A Martyr's Crown

church, tried to push the horrible images from her mind, but the more she tried to vanquish the thoughts, the more they kept replaying themselves. Picking up her rosary beads from the night stand, she tried to pray, tried to focus on the words. When a knock sounded at the front door a little while later, she jumped, startled. *That must be Raad,* she said to herself, tiptoeing from the room.

Nahida had already opened the door and locked it again, being sure to bolt it with both of the well-worn heavy chains. These were treacherous times, and they were careful to keep the place as secure as they could.

"What happened to the man who lives here?" a prying neighbor asked her one morning as she carried the trash outside. "We haven't seen much of him lately."

"He's not been feeling well," Nahida said as she hurried away.

Raad stepped inside the apartment and handed the white paper bag with the medicine from the pharmacy to Hanne. She peered at the label on the brown plastic bottle of pills, trying to read the instructions carefully. "To be taken every four hours as needed for pain. Do not operate machinery while taking this medication." *Not much chance of that—the man can hardly walk. Painkillers. Why didn't they have something that could numb the sorrow that had crushed her heart?* Even with her deep faith in God, she felt utterly despondent. The terrorists had robbed her of her daughter and it was all she could think of. It was as though she'd fallen into some sort of black hole and couldn't find her way to the top. Nothing made sense to her. She could barely speak.

Hanne gave the medicine to Nahida wordlessly and sat down on the sofa, feeling dazed. Her sister was discussing something with Raad, something about their mother, speaking as though their world hadn't stopped spinning, as though any sense of normalcy could ever return. What were they saying?

"So *Yemmi* wants to come over tomorrow to see Hanne and

Fadi," Nahida was asking. "Can you pick her up in the morning?"

"Of course," Raad answered. "I'll probably stop by the restaurant with her for a little breakfast first." Mariam was surely lonely, even though some of their cousins were staying with her. "I'll go say goodbye to Fadi," he said as he headed toward the bedroom.

"Here, he needs one of these," Nahida said, depositing the pill bottle in Raad's outstretched hand. "I'll bring a glass of water for him." Hanne rose from the sofa and stumbled down the hall, following Raad.

Fadi was lying there, staring up at the ceiling, feeling alone as he listened to the chatter in the other room. What would become of a man who could neither defend nor support his family? He needed a solution quickly. He couldn't stay an invalid much longer. Tomorrow he'd have to start trying to do more on his own, take less pain medication.

Hanne lay down on her side of the bed, exhausted.

Raad stood there, looking down at them both, wishing he could do something to ease their heartache.

"Here, Fadi," Nahida said, entering the room with a tall glass of cool water. "Sit up and take your medicine. It will ease the pain a bit, help you rest."

Fadi sat up slowly, swallowed one of the little blue pills gratefully and lay back down on the bed. "Thank you, Nahida. You're an angel to take care of us this way."

Nahida covered them both with the sheet and turned out the light. "It's good to have you home, Fadi."

"I'll be by tomorrow with Mariam," Raad said. Fadi nodded. He was sure his mother-in-law came to the hospital to visit him, but he couldn't remember. The 10 days since the attack were lost in a fog. He recalled only bits and pieces, fragments of time.

He reached for Hanne's gentle hand and kissed it. They'd always fallen asleep this way, holding hands. How he loved her—

### A Martyr's Crown

how he wished he could go back in time and save her from this nightmare. He would wait to tell her his thoughts about leaving Iraq.

*Why didn't I say something weeks ago, when I first thought of it?* It was too late for such thinking now. They had to deal with the current reality, make a plan of escape—it was the only way.

He would have to get stronger first, show that he could make the trip, that their future was in America, where they could live in freedom. In peace. Fadi closed his eyes, knowing that sleep was not far off, that he was home in the bed they shared, and that Hanne, dear Hanne, would never leave him.

כ כ כ כ כ כ כ

# Chapter 13
Phoenix
Saturday, December 19, 2009

Sarah showed up early at the Christmas party for the refugee children at Mar Ephrem. Father George told her the celebration began at 10 a.m., right after the kids finished their weekly catechism lessons.

Rick gave her the thumbs-up for a story on the party.

"It's the kind of thing our readers love, Sarah," he said when she told him she'd been invited to attend. "Make sure you get some good pictures. I can't send a photographer, but you've got a nice digital camera. This is the sort of event where the pics really tell the story."

Sarah parked and quickly checked her email before getting out. There was something from Sholeh.

*Great having a break from basketball and carpools, isn't it? I just wanted to tell you that the kids and I saw your Christmas lights last night and they look beautiful. We've never seen anything like it! Hope you're having a good day. Sholeh.*

Sarah smiled, pleased to hear from Sholeh who always seemed so upbeat. Javier was known around the neighborhood for the dazzling array of Christmas lights he set up each year—except for last year. He just couldn't bring himself to do it then, with it being the first Christmas since they'd lost Patrick. He'd merely

## A Martyr's Crown

hung a simple, illuminated Star of Bethlehem in the front yard. The neighbors understood why.

This year, the boys begged him to let them help with setting up the lights and he couldn't say no. It was an emotional day, but they'd gotten through it. Sarah made turkey soup, the way she always did, the way Patrick and the other boys liked it. There was comfort in family traditions.

Patrick was a boy who reveled in every holiday. With a pang, Sarah thought of the Veteran's Day years ago, when he was just 9 years old. He made a card for their elderly neighbor, a World War II combat vet, and left it by his front door with the newspaper.

"Thank you for all the sacrifices you made to protect our country," he'd scrawled in his little-boy handwriting. He'd colored a big American flag on the front of the card. Mr. Graziano told Sarah the card made him cry. "You're doing a fine job raising those boys, Sarah," he told her later, proudly showing her the card. "He's got a good heart, that Patrick."

Sarah got out of the van, trying to shake off the heavy feeling she felt descending on her at the thought of Patrick, and headed toward the church.

The first thing she noticed as she walked toward the dilapidated building was that the roof was falling apart and needed to be replaced. The place looked practically primeval, as though it were built long before Mr. Graziano was off fighting WWII. Then again, the Second World War was like yesterday to people whose homeland encompassed ancient Mesopotamia, she thought to herself, suppressing a laugh. In that first interview where he'd told her about the Chaldeans, Father George had actually begun a sentence by saying something like, "Recently—about two hundred years ago," which struck Sarah as rather ironic. Comparatively, America was still in its infancy.

She stood there in the morning sunlight, peering through the windows of the building. About a hundred kids were crammed into the tumbledown hall which stood a short distance from the church. In one corner with the youngest students, a college-age teacher was reading aloud from a book, the Bible maybe, and pointing to pictures. The kids sat cross-legged on the floor around her, listening quietly.

In another corner with slightly older students—fifth graders maybe—Sarah could see boys and girls bent over the tables where they sat, taking what looked like a test. Father Michael stood over them, watching them silently.

"Ah, there you are," Father George said, interrupting her thoughts. "You arrived here early."

"Hi there," Sarah said, extending her hand. "I thought I'd come before the party and see the kids in their catechism classes. I didn't realize they'd all be in one room together."

"Yes, it is unfortunate. We bought this church a couple years ago, hoping to improve on it," Father George said. "There is much repair work that must be done. We were thinking to do some remodeling or renovation, but we have no money to do so right now."

"Remodeling is expensive," Sarah agreed. "Are these kids all refugees?" Sarah asked.

"Many of them, yes, but not all. Some of them have seen horrible things before they got here. A couple of them once told me, they said, '*Aboona*, Father, when we leave our house in the morning to go to school, we see an arm here, a leg there.' It is terrible, what these children have witnessed. I worry about them."

Sarah thought about that for a moment. Looking at these kids, they seemed so young and innocent, but some of them had seen things no adult—much less a child—should ever see.

"That little boy there, the one in the brown jacket," Father George continued, "He was in his mother's arms when a bomb exploded. His mom, she was killed, but he survived. The father was killed in an earlier attack."

"So who takes care of him?" Sarah asked. "Who brought him

# A Martyr's Crown

here?"

"He and his sister live with an aunt. She brings the two of them to catechism school every Saturday."

"I had no idea kids like this lived here," Sarah said softly. "They look so...normal. It's heartbreaking to think of what they've been through."

"It is like I told you before," Father George said, "no one seems to know about us. We have about 500 families that belong to our church, but somehow we are invisible to others."

Sarah noticed the way he rolled his R's, almost the way Javier did when he spoke Spanish.

"Maybe this article will introduce your community to ours," Sarah said.

"Maybe. But part of the problem is the people here—they are sometimes afraid of us."

"Afraid of you? Why?" Sarah asked, puzzled.

"They maybe have this idea that everybody from the Middle East is a terrorist. Or that everyone from the Middle East is Muslim. Americans do not know about the Christians there. We were evangelized by the Apostle Thomas—we go back to the beginning of Christianity!"

"So you're saying that people are prejudiced against you because you're from the Middle East?"

"Well, yes, unfortunately. Some are. Or perhaps they are just uninformed. I've actually had people ask me if I'm a Muslim Catholic priest! It is like they cannot believe that we are really Christian. And a lot of Catholics have not heard of the Eastern Rite."

Sarah wasn't sure she had either, though it sounded vaguely familiar.

They were still standing near the corner where Father Michael's students were working on their test. Sarah could see a few of the kids were already finished, turning in their papers and gathering their things, pulling on their sweaters.

"Classes are over now," Father George said, looking at his watch. He opened the door to the hall and rang an old brass-colored hand bell. "Time to come outside for the party, kids," he announced.

A chorus of cheers went up from the musty-smelling room as the children swarmed the door to the courtyard, laughing and talking, some of the younger boys pushing past others to get outside first.

"Slow down, Sami," Father George told a little boy in a faded sweatshirt and jeans. "No need to hurry. We will not start until everyone is lined up outside."

"We have two hours for the games and activities before lunch," Father George told the children, once the volunteers were able to quiet them. "Wait a minute—look! It is *Baba Noel*," he said with a grin, pointing to the gate. The younger kids erupted in squeals of delight. Sarah pulled the camera from her purse and began taking pictures.

Right on cue, an older man dressed in a worn-out Santa suit came around the corner, carrying a sack. He was a little on the thin side, in Sarah's view, and a dubious pick for Santa, but the children rushed him anyway, hoping to be the first one to be greeted by *Baba Noel*.

"You need to line up and wait your turn, boys and girls," one of the volunteers told them. "Everyone will have a chance to talk to *Baba Noel*. The children crammed into line, anxious for their turn. One by one, the unlikely St. Nick reached into his sack and handed something small to each child.

"What's he giving them?" Sarah asked. "Candy?"

"Uh, no, those are holy cards," Father George said with a smile. He reached into his pocket, fished one out and gave it to Sarah. She looked at it, turning it over in her hands. It wasn't the most beautiful holy card she'd ever seen—in fact, it was downright

## A Martyr's Crown

flimsy in Sarah's estimation. She had seen this same image once before; it showed red and white rays emanating from the heart of Christ. The other side was completely blank.

Still, it was obvious that to these kids, a holy card received from *Baba Noel* was extraordinary, a thing to be treasured. They were thrilled to receive something—anything. After what they'd been through, this place was paradise. Tucking the card into her purse, Sarah felt a mixture of joy and sadness.

"Excuse me *Aboona*," one little girl in a threadbare pink jacket asked Father George, "but are we allowed to go in there?" She was pointing at a large red-and-yellow bounce house that was tied down with wooden stakes in one corner of the dead Bermuda grass.

"Of course you are, Rita," Father Rama told her kindly. "All these activities we have here today are for you to have fun." He turned to Sarah as the girl dashed toward the bounce house. "Such things seem extravagant to them still."

Some of the children were already peeling off their socks and shoes and tossing them in a big heap near the flap at the front. "Only three at a time," one of the volunteers, a college-age looking girl with long dark hair, was telling them patiently, though loudly. "You have to wait your turn. Sami, no pushing!" The kids stood there, practically on top of each other in line, straining to see the lucky ones who were already inside, tumbling and jumping until they emerged dizzy, sweaty and spent.

The older, bigger kids were clustered around a volunteer handing out big burlap bags for a sack race. Sarah tried to remember the last time she'd seen one of those. When she was a kid at St. Margaret's annual parish picnic, maybe? She wondered briefly then how suburban American kids—hers for that matter—would have viewed sack races, face painting and a Santa who only handed out holy cards, but she already knew the answer. *Sack races? Seriously, Mom?*

By lunchtime, Sarah was famished. The adults were setting up tables and chairs in the breezeway and a couple men carried in huge stacks of pizza boxes and coolers with drinks.

"Can you stay for lunch?" Father George asked Sarah. "We have plenty of food."

She looked at her watch; she still had some time before her mom would be at the house to bake Christmas cookies.

"OK, sure. That would be great," Sarah said. She was hungry and the pizza looked delicious, but more than that, she sensed a real joy here—it was actually palpable, the way the kids delighted in small pleasures. There was something so heartwarming about watching them enjoy a day of innocent fun.

Father George rang the bell again and said a blessing over the food. Then he asked the kids to pray the Our Father. "*Baban deele beshmaya...*" Sarah listened as the chorus of young voices filled the courtyard. To think that this was the language that Jesus and the Apostles spoke. It was rather amazing, she thought, to hear it half a world away in Phoenix, Arizona.

He motioned for Sarah to join him at the table with the teachers and volunteers and then made a brief announcement in their language. The women at the table looked at her with curiosity. A few smiled.

"I was telling them that you are a journalist who is writing an article about our community," he explained.

"Do they speak English?"

"Some do. Some have been here longer than others. And we all have to study a little English back home in Iraq."

"We were wondering who you were," one of the ladies said shyly as she handed Sarah a plate laden with pizza and fruit.

When they finished eating, Sarah reached into her purse and pulled out an envelope with the donation Sholeh had given her for Father George.

"I've got to get going now, Father," Sarah said as she handed

# A Martyr's Crown

the envelope to him, "but a friend of mine wanted me to give this to you. It's for the refugee children."

Father George arched an eyebrow, clearly surprised by the gesture. "This is very kind of your friend. You must have said something that touched her heart."

"Actually, she wanted me to tell you that she was raised as a Muslim but converted to Catholicism about 20 years ago," Sarah said. "She's from Iran."

At that, Father George's expression changed slightly. "She was Muslim?" he asked, somewhat incredulously. He knew what happened to Muslims who converted. More than a few of his parishioners had told him over the years about friends back home who secretly wanted to become Christians, but couldn't, certain they or their family would be killed. Was Sarah's friend for real?

"She converted after she left Iran," Sarah explained, "but the rest of her family didn't. I don't know much more about it than that."

"I see. Well, please tell your friend I said thank you for the generous gift," Father George said. "What is her name?"

"Sholeh," Sarah said. "Sholeh Kashani. She's a single mom and moved here with her kids over the summer from the East Coast. Our sons are on the same basketball team."

"So this is how you know her," Father George said. "Maybe she would like to visit us sometime."

"Maybe," Sarah said. "I'll ask her about that. You'd like her."

"I am sure she must be a very generous person to help people she does not even know."

"I haven't known her that long, but she seems very kind," Sarah said as she stood up to leave. "Thanks for having me here today, Father. It was nice to see the kids and learn a little more about them. "

"When will your article be in the newspaper?" Father George asked.

"Thursday," Sarah said. "It's a good story for Christmas Eve. I'll send you the link when it publishes and you can post it on your parish website. What's your email address?"

Father George handed her his business card. "Come see us again, Sarah," he said. He held her gaze for a moment, and Sarah had the odd feeling again that he was looking right into her soul. "You are always welcome here."

Sarah nodded silently, staring at the business card. Somehow, she knew he sensed the brokenness inside her, that she'd lost her way.

As she slowly walked away, she pondered what he said, that she should return, that she was always welcome at Mar Ephrem. Many years had passed since she felt welcome at church. St. Margaret's was her childhood parish and would forever hold a special place in her heart, but it was nowhere near their home. St. Clare's was huge and though they'd been attending there off and on for years, she hardly knew a soul. The same people sat near them, week after week, but she didn't even know their names.

"You should come to our women's Bible study," the mother of one of the kids' friends urged her one Sunday. "I guarantee you'd like it."

Sarah quickly invented an excuse. "Tuesday nights? Sorry. We've got basketball games."

"Are you able to volunteer at the parish picnic?" another mom asked her one day as they were leaving church.

"Sorry. Not this year."

She had no one to blame but herself for the loneliness she felt inside, the distance she felt between her and God. How had it happened? She knew it was true—she needed God now more than any other time in her life. But where was He?

It was undeniable: meeting Father George and hearing the struggles of his people stirred something deep within her, a longing for something. The more she learned of the Chaldeans and what

## A Martyr's Crown

they'd endured, the more she felt compelled to act, to obey that inner voice prompting her to not look away. It was the picture of the murdered baby that had awakened something in her. She felt as though she could hear the voice of the martyred imploring her to not forget the spilling of their blood. Maybe, just maybe, she should actually *do* something about what she'd learned this time — not simply write about it.

✡︎✡︎✡︎✡︎✡︎✡︎✡︎

Father George watched as Sarah walked back to her van. What was it about this American reporter lady? She smiled and seemed quite friendly, but he could tell she had some kind of sorrow in her life, some private agony that was holding her back. It was something in her eyes, he decided.

He could always tell the lukewarm Catholics. He was only 35, but in his 10 years of priesthood, he'd learned to notice the little things about people. Sarah had obviously been raised in the faith — he saw her make the sign of the cross — but it seemed to him she felt far from God. Maybe she was one of those poor souls who felt as though God had abandoned her. He could certainly identify with that. Whatever it was, someone or something had wounded Sarah, of that he was certain. Her spirit was broken. That had to be it.

"One of Your little lost sheep has found her way to my doorstep," Father George whispered as he knelt in the cool, dark chapel later that day for *Ramsha,* evening prayer. "Help me to lead her back to You."

✡︎✡︎✡︎✡︎✡︎✡︎✡︎

By the time she pulled up to the house, her mom's car was already parked out front at the curb. Kathleen Murphy had stressed the importance of punctuality when Sarah was growing up. "If you can't be on time, be early," she used to tell them.

"Hi, Mom," Sarah called out as she hurried through the backdoor, unzipping her jacket. She could hear her mom's musical laughter ringing out from the family room. "Ready to bake?"

"You bet I am!" Kathleen cried as she jumped to her feet to embrace Sarah. She had been sitting on the couch talking with Benny and Thomas while Zach and Andrew were out front shooting hoops.

"I was just telling the boys about your first Christmas when you and Javier went up to Flagstaff and cut down your own tree."

Sarah nodded, remembering when they'd driven a friend's beat-up pick-up truck four hours north to the White Mountains on a quest to find the perfect Christmas tree. They were in their early 20s, deeply in love and with hardly a dime to their names.

"Think we'll find a decent tree up here?" Sarah asked as they approached the mountains. So far, the pine trees looked fairly scraggly.

"Who cares? As long as we're together, that's all that matters," Javier said, squeezing her hand. "We could always get a fake tree, you know."

"I know. But this is an adventure. Something we'll tell our kids about one day."

Standing here all these years later, that first, innocent Christmas with Javier seemed a lifetime ago. *Would this be their last Christmas together?* Sarah quickly pushed the thought from her mind. The last thing she wanted was a grilling from her mother. The woman had a keen eye.

Kathleen was already in the kitchen, donning her red and green Christmas apron. She stood at the counter and began rolling out the dough. Sarah began pulling ingredients from the cabinets and lining them up on the island in the center of the kitchen.

"Here, Benny," Kathleen said, "Go load this CD in the stereo,

## A Martyr's Crown

would you?" She handed Benny a disc with Christmas carols and hymns. Sarah remembered listening to those familiar tunes on the family record player when she was growing up. No one could sing "Have a Holly, Jolly Christmas" like Burl Ives.

"So what's Javier up to today?" Kathleen asked casually as she began cutting out cookies.

"Oh, he's at the office, catching up on work before the Christmas holiday," Sarah said, a little too quickly perhaps.

"Really? On a Saturday? Oh, that's too bad," Kathleen said with a slight frown. "He really works hard, doesn't he?"

"So do I, Mom," Sarah answered. "We've got all those boys to feed, you know. Not to mention college."

"I know," Kathleen answered, lowering her voice. "But still. Are you sure everything's OK between you two?"

The grilling had commenced. And Kathleen Murphy could spot phony baloney from miles away.

"Well..." Sarah began. "It hasn't been easy. We've been under a lot of stress."

Kathleen nodded. "I know, honey. These last couple years have been incredibly difficult for you guys." She put down the cookie cutter and came over to Sarah. Placing her hand on Sarah's cheek, she looked her square in the eye. "Promise me you won't let what happened tear you two apart."

Sarah pulled away. "Mom, we talked about this before. You don't understand what it's like. You couldn't possibly know what we've been through."

"You're right, Sarah," Kathleen said softly. "I never lost a son the way you did. But your father and I had other heartaches, other challenges. And we tried to face them together. In the end, all you really have is each other. That and your faith." Kathleen sighed and returned to rolling out dough.

"You were so young when we had all those problems with Susan, but believe me, it was really hard. There were some tough years there for a while," Kathleen said. "And when your dad got hurt and I had to go back to work, well, that was rough, too. You younger kids were still so little, but what could we do? Someone had to run the business."

Sarah didn't remember any of it. She had vague memories of her early childhood and her troubled sister, Susan. She did remember clearly, however, the awful moment when her dad fell from a ladder one day while fixing a ceiling fan in the living room. He'd broken his collar bone and arm in two places and was out of work for some time, undergoing many months of therapy and rehabilitation.

Mom, who had always stayed home with the children, had to learn how to run the bookstore she and Dad owned. At the same time, she had to take care of an invalid husband's needs and manage a houseful of small children. Sarah wasn't sure how her mom had been able to do all that and stay sane.

"We were a united front, no matter what, your father and I," Kathleen said. "It's the only way. You've got to talk out your differences."

"It's not as easy as that, Mom," Sarah said, a bit dismissively. "Can we please talk about something else?"

"I'm glad we're going to church together tonight," Kathleen said as she placed gingerbread men on the cookie sheet. "I really like your new pastor over at St. Clare's." She cast a sidelong glance at Sarah. "What do you think of him?"

"He's alright I guess," Sarah said casually. She didn't mention that their attendance lately had been spotty. And it wasn't as though they sat on the edge of their seats listening to the homily when they did attend. Javier often dozed off and Sarah found her mind wandered. Sort of like it was now.

"…and Margaret Duffy tells me her grandsons go to the youth group there. Maybe your boys would like it," Kathleen was saying as she slid the pan of cookies into the oven.

# A Martyr's Crown

"Maybe," Sarah said noncommittally. She wasn't about to get into that discussion. The boys were busy with sports and school. Still, Sholeh's son, Andrew, belonged to the group. Maybe Zach might be interested after all.

"Now then," Kathleen continued, "let's talk about Christmas Eve. We'll all meet at St. Margaret's for 5 o'clock Mass as usual. Would you and Javier be able to pick me up beforehand? Bridget just had a baby and I don't want to ask her and Mark," Kathleen said as she expertly cut out a few more cookies. She didn't like driving at night anymore.

"Of course we will, Mom. You're right on our way," Sarah said as she placed gingerbread men, one by one, on a wire rack to cool. She offered her mom one of the warm cookies.

"It's always nice to have all you kids and your families back at St. Margaret's," Kathleen said, nibbling on the cookie. "These are delicious! Now then, remember, we'll need to get there early so we can get good seats."

Sarah laughed. "Make sure you tell Joe it's 4:30 Mass this year," she joked. Her brother was perpetually late and it was the family custom to give him an earlier start time for get-togethers.

With such a large extended family, the Murphy siblings and their spouses took turns each year hosting Christmas Eve dinner. This year it fell to Matt and his wife Amy to host. Sarah was glad her turn wouldn't come up for a while. The thought of having to plan such a huge gathering when she and Javier and the boys were still reeling from what happened…well, it was just too much to fathom. She tried not to think about how she and Javier would be doing by the time their turn to host rolled around. Her mom was singing along with Burl Ives now and cutting out another batch of cookies.

Sarah scooped out the last few spoonfuls of oatmeal cookie dough and placed them on the baking sheet in neat rows. Then she thought of the refugee children she'd seen this morning, with their smiles and laughter in spite of all they'd experienced. She thought of Father George and the grief she knew he bore.

"Father Ameer was dear to me," he'd said, looking away when she'd asked him about his friend. "We knew each other our whole lives. He was the one who consoled me the most after the kidnapping."

Even with all that grief, she saw a quiet determination in the young priest, a sense of peace in spite of everything he'd endured. What was his secret?

Maybe this Christmas would be different after all. She felt as though she was at a crossroads, poised like Robert Frost at the fork of two roads diverged in a wood. How her father had loved that poem! She remembered the first time he read it to her and with a stab, thought of what he'd told her then, that life was a process of choosing, always choosing, the right path.

"Quite often, my dear, it's the one less travelled," he said as he closed the book and replaced it on the shelf near the cash register.

ש ש ש ש ש ש ש

A Martyr's Crown

# Chapter 14
Mosul
Thursday, December 24, 2009

Fadi grimaced as he stood from the couch—he still needed someone's help to get up—but he was feeling a little stronger with each passing day. The rickety wheelchair was off in the corner, waiting for Raad to return it to the hospital. Nora was not about to let Fadi lie in bed all day, even though that's really all he wanted to do.

"You'll never get your strength back if you don't get up and walk a bit."

"Just let me rest!" he told her, irritated at her demands.

"Look, I know you don't feel like it, Fadi, but you've got to get up and move around!"

He complained at first, but she insisted that he get up and take laps around the apartment at regular intervals throughout the day. "The longer you stay in bed, the longer it's going to take you to recover," she told him kindly but firmly. He knew she was right but he hated feeling like a useless invalid.

Sleep was one way to try and escape the horrible memories, the enormous sorrow weighing on his heart. How it grieved him to see Hanne so bereft, knowing that there was nothing at all he could do to fix this. And isn't that what a man did? Fix things? But there was nothing he could say or do. They just had to get through the days. Sleep, when it came, seemed the only way, at least until a flashback or nightmare ruptured the relative calm.

When he wasn't immersed in the grief, there was the tremendous anger burning in his belly over what happened. He wanted to pound his fists, to yell, to scream, to punish the men who had done this to their family. Instead, he sat there in his apartment, captive. It was eating away at him, this rage.

Hanne seemed to be constantly on the verge of tears, though having her sisters stay at the apartment was a source of comfort. They tried to keep her distracted, giving her small tasks in the kitchen.

"Help us cut up this fruit, won't you, Hanne dear?" Nahida asked sweetly. "Come on. We'll make a nice platter of fruit for the table."

Hanne obliged, though it exhausted her. Every once in a while, she would go and sit next to the crib in the room where Noor used to sleep. One afternoon, Fadi found her in there leaning against the wall, pressing Noor's pink blanket to her cheek. She didn't look up when he entered the room.

"Oh, Fadi!" Hanne sobbed. "Our baby! Our poor baby!"

He held her then, tried to comfort her, but it was no use.

He'd been home for almost a week and they still had not ventured from the apartment, but tonight they would attend Christmas Eve Mass together at the cathedral.

"They say there will be heavy security," Raad said gravely. "But if you'd rather stay home..." his voice trailed off.

"No, no," Fadi answered. "It will do us some good to get out of here for a bit. We'll be fine."

Hanne wasn't so sure.

Navigating their way through the crowded cathedral was going to be tricky. Hanne held onto Fadi's arm as they made their way into the church that night.

"Let's sit in the back. Right here," Hanne whispered as they

## A Martyr's Crown

came to the last pew.

The scene of the funeral, which had only taken place a week ago in this same church, was still sharp in her mind. Hanne held her head high, determined to show strength and grace and dignity in spite of how she felt inside. She would be strong for Fadi, for the others.

When it came time for the homily, Bishop Abbo took his place at the ambo and looked out over the crowd. Despite what his flock had been through, they were still here, in large numbers, just as he'd hoped, to worship on Christmas Eve.

"My dear brothers and sisters in Christ," the bishop began. "Tonight we recall that moment in time when our God, the King of kings and Lord of lords, took on flesh and was born of the Virgin Mary in the humble circumstances of Bethlehem.

"From the beginning, those who have chosen to follow Christ have often had to lay down their lives, just as the Master and Lord of all taught us to do. The road to the cross began right there in Bethlehem, at the Savior's birth, when the Holy Family had to flee persecution and journey to a foreign land.

"My dear brothers and sisters in Christ, no matter what they do to us, they will not destroy our faith. We will follow the way of the cross, wherever it leads."

The congregation was hanging on every word the bishop spoke and when he was finished, there were muffled sobs. Bishop Abbo was a man of great courage, a leader the people respected. His fiery words, they knew, were spoken from the heart. His uncle, a priest, had been arrested and tortured for the faith years ago when he refused to break the seal of the confessional.

"You're coming back to my house, aren't you?" Mariam asked them when the Mass ended.

"Of course, *Yemmi*. It's Christmas," Hanne said.

"Good. I've made *pacha*. You're looking a bit thin, *azizta*. We need to get you to eat more, I think." Turning to Nora and Nahida, she furrowed her brow. "What? Didn't I teach you girls to cook?"

It was a good sign. Mariam's feistiness was coming back.

After dinner they gathered in the living room to exchange a few gifts. Mariam gave Hanne a small box wrapped in red and white paper.

Hanne opened the package, being careful not to rip the paper, knowing her mother would want to reuse it. She lifted the lid and beheld a delicate gold chain with a tiny, ornately fashioned gold crucifix. She let out a gasp of wonder.

"*Yemmi*!" Hanne cried, "It's beautiful. Here, Fadi, help me put it on," she said with the faintest glimmer of a smile. It was the first time anyone had seen the light in her eyes in weeks.

"That cross belonged to your grandmother," Mariam said. "She would have wanted you to have it, Hanne dear."

"Thank you, *Yemmi*," Hanne said, rising from the couch to embrace her mother. "It's beautiful," Hanne said wistfully. "I remember Grandmother wearing this to church." Mariam smiled. To see her daughter smile, if only for an instant, was consolation.

When all the presents had been opened, the family sat talking and telling stories about the old times, the years between the wars when things were better. Mariam talked about the day the family restaurant opened, when Hanne's father first invited people in the neighborhood to taste the fine food prepared by his wife.

"Your father and I, we worked from sunrise until long into the night for the first couple years to get the restaurant established," Mariam recalled.

"And you're still on staff as our official taste tester," Saeed joked. Mariam had no qualms about dishing out plenty of advice to the cook, even though Raad and Saeed had long since taken over the business.

Fadi tried to listen to the banter and smile, but he felt himself growing sleepy. His side was beginning to ache and he couldn't

## A Martyr's Crown

wait to get home and lie down. He squeezed Hanne's hand and she knew instinctively it was time to leave.

Raad drove them back to the apartment, along with Nora and Nahida, who planned to stay with Hanne and Fadi for a few more days.

Hanne took off the cross her mother had given her and put it away safely in her jewelry box on the bureau. She crawled into bed beside Fadi, already drifting off to sleep, and closed her eyes. This Christmas was not at all what they had expected. Less than three months ago, she'd given birth to beautiful Noor. She felt the tears forming in her eyes, spilling down her cheeks.

"Hanne, love," Fadi said, "let me hold you, my sweet. There, there now. I am here."

Hanne sniffled. "Oh, Fadi," she cried. "I miss her so much!"

"I know, *azizta*, we both do," Fadi sighed. "We both do."

They stayed quiet like that for a few minutes there in the dark, holding each other, wishing they could go back in time, that they could erase that horror in the church, go back to the way it was before everything fell apart.

"Hanne," Fadi began slowly, "I've been thinking: life for us here in Mosul will never be the same. Not now. Not ever. I don't feel safe here anymore, not with those fanatics out there."

Hanne listened quietly. She could feel the steady beat of his heart and it comforted her. She knew Fadi's work had put them in danger. "I don't want to think about that right now, Fadi. I just can't," she said turning her head away.

Fadi understood, but he also knew he would have to bring it up again—and soon. The insurgents would eventually discover he'd cooperated with the U.S. and they'd be only too glad to kill him— or Hanne. He wasn't going to let them near his family ever again.

# Chapter 15
Phoenix
Thursday, December 24, 2009

Sarah sat in the upholstered pew next to Javier and Kathleen, waiting for the rest of the Murphys to arrive and caught up in the memories of Christmas Eves past at St. Margaret's. In some ways, tonight was not much different from many of them. Pine trees illuminated by hundreds of tiny white lights lit up the sanctuary and a life-sized Nativity set—the same one Sarah remembered as a child—was just to the right of the altar.

The three Castillo boys, saving seats in the pew in front of them, were dressed in long-sleeved dress shirts and slacks, each wearing neckties, a once-a-year fulfillment of Sarah's wishes. Kathleen sat busily fanning herself, watching the young family to the left of them with amusement. A young mother and father were attempting, so far unsuccessfully, to get their twin toddler boys to sit beside them quietly until Mass began. The father was holding a baby girl who looked to be about 8 months old.

"Here. Let's read this book about St. Nicholas," the mother was saying patiently.

"Need go bathroom," one boy was saying.

"Me too," the other announced automatically.

"Here," the father said, handing his wife the baby. "I'll take them."

## A Martyr's Crown

The Murphy brothers and sisters and their children slowly began trickling in, a few at a time, exchanging hushed, church-voice greetings and filling up the pews. Between the seven siblings and their spouses, there were 19 grandchildren. *Twenty if you counted Patrick*, Sarah thought to herself wistfully. She watched Bridget soothing her newborn daughter, Emma, and remembered Patrick's first Christmas, when she'd dressed him up in the Santa suit her mom had given him. He'd slept through the entire Mass.

Seeing Bridget made her think of Hanne, the mother of the newborn baby who was killed in the church in Mosul. *Her first Christmas after,* Sarah thought. *That poor woman.* She found herself praying for Hanne then, asking God to comfort her and give her strength.

"Oh, look," Kathleen whispered excitedly to Sarah, "It's Father Tom." The soft-spoken priest captured Sarah's attention—and doubtless that of many others, too—since last Mother's Day when he described in detail his rebel years and the many mistakes he'd made before he rediscovered his faith. "I violated every one of the Ten Commandments, and then some," he quipped. "I put my dear mother through some very difficult times, but she never stopped praying for me."

At the end of the homily, he had his mother stand up so everyone could see her. Sarah remembered the congregation giving the elderly, frail-looking woman a standing ovation.

Sarah had never heard such a story from a priest before, and it stayed with her. As Father Tom made his way toward the altar, it suddenly occurred to her that she wished Patrick could have had a chance to meet him. *Maybe he would have changed, too, if he had lived. He was a good-hearted kid, in spite of everything.*

Sarah herself didn't have any wild teen years—her sister Susan had taken that unfortunate role in the Murphy family—so she was both alternately perplexed and angered by Patrick's rebellious behavior. She wondered what she would have thought of Father

Tom's story if she'd heard it when they were in the midst of all that craziness. His experience was probably something that encouraged a lot of parents of wayward teens, but it was too late for Patrick.

The stubborn doubts still nagged at her, two years later. She thought she'd been doing a good job as a mother, but then she had this strong-willed child who wouldn't listen to her or Javier, who regularly got drunk with his friends, who often smoked pot and stayed out past his curfew. They'd tried everything to get through to him. Here it was, Christmas Eve—what should have been one of the happiest nights of the year—and Sarah was still mulling over her last tug-of-war with Patrick.

"What are you doing after the game tonight?" she'd asked him that evening.

"Blake's house. I'll be home by midnight, don't worry."

"I always worry with you. I'll be waiting up. Make sure you're home by 12."

"You treat me like a baby, Mom. I'm 18! Nobody else on the team has a curfew except me!"

"If you want to be treated like an adult, you have to act like one first," she'd shot back. "Getting drunk, smoking pot—that's kid stuff, Patrick! When are you going to start acting like a man?"

"Get off my back!"

He stormed out of the house before she could say anything else.

How she wished she could go back, insist that she talk to Blake's parents to make sure they'd be home that night. Perhaps if she'd done that, Patrick would be here with them now. *Why did God let him die?*

She felt the anger and guilt just below the surface, every time she relived that last conversation, those final moments with Patrick. It was as though she was being tortured by some sort of inner demon that taunted her, blamed her, condemned her for being a complete and utter failure as a mother. *How else can you explain having an uncontrollable child? Only an incompetent mother*

## A Martyr's Crown

*would have such a child. Why weren't my last words to him—in my last moments with him—words of love instead of criticism?*

*And Javier? How could he let Patrick drive around with an airbag that didn't work? How* could *he?*

The man behind her sneezed and Sarah was suddenly thrust back into the present.

"And so, my brothers and sisters," the priest was saying as he wrapped up his homily, "We celebrate the birth of our Lord and Savior, recalling His birth in the utter simplicity and poverty of the stable in Bethlehem."

Sarah snapped out of her little reverie. She glanced at Javier; he looked as though he'd been lost in thought, too. Or had he fallen asleep? Sarah wondered if he was really thinking about going back to Puerto Rico when the Christmas holidays were over. *Good grief. What would she tell the boys?*

They left the crowded church and Sarah welcomed the stillness of the cold, starlit night. Matt and Amy's house was on a quiet, tree-lined street in a neighborhood near St. Margaret's, not far from their childhood home where Kathleen still lived.

Sarah shoved her potato casserole in the oven and set the timer, resisting the urge she felt to disappear, to shut herself up in the den, looking through Matt's books. She didn't feel all that sociable, but she would force herself to make small talk, to smile and laugh, pretend like everything was fine. Javier, she noticed, was already deep in conversation with her brothers. Football, she hoped, and not politics.

"What can I do to help?" she asked Amy, hoping to be given something, anything to keep busy.

Amy reached into the fridge and gathered some large bags of vegetables. "Here," she said to Sarah, handing them to her, "maybe you could arrange these on trays for me."

Kathleen, standing at the stove stirring gravy, was watching Sarah carefully, thinking about the gift she planned to give her tonight in private. She'd noticed that Sarah and Javier were barely speaking to each other lately and it worried her. Later, when they went to drop her off, she would present it to her.

Sitting around the Christmas tree after dinner in Matt and Amy's expansive living room, they exchanged gifts. Years ago, one of the girls—Maggie, maybe—came up with the idea that the adult Murphys should draw names. The rule was that they weren't supposed to spend more than $35 per gift.

Sarah was opening a package from Bridget. As she lifted the tissue paper in the box, her face lit up in delight.

"The Poetry of Robert Frost, unabridged edition," Sarah read aloud, holding it up so everyone could see. "I hope you bought it from Murphy Book Sellers," Sarah joked.

Opening the volume to the middle, Sarah was touched to see she had stumbled upon "The Road Not Taken," her personal favorite, the one that always made her think of her father.

"Here, let me hold Emma," Kathleen said to Bridget, sitting down beside Sarah. They were all taking turns holding the newest member of the Murphy clan, giving Bridget and Mark a much-needed break.

The younger kids were sprawled on the floor, immersed in "How the Grinch Stole Christmas" on the big screen TV. Sarah remembered how her family used to watch it every year together and it was good to see Matt carrying on the tradition.

In spite of the music and the laughter, Sarah heard an incoming text message on her cell phone. She pulled it from her pocket and lit up the display. It was from Father George.

"Merry Christmas, Sarah, to you and your family. I hope it is filled with many blessings and great peace. Never forget how much God loves you. He is waiting with open arms. All you need to do is open the door."

*That's a first. I've never had a priest text me before. But then, I've never really gotten to know one before either.* Father George,

## A Martyr's Crown

she could tell, was not the sort of person who was too busy to develop relationships with people. It was the way he listened, really listened, when people spoke to him that impressed Sarah. He didn't interrupt them or try to hurry them along.

Sarah texted him back, wishing him a Merry Christmas, remarking how nice it was to hear from him. In a matter of seconds, she heard another incoming message.

"I will be near to your neighborhood on Saturday morning to visit a parishioner in the hospital. May I stop by to visit your family?"

*A priest? In their house?*

"Sure, Father. We'd love to have you," Sarah answered, feeling a bit nervous but not sure why. She hardly knew what to think. No priest had ever crossed their threshold and she worried, briefly, what he might think of their family and their home. What would Javier say?

"When you drop me off tonight, I want you to come with me in the house for a few minutes. I've got something special for you," Kathleen whispered to Sarah as she stroked Emma's arm.

"But, Mom, you already gave me a gift," Sarah protested. Kathleen presented each of her children and their families a generous check at Christmas. "I'm too old to be out shopping, trying to figure out what you kids want," she would tell them. "Now don't use this to pay bills! Do something nice for yourselves."

Sarah and Javier usually took the boys out for a meal at a good restaurant, the kind of place they wouldn't normally go. Last year, Kathleen joined them.

"Well, let's just say this is a little something from your father," Kathleen said quietly.

Sarah wondered what that could mean. Her dad had been gone over a year now and she couldn't imagine what her mom had in mind.

## Joyce Coronel

By the time people began gathering their gifts and coats and empty platters, it was nearly midnight. Javier pulled up to Kathleen's house and they went inside.

"We'll just be a few minutes," Kathleen told Javier as he and the boys sat down in the living room. "There's something in my room I want to show Sarah."

When they entered the bedroom, Sarah noticed that it still looked and smelled just as it always had. She spied the half-empty bottle of Dad's Aramis cologne sitting on top of the dresser, his old-fashioned alarm clock on the nightstand. She knew her mom had not yet gone through the closet and given away his clothes. Kathleen opened the top drawer in the tall bureau and pulled out a rather hefty, leather-bound book. She handed it to Sarah.

"What's this?" Sarah said, feeling the weight of it in her hands. She felt overcome as she held it, and she wasn't sure why.

Her mom's eyes were shining. "All those hours your father spent among books, well, he'd always wished he'd written one himself. He kept this journal for many years," Kathleen explained. "He didn't write in it every day, but he did write in it regularly, especially after his accident, when he couldn't work. Helped him deal with things, sort out his thoughts, he said.

"He never let me read it while he was alive, but after he died, well..." Kathleen's voice trailed off. "I've been reading it slowly over the last year and it seems to me, Sarah, that you're the one who should have it. You're the only one in the family who became a writer," she said. "He was so proud of you, honey."

Sarah set the book down on the bureau and put her arms around Kathleen. She knew she'd been given something precious— something sacred. All her life her father had been her hero. Having his journal was like having a visit from him, one last chance to hear his thoughts.

"I love you, Mom," Sarah said, swallowing the lump in her throat. "You know how much this means to me. I didn't even know

## A Martyr's Crown

he had a journal."

"I used to see him sitting right there at that desk at night, writing in it," Kathleen said, eyeing the mahogany roll-top desk in the corner of the room. "It was comforting to him somehow."

"Writing usually makes me feel better, too. I guess we were the same that way."

"You're a lot like him, Sarah. You know that. You inherited his gift for words."

"This has to be one of the best gifts I've ever received," Sarah said as she picked up the journal and held it close to her heart. "Thank you for giving me this tonight, on Christmas. It's kind of like having part of him here with us right now."

Standing there in the dimly lit bedroom, Sarah thought of her dad holding this very book, pouring out his thoughts, his worries and dreams within its pages. Seeing the world through his eyes this way would be something to savor. What would he say if he knew Javier was talking about leaving? How she wished she could ask his advice one last time. Perhaps there was some nugget of wisdom within the pages of his journal, something to guide her.

"What was that all about?" Javier asked as they drove away from the house, waving to Kathleen, who stood by the front door waving and blowing kisses.

"Oh, just a little something from my father," Sarah said as she clasped the journal, anxious to see what its contents might reveal.

"Something from Granddad?" Zach asked from the backseat, instantly curious.

"His journal. Grandmom gave me his journal."

She remembered then the Christmas *her* grandfather sat at the table with all the other grownups and talked about his inevitable demise.

"Yep. I'm gettin' old. All these medications I take," her grandfather said scornfully as he took a long drag from his cigarette.

## Joyce Coronel

"You would live a little longer if you'd give up those things," Sarah's grandmother said worriedly, knitting her brow.

"What? And be miserable? My days will soon be over," he said simply, as if it were nothing, as if the end of one's earthly existence was not something catastrophic.

Sarah, who at the time was only 10, rushed from the table and went to sit by herself in the garden. She was scared and worried and confused all at once.

A few minutes later, her father stood before her, his eyes filled with sympathy.

"I'll be around for a long time, Sarah," he said, sensing her fear. "Don't worry," he said as he embraced her.

Sarah nodded her head and stayed there in his arms until her sobs subsided. How had he known what she was feeling? She'd hardly been able to understand it herself, the terror of a world without her father. The thought of it now brought tears to her eyes.

Though he'd lived many years after that night in the garden, Sarah still missed him, still longed for his gentle wisdom, especially as she faced the all-too-real possibility of the death of her marriage.

Would this be her last Christmas with Javier?

שׁ שׁ שׁ שׁ שׁ שׁ שׁ

# Chapter 16
Mosul
Saturday, December 26, 2009

"Don't worry about a thing," Nahida told Hanne as she buttoned her sweater. "Try to relax while I'm gone. I'll help you fix dinner when I get back later on this afternoon."

Raad was on his way to the apartment to take her and Nora to visit Mariam. They noticed their mother seemed a little more tired than usual and they were worried about her. Nora remembered reading that extreme distress could trigger serious health problems in the elderly and she planned to stay with Mariam and keep a closer eye on the situation. "It's probably from all the grieving," she told Nahida. "She's exhausted—at least that's what I think."

"Are you sure you don't want to come with us?" Nahida asked worriedly.

Hanne shook her head. She and Fadi were worn out and hoping for some quiet time. Fadi was feeling a little stronger each day, but Hanne didn't want him to overdo it. And she certainly wasn't going to leave him there in the apartment alone.

After they left, Hanne stood up from the couch and went to the kitchen where Fadi sat at the table, drinking a cup of tea and looking at something on his laptop. He was completely engrossed in what he was reading but as Hanne entered the room, he looked up and smiled.

"Hanne, dear," Fadi said with a smile. "I'm glad you stayed here with me." He was watching her, waiting for the right moment to broach the subject.

"I don't feel up to much today," she said with a sigh. "Maybe I'll cut up some of these oranges," she said eyeing the fruit gathered from Mariam's tree. In spite of the war and the turmoil in their homeland, the tree still bore its sweet fruit and *Yemmi* had given them a good-sized bag last night. "You need to eat, child. You're too thin," her mother said as she placed the last orange in the bag.

Hanne brought the plate of orange slices over and set it on the table next to the bread and cheese. She sat down in the chair beside Fadi and poured herself a cup of tea.

"Thank you, *azizta*," Fadi said as he helped himself to some of the fruit.

"What are you looking at on the Internet?" Hanne asked.

"Different things," Fadi said carefully. "I got an email from my cousin Remza in America today."

"Oh? How's she doing?" Hanne asked innocently.

"She's fine," Fadi said. "She sends her love, says that she misses us."

"Hmmm," Hanne said, stirring her tea. "How are her parents?" Fadi's aunt and uncle owned a small grocery store, a mom-and-pop kind of place, in Phoenix.

"They're doing well, she said," Fadi answered. "They're working hard and Remza is helping them, too. They own two little stores now and I guess they're getting used to the United States. Seems they like it there."

"I suppose it all worked out well for them then," Hanne said, absentmindedly sipping her tea.

"Remza said it was difficult in the beginning, but they are doing better now. They live near one of the biggest universities in the U.S.," Fadi said. "I was checking the school's website and they

## A Martyr's Crown

offer a certificate in Arabic studies." Fadi clicked on the webpage and read aloud: "'Students must demonstrate proficiency in the Arabic language at the intermediate level.' Who knows? Maybe there's an opportunity there for me."

Hanne put down her teacup. "What are you getting at, Fadi?" she asked worriedly. "Are you telling me that you're honestly thinking of moving us there?"

"Hanne, dear, you must realize by now that there's no future for us here in Iraq," Fadi said softly as he closed the laptop and took her hands in his.

"What do you mean?" Hanne cried, yanking her hands away, her eyes full of fear. "What do you mean we don't have a future here? What are you saying? What about your job at the university?"

"I'm saying that maybe it's time for us to follow my aunt and uncle and cousin to America," Fadi said quietly. "Hanne, the work that I do for the Americans here—it's put us in a lot of danger. Those terrorists aren't going to stop. You know as well as I do, things are getting worse, not better."

Hanne rubbed her forehead. "But my family, Fadi. My mom! And what about my brothers and sisters and all my friends—I can't leave them. I can't! We've buried our daughter here! I can't leave—it's impossible," Hanne cried, her voice rising. "I can't believe you're even considering it! That you'd even think of making me give up our home!" Hanne stood up and poured her tea down the sink. Her back was to him now; how she hated quarreling. She willed herself not to cry.

"But maybe our families will join us eventually, Hanne. Lots of our people are settling in America," Fadi said matter-of-factly. "Just think of it. We're young. We're educated. We have relatives there. And we'll be safe."

Hanne spun around, hands on her hips, eyes flashing. "Now you listen to me, Fadi," she practically shouted. "I can't do this right now. You can't make me. Oh! I can't *believe* you!" She had to get away from this discussion. She felt like she was suffocating. She dashed out of the kitchen and hurried down the hall.

Fadi heard their bedroom door shut, hard. He knew his words had just poured acid on her open wounds. It was best to let her have some space—he'd never seen her angry like that before. Guiltily, he admitted to himself that he probably shouldn't have brought up the subject of leaving Iraq. Not today anyway. *What was I thinking, upsetting her like that? Still, we've got to face facts. What am I supposed to do? Ignore the dangers we're facing?*

Hanne lay down on the bed and closed her eyes. She was angry and sad all at once. She drew her knees up to her chest and wished with all her heart that they could go back to the way things were. They hadn't understood then how tenuous this life is, how uncertain. That everything could change in a matter of moments. *Why did they have to take Noor from us? Why?* Hanne felt hot tears running down her cheeks now and she let them. To have had her beautiful baby daughter torn from them and now to face the prospect of having to leave all she'd ever known—it was too much to bear.

Finally, after her sobs subsided, she lay there, clutching the blanket under her chin, its bunched-up folds damp with her tears. Deep down, if she was completely honest with herself, she knew Fadi was probably right. Though she didn't know the details of his work or what he did out there, she knew he was helping the U.S. military. That alone made them targets for the terrorists. The fact that they were Christian only made matters worse. But she couldn't allow herself to think of it, not now.

The only thing she wanted to do was to stay in their quiet apartment and not contemplate the madness outside. Lying there in the darkened bedroom, she could hear the wind blowing, whistling around the corner of their apartment complex. After a while, she drifted off to an uneasy sleep, exhausted by grief and

## A Martyr's Crown

the gnawing anxiety she felt growing inside her.

Fadi, meanwhile, had opened his computer again and sat hunched over the keyboard, reading the news, trying to learn more about Arizona. He regretted having upset Hanne, but he knew he had to think clearly about their prospects. It was his responsibility to protect her and he didn't see much chance of that happening as long as they stayed in Iraq.

'Three more interpreters killed' one news service website proclaimed. "The three men were killed by a roadside bomb while out on patrol in their Humvee with members of the U.S. Army. No troops were killed in the attack."

None of his neighbors in the apartment building where he and Hanne lived knew that he was helping the U.S. The imams said that those who cooperated with the Americans were traitors and spies. Fadi was careful to vary his routine and keep his guard up, forever on the lookout for someone who might want to harm him.

His work as a language professor at the University of Mosul was tenuous at best. Classes hadn't been in session for months and when the opportunity came up to do some interpreting, he simply couldn't refuse. They needed the money—Hanne's mother depended on them for financial help.

Many mornings during the last year, usually before Hanne even awoke, he went door-to-door in the more violent neighborhoods of Mosul, accompanying heavily armed soldiers, looking for insurgents. He was fluent in English, and the soldiers depended on his expertise in being able to accurately and quickly translate Arabic to English and vice versa.

The pay was good, much better than the paltry salary the university paid him. With classes canceled, they hadn't paid him in months. Before he began helping the Americans, he watched with rising panic as their savings dwindled down to almost nothing. The average Iraqi worker brought home maybe $100 a month. With the U.S. paying him more than six times that, it was hard to pass up the interpreting job, even though it was dangerous.

He'd seen some terrible things out there, helping to hunt down terrorists. Like last year, when that young American soldier was killed right in front of him.

"I want you to have this gun, Fadi," Jake told him, just days before his death. "You never know when you might need it out there to defend yourself."

He came home badly shaken after seeing Jacob's head blown off by a sniper, across the street from where he stood inside a doorway, consulting with another soldier. Even though Hanne pressed him for details, he never spoke about it to her, knowing she would be horrified. He didn't want to worry her and he could barely cope with the memory himself. He tried to forget the bloody images that sprang to mind every time he recalled that last, terrible afternoon with Jake.

Hanne knew the work he did was risky, but Fadi now realized that she didn't quite understand just how dangerous it really was. She was extremely close to her sisters and he knew the thought of leaving them was tearing her up inside. He didn't blame her after all they'd been through.

He clicked on the email from his cousin again.

"Come to America, Fadi," Remza urged him. "Life here is good. You'll be safe. And you can work for the university here."

Fadi thought about that for a moment. He didn't really need further evidence to convince him that life in America was their only option. He loved his country, but there was no way they could stay here anymore. It was Hanne who needed to understand that their very survival meant having to flee Iraq. Fadi closed his eyes and leaned back in the chair.

"Help me, Lord," Fadi prayed. "Please. I don't know how to convince her. Show me what to do."

☙☙☙☙☙☙

### A Martyr's Crown

# Chapter 17
Phoenix
Saturday, December 26, 2009

As soon as she opened her eyes, Sarah saw that Javier was gone, but she remembered with a sigh of relief that it was probably only as far as the local gym. Holding her breath, she looked in his side of the closet and noticed his running shoes were missing. Perhaps he would remember to be home later for Father George's visit. She could feel a nasty knot growing in her belly, realizing that a week from now, Javier might be gone altogether. *How am I going to explain that to the kids? To my mother? Is he really going to leave us?*

She came down the stairs slowly, rubbing her eyes, and beheld the relative chaos that was their living room. Crumpled-up wrapping paper, bows and assorted gifts were strewn about the floor and heaped on the couches and coffee table. The star atop the Christmas tree was crooked and someone had left a sticky, half-eaten candy cane on one of the end tables. Reilly slept peacefully, curled up in a ball amidst some wrinkled red tissue paper, oblivious to it all.

After her morning coffee, Sarah set about tidying the living room, trying in vain to eliminate the trail of glitter that must have come from one of the packages the kids had torn open yesterday. The sparkly stuff was now deposited throughout the downstairs and she had a pretty good idea that Reilly had laid down in it at some point and helped with the generous distribution.

When the doorbell rang later that morning, Sarah folded up the newspaper and peered through the window by the front door. There stood Father George, dressed in his clerics and holding a small package—a Christmas present for their family, no doubt. She reproached herself, wishing she had been thoughtful enough to have something for him. At least she'd set aside extra tins of her homemade Christmas cookies.

"Hi there, Father George," Sarah said as she ushered him through the door, noticing that his limp seemed even more pronounced today. *Was he in pain?* "Come on in and make yourself at home. Kids!" she called up the stairs. "Here, Father, I'll take your coat for you," Sarah said. She hung it in the closet and showed him into the living room which, by her estimation anyway, looked remarkably improved from the shambles of earlier in the day.

"Here—I brought this for you and your family," Father George said, handing her the package. "It is a recording of Chaldean music. I thought you maybe will enjoy it."

"Oh, thank you. That's very thoughtful. So this is singing in Aramaic?"

"Yes. If you listen to it enough, maybe you will learn a little of our language, too."

"I suppose that's possible," Sarah said with a grin. "I do have a thing for languages."

Zach, Thomas and Benny came down the stairs, curious to meet the priest who was standing in their living room. As far as they knew, a priest was someone who said Mass on Sundays. To see one standing here in their house, seemingly out of context—at least in their opinion—was unprecedented. And why did he have that terrible scar on his face? Benny tried not to stare.

"Boys, I'd like you to meet Father George, the priest I was

telling you about, the one I wrote about for the newspaper," Sarah said.

Father George looked each of the boys in the eye and shook their hands warmly. "You must be the oldest," he said to Zach. "What is your name?"

A cloud passed over Zach's face, but then quickly dissipated.

"I'm Zach. I'm a senior this year."

"A senior. I see. And how about you?" Father George said, shifting to Thomas.

"I'm Thomas and I'm a sophomore."

"And I'm Ben and I'm in eighth grade."

"All boys. This is wonderful. I have three brothers myself. And three sisters, too," Father George added. "Now, where is your father?" he asked, looking at Sarah quizzically. The boys looked at each other, not sure what to say.

"I think he's at the gym," Thomas ventured.

"Oh, yeah, he's been there since this morning," Sarah hastened to add, blushing. "He really tries to take care of his health. I thought he'd be home by now. Can I get you something to drink, Father George?" Sarah asked.

"Water would be great, thank you."

"Mom, is it OK if we go shoot some hoops out front?" Thomas asked, following her into the kitchen.

"Sure. Benny, are you going, too?"

"Nope. I was reading in my room though."

"Impossible. You? Wrapped up in a book?" Sarah said teasingly. She took a glass from the cabinet, making sure there were no spots, then filled it with cold water from a pitcher. "That's fine, Benny. Enjoy."

She carried the water and a plate of cookies into the living room and stopped when she saw Father George standing in front of the table in the corner, the one with the candle and all the pictures and memorabilia. He looked up as she entered the room and saw her face, and in that moment, it clicked.

Sarah placed the glass of water and the cookies on the coffee table and sat down stiffly on the rose-colored wingback chair. She figured this conversation would happen eventually, just not so suddenly.

"That's our son, Patrick," she said quietly. "Our firstborn. We lost him a couple years ago."

"Oh, Sarah, I am so sorry to hear this. I had no idea," Father George said kindly as he eased himself onto the couch. His leg was bothering him today and it grieved her to know that someone, some cruel person, had caused this suffering in him.

"It will be two years on January 8. But in some ways, it feels like it just happened."

"I am very sorry for your loss," Father George said, looking at Patrick's memorial. "It is good the way you have his picture and some of his things here. You must have been very proud of him."

Sarah smiled sadly. "If you only knew. Would you like to rest your leg on the coffee table? It seems like you're in some pain today."

"A little. Some days it is worse. Too much walking at the hospital this morning. So it is alright for me to rest my leg there? This would be considered rude in my culture."

"Please. Of course it's alright."

"Thank you. Now, what was Patrick like? Tell me about him."

"You really want to know?"

"If you feel like talking about him, sure."

"Actually," Sarah said slowly, "I don't talk about him very often, but it might be good to talk about what happened with you. You seem easy to talk to."

"I am here to listen, Sarah," Father George said, looking at her intently.

Sarah leaned back in the chair, thinking back to the moment their lives were changed forever. It had started out like an ordinary

## A Martyr's Crown

day.

"Well, it happened when Patrick was a senior in high school. He wasn't that great of a student, mostly B's and C's, but on the basketball court, he was fantastic. A couple of colleges were interested in him," Sarah said, looking down at her hands.

"The thing was, he sometimes got into trouble — staying out past his curfew, drinking, smoking pot, that kind of thing. It wasn't like he was drinking every day — just from time to time. But we absolutely did not approve and we made that very clear to him, of course. We tried everything to get him to behave, but nothing seemed to work," Sarah stared out the window, watching as Zach dribbled the ball past Thomas.

"We lectured him, grounded him, took away his cell phone, but it was no use. We tried counseling, but he hated it. He kept telling us other kids were doing much worse stuff than he was. As if that mattered to us. 'We're not their parents,' we told him," Sarah shook her head. "He wouldn't listen.

"Anyway, one night after his team won a big game, he went to a friend's house. The parents weren't home and a whole bunch of kids showed up. These people lived in our neighborhood, only about a half mile away.

"Somebody brought beer, and Patrick had too much to drink. He got into an argument with another kid and he wanted to leave. His friends told him he shouldn't drive, but Patrick was stubborn. 'I live right around the corner,' he told them, 'I'll be fine.'

"Well, he wasn't fine," Sarah said, her voice breaking. She paused to compose herself. "He lost control of the car at a bend in the road and crashed into a big tree. He wasn't wearing his seatbelt and went right through the windshield.

"The paramedics took him to the hospital, but there was nothing they could do." Sarah broke down at this point, covering her face with her hands.

Father George sat quietly waiting. Eventually Sarah looked up.

"I'm sorry—this is still so hard to talk about," Sarah said, shaking her head. Father George reached into his pocket and handed her a folded-up tissue. He heard his parishioners' sorrows day after day and he knew it was important to listen carefully, to allow the person to fully express the pain.

"You and your family have been through a very difficult time," he said. "God bless you all. It must be really hard for you and your husband."

Sarah sniffled and dabbed at her eyes, certain that she looked like a wreck, surprised that Father George had zeroed in on what was weighing so heavily on her heart. "It's definitely caused a rift between us. It sounds crazy, but I've been blaming him for Patrick's death."

"But this accident—how is it his fault?" Father George asked, puzzled by the notion that Sarah's husband could be responsible for such a tragedy.

"The thing is, he likes to fix cars. And he's pretty good at it," Sarah explained. "Actually, he's very good at it. The car that Patrick was driving that night was one that the two of them had just finished fixing up a few weeks earlier. Only Javier never got the airbag checked out, even though there was a light on the dashboard that said he should. He just never got around to having a technician inspect it. And it seemed to me that if that stupid air bag had worked, Patrick would still be here. At least that's how I looked at it. Who knows?" Sarah said, blowing her nose. "I mean, really. It's like I needed someone to blame and Javier was the most convenient target."

"And now you feel differently?" Father George prodded.

"Well, sort of. I guess I realized that it was wrong for me to blame him. Javier loved Patrick—he would have done anything for him. I kept him so busy with stuff around the house, and he works so hard to take care of us all—he never had a chance to catch his breath. It wasn't his fault Patrick got drunk and drove the car. He shouldn't have done that. He knew better. We told him a million times not to drink and drive. A million times!"

"It is just my opinion, but I am thinking that Javier, he was already blaming himself for what happened."

"I think you're right about that," Sarah said. "In fact, he told me that one night after we had an argument."

"So it is stressful here in your home since the accident. You two are maybe not talking so much, maybe arguing many times."

"Definitely."

"Is this why he is not here today?"

Sarah took a deep breath and wondered if she should admit it. Father George was only trying to help.

"Actually, he told me a couple weeks ago that he's going to go back to Puerto Rico after the holidays. He's from there and he misses it."

Hearing the words out loud for the first time, Sarah realized she'd barely been able to believe them. Now they were out there and no longer able to be denied.

"I see. It is hard to be away from one's homeland. Believe me, I know."

"I don't know why I'm telling you all this. I mean, I barely admit these things to myself, really. But you're a good listener."

"Sarah, I think God, He brings us into each other's lives for a reason."

"You do?" Sarah said, surprised by the suggestion.

"Nothing happens by coincidence. Everything unfolds under the loving providence of God. You did not realize this?"

Sarah pursed her lips. "Providence? I guess I never thought of things that way. I don't know if you've ever heard the phrase, but there's this saying about Murphy's Law. Murphy was my name before I got married, by the way."

"Murphy's Law?"

"It's kind of this cynical expression that means if something can go wrong, it will."

"This expression, it does not sound very hopeful."

"Hope's in short supply around here these days, Father."

The priest nodded his head. "I understand. But, He is waiting for you, you know."

"Who is?"

"God. He is always standing at the door, waiting for us to turn around and run back to Him. Entrust your marriage to him, Sarah. Ask Him to heal it. And ask Javier to forgive you."

"Forgive *me*?"

"Yes, you. To hold onto this anger so long—this is not love. You must know that somehow, deep in your heart."

Sarah sat there, feeling stunned. Here this priest she hardly knew had walked into her house and was readily dispensing advice. *What did he know about marriage? How could he understand what it was like? How could he understand the loss of a child?*

"I counsel many couples, Sarah. And what I see is that every marriage has its seasons. Some years, they are more difficult than others. The important thing is to be patient with each other. You must forgive each other and face your issues together."

Sarah didn't really want to admit it, but she knew he was right. He had put his finger on the center of the problem and it was unavoidable now, this obligation of hers to forgive, to try to patch things up with Javier.

"But where do I start? What if he won't listen to me, Father?" Then what am I supposed to do?"

"Start at the beginning. First, we pray. We ask God to bless you and give you both the grace and the strength to forgive each other,"

Sarah nodded her head, but she wasn't so sure.

"Marriage is like that, you see. Love grows, love changes through the years, through the children, then the grandchildren. But all the while, if you nurture it, love will grow. If you embrace the cross together, then love grows strong."

"I love him, Father. He's a good man," Sarah said, drying her eyes. "We've just lost our way it seems."

"This can happen. But there is always a way back. You must never give up hope."

"I wish he were here now so you could meet him. You'd like him."

"Next time then. Talk to him, Sarah. I feel he does not want to leave you, even though he says these things."

"Why's that?"

"If he was going to leave you, he would have already done it. Christmas was just a way to put it off."

♕ ♕ ♕ ♕ ♕ ♕ ♕

Father George sat alone in the darkened chapel back at Mar Ephrem, praying for Sarah and Javier, praying for all troubled souls who shared their burdens and sorrows with him. He'd listened to many couples through the years, here and back home in Iraq, who had struggled with their marriages.

"Be patient," he told all of them. "Forgive. Remember your vows that you made."

His leg was throbbing now and the images that forever haunted him came crashing through his mind, disrupting his prayer: the seething hatred of the men who had kidnapped him that day, their rage as they smashed his leg over and over with a hammer. He remembered passing out from the pain and awakening hours later, bleeding and shackled to a steel beam inside the empty, stifling hot warehouse.

*Forgiveness is an act of the will. I forgive them, Lord, yet I cannot forget what they did to me.* Again and again he pondered Jesus' words from the cross, "Father, forgive them," and each time he meditated on those words, he was humbled. *Let my love be as Yours, O Lord. Let me forgive and love the way You do."*

On days like this, when the pain in his leg was unbearable, it was especially hard to pray that way. Each time he felt the anger burn in his chest, he tried to take a deep breath, to dismiss the desire for revenge that resurfaced from time to time. After what they'd done to him, it was only natural to want to strike back. Bishop Abbo had told him so.

"My son, you are human. You must take it slowly. Rest. Allow for time for God to heal your mind and soul."

In the months after the old woman saw him lying there in the street, he daydreamed about finding his torturers and throttling them for what they'd done, for what they'd taken from him. Bishop Abbo had him transferred to America after a year, thinking that here in a new country, he might more easily forget what had happened, that he might relinquish this desire for vengeance.

He still struggled with it.

It was infinitely easier to preach about forgiveness than it was to actually live it. He tried to offer his pain for the sake of this couple who'd wandered into his life by some design of Providence. Though the suffering he endured was physical, he struggled even more with the emotional trauma that reignited every time he looked in the mirror. He worried that he frightened people, especially children.

"Don't stare!" he heard their mothers whisper behind his back.

How he loathed the jagged scar that bisected his face. As far as he was concerned, it was far worse than the limp. He thought so even on the days his leg felt like a 50 pound weight. He avoided mirrors; every time he beheld his countenance, he was instantly propelled back to an excruciating moment that last day in captivity. Two of the men—he didn't know any of their names—held him down while a third sliced into his cheek deeply. *"So you never forget us, priest!* As if that were possible.

## A Martyr's Crown

Although Javier and Sarah weren't members of his parish, Father George felt responsible for them now that Sarah had told him of their imminent separation. He could tell Sarah hadn't spoken to anyone about all the guilt and anger she was feeling, and he knew from experience that those feelings had a way of crushing the spirit.

He thought then of Ameer, and that they would not speak again on this earth. When things were at their worst, in the days following his release, when he refused to get out of bed, it was Ameer who sat beside him, listening as he poured out his heart.

"It's very understandable, what you're feeling," Ameer would say, his eyes filled with concern. "Do not despair. 'God is close to the brokenhearted.'"

"He doesn't feel close, Ameer. He doesn't even seem real," Father George answered. "Why did He let this happen to me? Look at me! Why didn't they just kill me and finish what they started? I must go through life now, half a man."

"One day you will see. There will be justice. Our God will wipe away every tear."

"I once believed that. But I cannot pray. They took my last hope from me."

"It is enough that you wish it were not so. Do not worry, George. I will pray for you, that God will heal your wounds, that He will console you. It is normal, what you are feeling."

Father George thought of those words now, sitting here in this hushed chapel, thousands of miles away from the clinic in Mosul where they'd tried to fix his leg and attend to the knife wound in his face.

"Pray for me, Ameer, you who wear a martyr's crown. Ask God to heal me, to help me forgive."

He thought then of Sarah, this journalist who could not forgive her husband, and in his mind he knew what he had to do. His faith had been weakened, to be sure, since the kidnapping and all he'd endured, but God was no longer silent. Perhaps God would use him—use his suffering—to help heal her marriage and draw her and Javier into a deeper life of faith.

"My grace is sufficient for you, for power is made perfect in weakness." The words of St. Paul came back to him in all their consolation. God would use his very weakness, humbly submitted to Him in an offering for this lost sheep of His.

שׁ שׁ שׁ שׁ שׁ שׁ שׁ

Sarah sat there in the den after Father George left, remembering what he'd said. She hoped he was right, that Javier was looking for a reason to stay around, to work things out.

Picking up her father's journal, she opened it to the first page and noted that it dated back to 1960, a few years before she was born. Her father was a young man then.

Reading through some of the entries, Sarah was amazed to discover that he sounded so much like the person he was decades later, in his 70s and 80s. Robert Murphy's trademark positive outlook and gentle spirit rose from the pages, making her feel as though he were right there in the room with her. She wondered what it would have been like to know him as a contemporary. She had no doubt that they would have been friends.

One entry, dated November 23, 1960, caught her by surprise.

*"Business is bad,"* he wrote. *"We have fewer and fewer customers each day and I'm not sure how we're going to make the rent on this place next week. Most people come into the store to browse, but they usually leave without buying anything. I know Kathleen is worried, what with another baby on the way this spring. Lord, help me to take care of my family, the beautiful children You've given us. If I have to take a second job, I will."*

Sarah didn't realize her parents had struggled in business. By the time she was old enough to understand things, her father's store

## A Martyr's Crown

was a very successful enterprise. He'd been able to send all seven of them to St. Margaret's school and then on to St. Dominic's High School. They'd all gone on to college, too, without having to take out student loans. Well, most of them earned scholarships, but still, her father's financial success was impressive. Sarah didn't have to worry, as some kids did, that her dad might lose his job and they'd have to quit school. He was his own boss.

A little further on, she found an entry from when her brother Matt was born:

*"Today Kathleen gave birth to our fourth son whom we named Matthew, after his grandfather. He's got a healthy set of lungs and let his parents know about it right away."*

Sarah thought about Matt for a moment; he had been close to their dad, too, and he was the one who kept up the book store's success. As the youngest child in the family, Sarah didn't remember her brothers and sisters being born and coming home from the hospital. She envisioned Maggie, her oldest sister, holding Matt as a baby and hearing him cry. It was strange to think of it, her giant of a brother as a newborn baby. She turned the page.

*"We had an argument today and I'm still so angry!"* her father had scrawled across the page. Sarah wondered what could have set him off; she'd never seen her father lose his temper. He was reserved, a man who rarely raised his voice. Her mother often said that Dad had enough patience for both of them. Sarah read on a little further.

*"...to think of all we've done for her—and this is how she repays us, with sorrow and shame! Kathleen and I can't seem to control her and she's ruining our family. I'm not sure what to do with this girl. She won't listen to us or her teachers. And that boyfriend! If I catch him around here again there's going to be trouble."*

Sarah reread the words, thinking of how hurt her dad must have felt as he wrote them. Though she'd always known that Susan had caused a fair amount of trouble during her high school and college years, she hadn't quite realized the depth of consternation it caused her parents. Suddenly, it clicked. Perhaps that was why they tried so many times to reassure her about Patrick. They could see what was happening. They knew what it was like to have a troubled teen.

"Just keep loving him, honey, and holding him accountable," Mom would say. "We're praying for him," her father would add. "Don't give up on him, Sarah. He's young. He'll figure it out sooner or later."

Patrick could be very charming with his good looks and gift for cracking jokes, making people laugh, the same way Javier did. Her mother had no idea the sleepless nights, the quarrels they'd had over this eldest son. Then again, with a troubled daughter, she probably knew precisely what they were up against. Susan had apparently been caught stealing money from the cash register at the book store. And it wasn't just a one-time thing.

*"There was money missing from the drawer again today,"* her father wrote in the journal. *"Why is she doing this to us? I'm going to have to tell her she can't work at the store anymore. She'll have to find another job."*

Sarah could only imagine the scene that would have caused. Her sister had a real temper, and on more than one occasion, she overheard the shouting matches between her parents and Susan.

Honesty was one of the virtues her father prized the most, so Susan's transgression had to be heartrending. Sarah remembered the day she came home from fifth grade with a writing assignment.

"Sister says we have to write an essay about what it means to be a person of integrity, but I don't even know what it is," Sarah told her mother.

"That's easy," Kathleen said. "She means someone like your father."

Sarah knew exactly what that meant.

She was up to 1962 in the journal now. Her dad seemed to go

through phases where he would write more and then there would be long stretches with very few or no notations at all. The one thing that kept surfacing in his musings was how much volunteer work her father did with the St. Vincent de Paul Society.

*"Visited a new family today. The father has been out of work for months and they've got six kids. Will try to see if anyone I know might be looking for an electrician. Thank you, Lord, for helping my business to prosper. Things are finally going better at the store."*

What Sarah recalled more than anything as she paged through the journal was that she loved her dad so deeply that she never wanted to disappoint him.

She pondered briefly then what her dad would have said about the trouble she and Javier were having, but she knew the truth: he would be sympathetic, but at the same time, adamant that they work things out — that they find a way to stay together somehow. "It's the hand you've been dealt," he would often say if someone brought up this or that hardship or difficulty. "Accept it." Robert Murphy believed in marriage, for better or worse. And he lived it right in front of them, for 53 years.

And whether it was the memory of her father, or what Father George had said about forgiveness and Divine Providence, Sarah decided right then she would try to forgive Javier, to make things right with him. It's what Dad would have expected of her. Father George, she knew, would be checking up on her too.

Then she heard it: the unmistakable hum of the garage door as it rolled up. Perhaps Javier had returned home. Rising from her chair, she hurried toward the back door.

# Chapter 18
Mosul
Monday, January 4, 2010

Four weeks had passed since the attack inside Mar Addai Church and Fadi was feeling restless. He wasn't used to being cooped up inside the apartment all day. Not that he missed going out on patrol with the Americans. The pain in his side from where he'd been shot was still there, but it was more or less tolerable. He'd stopped taking the medications the doctor prescribed, trying to tough it out.

"I'd rather deal with the pain than the nausea," he told Hanne ruefully.

Twice Saeed had taken him to the university hospital for physical therapy but Fadi realized he could just as easily exercise at home.

"Why should I come all the way over here and pay for therapy when I can walk around my own apartment building and build my strength?" he told Saeed impatiently after his last appointment. Really, it was his heart and soul that needed healing. He knew that wouldn't come in the form of any pill or physical therapy session.

Fadi was worried about Hanne, too. He decided both of them could use a change of scenery, if only for the afternoon. The holidays were finally over and the days seemed to drag by with no meaning, no focus. It had been more than a week since their heated discussion and he could tell she was still on edge.

"Where are you going?" he asked her one night as she crept from their moonlit bedroom.

"Oh! I thought you were asleep. You scared me!"

"Sorry about that. What are you doing?"

"It's that clock ticking. I can't stand it anymore."

She'd never noticed before how loud, how annoying the tick, tick, tick of a clock could be. She stood on a chair to take down the timepiece, a wedding gift, from where it hung in the hallway and shoved it into the coat closet under some blankets.

Sitting on the floor with her back leaning against the closet door, she thought about how empty life seemed. Without little Noor to care for, the hours crawled by. The baby's sweetness—her complete innocence—brought them such joy. The way her delicate hands grasped their fingers, the way she fed as though nothing else in the world existed, the ease with which she fell asleep curled up in their arms, soft and warm, her long, dark lashes shut tight against the pale curve of her cheek. Somehow, they would have to go on without her, but how?

"Lunch," Fadi announced the next day. "We're having lunch at the restaurant with your family."

Hanne, who would have rather napped on the couch all afternoon, pulled on her black sweater with a sigh. Fingering the gold cross *Yemmi* had given her at Christmas, she thought of what Father Ameer used to say. "No cross, no crown. No Good Friday, no Easter. If we don't share in Christ's suffering, we won't share in His glory."

*But why* this *cross, Lord? Why did Noor have to die?* There were simply no answers, except to trust that God still held them in the palm of His hand.

"He is with us in the midst of the storm," was what *Yemmi* used to say when all seemed lost, when they heard the thunder of planes overhead, smelled burning flesh as war threatened to end their lives. *Where are you, God?*

Life marched on, in spite of her pleas, and Hanne wished she could curl herself into a ball and go to sleep forever.

"Time to go, *azizta*," Fadi said softly.

Saeed greeted them at the door of the restaurant. He'd asked the cook to prepare the family a special meal of *sulafa roumaya*, curry beef stew. As they sat around the table chatting and enjoying the tasty concoction, Fadi caught a glimpse of Hanne almost smiling, if only for a few seconds, as she talked with Nahida.

"*Yemmi's* birthday is next week," Nahida whispered.

"Are we going to bake a cake for her?"

"Of course we are! We thought we'd do it at your apartment."

There were still occasions to celebrate, Fadi realized, even after all they'd been through. The world went on, whether one wished it so or not.

"Thank you, Saeed," Nora said when her brother emerged from the kitchen and came to sit with them at the table. "Tell the cook he outdid himself today. The stew was delicious."

Mariam agreed, with a minor reservation. "Tasty, yes, though perhaps a little less salt next time would be in order," she recommended. Everyone laughed. Mariam was known for her expertise in the kitchen and Saeed was certain his mother's recipes were in no small measure chiefly responsible for the restaurant's popularity.

Afterward, when they were done talking and the tea and desserts had been shared, Raad rose to drive them all home.

"Nap time," Fadi said. "That was a heavy meal."

Hanne nodded, feeling drowsy. She'd lain awake for hours last night, unable to fall asleep after hiding the clock in the closet.

Fadi was glad Raad was the one driving. His side was beginning to ache and he still didn't feel up to driving. They dropped off Mariam and Nora first.

# A Martyr's Crown

As they rounded the block and headed toward the apartment complex, Fadi felt uneasy. Something didn't seem right on the street, but he couldn't put his finger on it.

"Slow down," he told Raad.

"Why? Something wrong?"

"I don't know. Just a hunch. Something doesn't feel right."

"Fadi, what is it?" Hanne asked from the back seat.

"Probably nothing, *azizta*. Just feeling cautious today."

*Why did the streets look so empty?*

Raad drove up to the front of the building, and out of the corner of his eye, Fadi spotted a small group of young, bearded men—strangers—lurking just inside the entrance to the parking garage. One of the men reached for something in his pocket, motioning to his companions to spread out.

"Get down," Fadi hissed at Hanne and Nahida, "Now!"

Hanne and Nahida immediately crouched down on the floor of the car. Fadi slouched down on his seat. Raad made a quick u-turn and floored it. Behind them, they heard the pop, pop, pop of gunfire.

As Raad sped away from the apartment complex, Hanne's heart thudded in her chest. Who were those men? The thought that they were in danger again was terrifying. In an instant, she was back inside Mar Addai, holding little Noor's broken body, the world spinning out of control, one of the terrorists screaming at her, yanking her hair. She covered her ears, sobbing. Nahida put her arms around Hanne, trying in vain to calm her.

"We got away from them, Hanne, dear. We're OK now, I promise."

Fadi wasn't so sure.

"There's no way we can go back to the apartment," he told Raad, clenching his teeth and clutching the armrest. "I've been discovered."

Hanne's heart froze. *Not go home? What on earth were they going to do?*

"I don't know where we can go, but we've got to get away from here!" Fadi said as they raced up the next street, blowing past a stop sign. "Faster, Raad! Don't stop!"

"But where do we go?" Raad pleaded. "Want me to head north?"

"North, south—I don't care! Just get us out of here," Fadi cried. "I don't want to be out on the edge of town after dark!"

"Who were those guys?"

"I have no idea. But they better stay away from my family."

After zig-zagging through the city streets for over an hour, they finally felt as though whoever was chasing them was long gone.

"If we can't go back to your apartment, where do we go?" Raad finally asked. *"Yemmi's?"*

"I don't think that's a good idea right now," Fadi said. "Mariam's house is too close to the apartment."

"I know where we can go," Nahida said suddenly. "We're near the Paulus' house. Why don't we visit them?"

Raad looked at Fadi, who nodded his head. "Fine. The Paulus' house it is then."

Nahida was hoping Margueritte Paulus, Hanne's old friend, would be there when they arrived. Margueritte was a serene soul, someone Nahida thought might help distract Hanne, take her mind off the chaos their life had become.

Hanne sat beside Nahida, leaning her head on her shoulder as the car chugged along, her eyes shut tightly, as if she could, by pure force of will, remove herself from the spreading disaster of their lives.

They pulled up in front of the Paulus' home and parked. Raad knocked on the front door tentatively, waiting to see if anyone was home. Yawsip Paulus, the patriarch of the family, carefully peered out from behind the blinds in the window by the door. When he saw it was Raad, the old man grinned and threw open the door.

*"Shlama!"* he cried. "Hello! Good to see you, my friend!"

Raad waved to the car, motioning for the others to join him.

### A Martyr's Crown

They'd be able to spend some time here among trusted friends and decide what to do next. The gang of men who were lying in wait for Fadi and had shot at their car were not to be trifled with, of that Raad was convinced.

🙚🙚🙚🙚🙚🙚🙚

# Chapter 19
Phoenix
Monday January 4, 2010

When Sarah woke up that morning, Javier had already left for work. She sat on the edge of the bed, rubbing her eyes, wishing she could crawl back under the covers.

She checked her email. There was something from Father George.

*Sarah, I was praying for you and Javier and I remembered the words that Blessed John Paul said when he began his pontificate: 'Do not be afraid. Open wide the doors for Christ.' Do not be afraid, Sarah. Surrender everything to God. Keep your eyes on Jesus and everything is going to work out. Trust Him.*

Sarah printed out the email and placed it on top of a mound of paperwork from the kids' schools. *I'll try. I really will.*

"How did it go?" Father George asked when he called later on that day.

"We didn't talk about it. But I've been trying to be really nice to him."

"Nice to him? This is not a solution. Apologize to him, Sarah. Ask him to forgive you. It may take him a while, but I believe he will."

"You make it sound so easy."

"The first thing you must do is humble yourself. And then pray that he opens his heart."

"OK. I'll do it tonight, Father. I really will."

"Good, Sarah. I will be praying for you both. Let me know what happens."

Sarah went upstairs and changed out of the sweat suit that comprised her work-from-home wardrobe and put on one of her better outfits. She styled her hair and even put on earrings.

"Going somewhere tonight?" Javier asked as he came through the door after work, exhausted.

"No," Sarah answered, innocently. "Actually, I thought I'd go sit on the patio and have a glass of wine. Care to join me?"

"But the game already started."

"Oh. Well, I guess I could sit down and watch some of it with you."

"But you hate TV. Especially sports."

Sarah laughed nervously. "True. I just thought it would be nice to be together."

"Where are the boys?"

"Upstairs doing homework."

Javier folded his arms across his chest. Something seemed strange. "What's going on, Sarah? What are you not telling me? Did you dent the car again? Wait a minute—did you lose your job?"

"No, no. That's not it at all. It's just...well, I've been thinking about things, Javier, and I realize now how wrong I was," Sarah blurted out. "The accident wasn't your fault. I know that now. I sincerely hope you can find it in your heart to forgive me."

Javier stood there, looking at her, not sure how he felt about this sudden repentance after two years. It seemed too little, too late.

"It's not that simple, Sarah," he finally managed. "You can't just say 'sorry' and think everything is going to be alright." He turned away, shaking his head.

"Please, Javier," Sarah said, following him into the living room, trying not to sound too desperate. "I'm sure we can work things out. I don't know what I'll do if you leave!"

"Sarah, I'm just not ready to talk about it right now. You're going to have to give me some time." He sat down on the couch, picked up the remote and turned on the game.

Feeling stung, Sarah retreated to the den. She didn't want their marriage to end, but she wasn't sure how they'd put things back together either. If Javier left the country, it was going to be difficult — probably impossible.

*I am not going to cry.*

She emailed Father George to tell him what happened.

"I did exactly what you said — I asked him to forgive me," Sarah wrote. "But it didn't turn out the way I hoped. He said he needs time."

Within minutes, there was a reply from Father George.

*"Remember the other part of what I told you: you have to pray and be patient, Sarah. Your marriage problems did not develop quickly and solving them is not going to happen quickly, either. I am praying for you both. Now stop worrying! Try saying this simple prayer: 'Jesus, I trust in You.'"*

Sarah stayed in the den, unwilling to go through the charade of normalcy for the boys' sake. She could hear them out in the living room, enjoying the game with Javier, whistling and cheering wildly. It helped to know that Father George was praying for her, but the uncertainty of what lay ahead still troubled her heart.

"I wish you were here, Dad. You always knew just what to say," Sarah said out loud, looking at the picture she kept on her desk of her parents at their 50th wedding anniversary. Someone told her once, she couldn't remember who, that people who have died can hear what their loved ones say out loud.

"I don't know if you can hear me or not, Dad," Sarah said softly, "but I need your prayers. I need your wisdom. Things have really fallen apart around here. I'm afraid."

## A Martyr's Crown

Picking up his journal, she began thumbing through the pages, hoping to find some word of consolation. The corner of the page dated April 1966 was dog-eared.

*Kathleen has forgiven me at last... I don't deserve her forgiveness, but she has given it. In some small way, I realize now just how great a gift God's forgiveness of us is... He loves us in spite of ourselves...*

Sarah was stunned by the entry. As far as she knew, the only disagreements her parents had were over politics. She turned back several pages in the journal, realizing she must have missed something.

*...I told Margaret, if Susan won't stop taking drugs, we'll have to send her away. We have younger children in the home to worry about.*

Then further on, another revelation:

*I told Susan I was sending her to a boarding school back East, a place that would help her straighten out her life, but I should have talked it over with Kathleen first. Susan got angry, said she didn't need our help, that she wasn't going to any reform school. Before I could talk sense into her, she ran away. We've looked everywhere, but she's gone. Kathleen won't even speak to me.... She's talking about going to stay with her mother in Chicago.*

Bits and pieces were coming back to her now as she read the journal: her parents' evasive answers when she asked them over the weeks and months where Susan was. Their nervousness every time the phone rang. The sound of the doorbell late one night, months later. Overhearing the police officer as he explained that he'd found Susan sleeping on a park bench across town.

Sarah remembered the way Susan looked the next morning: painfully thin, her once beautiful hair scraggly and lifeless. People at St. Margaret's must have known what happened, too, the way people in tight-knight communities tend to know each other's business. Sarah imagined her parents' embarrassment and sorrow over Susan's disappearance, the strain it must have caused on their marriage.

Benny interrupted her reverie.

"The game's over."

"Great. Did you make your lunch for tomorrow?"

"We're out of peanut butter."

"I'll put it on my list," Sarah answered. "You could pack a turkey sandwich, you know."

"Zach took the last piece."

Sarah got up to investigate. Benny was right. She reached into her purse to dig out lunch money for Benny and her running grocery list. As she pulled the notebook out of her bag, the holy card Father George had given her fell from its pages and fluttered to the floor. Sarah bent down and picked it up. She hadn't really looked at it since that day at the Christmas party for the refugee kids.

It was a picture of Jesus, dressed in a flowing white robe, with red and white rays emanating from His heart. Printed at the bottom were the words, "Jesus, I trust in You." *Wasn't that the prayer Father George had asked her to say?*

Trust in God; it wasn't something Sarah had ever really tried —not completely anyway. There was something scary about surrendering everything to Him, but even as that thought entered her mind, Sarah realized how preposterous it sounded. How could she possibly think that she was more capable of solving a problem than God?

She said goodnight to the kids and went back into the den. Javier had already gone upstairs and Sarah knew he was in no mood to talk. Kneeling down beside her desk, she closed her eyes and offered the most heartfelt prayer of her entire life.

"Dear God, I know I've made a lot of mistakes. I've really blown it down here and it looks like Javier might leave me. I don't know how to fix this mess, dear God, so I'm just going to give

## A Martyr's Crown

everything to You: my past, my present, my future—my marriage, all my problems and worries—everything. You're the only one who can save me."

She sat there in the dark and stillness of the den for a long time after that, wondering if God heard her prayer and if He really would salvage her marriage. She thought of Father George and all he had suffered for his faith in God.

*I don't have faith like that. I'm weak. I'm a failure!*

She drifted off to sleep in her chair in front of the computer, thinking of Father George's courage, of her father's love.

*They were in the backyard, working in the garden, digging in the soft, brown dirt under a robin's egg blue sky. The father turned and scooped something up with his gentle hands, the hands with the big blue veins that held hers when she was afraid.*

*"Look," he said to the little girl, holding out his hand for her to see.*

*"What are they, Daddy?"*

*"These are mustard seeds, the smallest seeds of all." He placed one of them in the girl's hand and she felt its smallness for herself.*

*"Jesus said that if you have faith the size of a mustard seed, nothing will be impossible for you."*

*"Nothing?"*

*"Nothing."*

Sarah awoke with a start. She could hear the boys upstairs, getting ready for school. She hurried up the stairs, hoping he would be there, but Javier was gone.

When she arrived at the office later on that morning, there was a small blue envelope sitting in the middle of her desk, her name and address penned in bold capital letters. Sarah slit open the envelope and found a letter from a Captain Peter Franklin of the Army National Guard.

*"Dear Ms. Castillo,"* the letter began, *"I served three tours of duty in Iraq and am now home in Phoenix with my wife and*

*children for what I hope will be a long break.*

"*I read your story about the Chaldean Catholic Church in Phoenix and would like to help. I tried to contact the pastor, Father George Rama, but have not heard back from him. Maybe he is suspicious of a U.S. soldier offering to help his community. I saw some terrible things when I was overseas and I really do want to do what I can to assist Father Rama's people. Would you please let him know I am serious? Sincerely, Capt. Peter C. Franklin.*"

Sarah folded the letter and placed it back in the envelope. It would be nice to give Father George some happy news. She was sure he heard enough of people's problems all day long.

There was an envelope from Dr. Emily Shallal, too, which Sarah assumed was probably a thank-you note for the story about the free medical clinic she founded.

*Dear Sarah,* the letter began, "*I'm writing to thank you for the wonderful article you wrote about our clinic. We've received many calls from doctors and nurses who would like to volunteer here.*

"*I also want to say that I was very moved by your story about the Chaldean refugee community. My husband's parents emigrated from Iraq in the 1950s. Please tell Father Rama that I would be happy to treat members of his church. I'm sure many of them are in need of medical services.*"

Two letters in one day commenting on an article and offering help.

"Nice way to start the day," Sarah said under her breath.

As she logged on to check her email, she saw there was something from Sholeh.

"*I saw your article about the Chaldeans, Sarah. It was just heartbreaking to read what these dear people have experienced. Andrew's youth group is looking for a service project and I was wondering if maybe they could do something out at the Chaldean church. What do you think? It would be great if you could be there with us since you know Father Rama. Maybe we can talk about it*

## A Martyr's Crown

*at the game tomorrow."*

Sarah had never become involved with a group or church after writing about them, but it was different with Father George. She saw in him a wisdom borne of suffering, the authenticity of a faith lived in the shadow of persecution. What began as a mere phone call for a quote was slowly blossoming into a friendship. Father George was trying to save her marriage, but it was more than that: he wanted to save her soul. And it needed saving, she realized. She'd wandered off the path somehow.

"The 'Hound of Heaven,'" Robert Murphy was fond of saying, "never tires in His pursuit of us. He will not give up until we fly to His love. Remember that, Sarah." Somewhere at home, in the crowded shelves that lined the walls of the den, was the book from her father that contained the stirring poem. She hadn't thought of it in years. Perhaps God had sent Father George into her life to pull her back from the precipice.

Her mind turned again to the image of the murdered baby, an innocent child torn from her mother's arms, and all the other innocent people who were inside the church the day the terrorists unleashed their fury.

She thought of Hanne, the baby's mother, and though she'd never done so at work before, Sarah closed her eyes for a moment and prayed, prayed that God would console this grieving mother in the agony of her loss.

A thought came to her then, as though a veil had been lifted. Although there was no way to make sense of the tragic loss of a child, there was an opportunity to see life differently, to realize its preciousness, to make the most of the days that remain.

*Whatever time I have left on this earth, dear God, let it be for good. Let me make the most of the gift of life. Let it be that when I'm gone from here, I will have brought some comfort to the voiceless and forgotten.*

When she opened her eyes, the first thing that came into her mind was a wish.

*If only I could reach out to Hanne, let her know that what happened to her and her baby is never far from my mind. I would tell her that I'm praying for her, that I know what it's like to lose a child. But it's impossible! She's 8,000 miles away in the middle of a war.*

♛ ♛ ♛ ♛ ♛ ♛

A Martyr's Crown

# Chapter 20
Mosul
Thursday, January 7, 2010

"Come in, come in," Yawsip cried when he saw them standing outside the front door. "So glad you could visit us. Margueritte, please go prepare our guests some tea," he said to his daughter.

They sat down in the family room, glad to finally be out of the car after circling the city streets, trying to figure out what to do next.

"These are trying times," Yawsip said. "Your family has been through so much," he added sympathetically. "How are you feeling?"

"I'm getting better, little by little," Fadi said, "but it's been difficult."

Hanne sat there beside him, eyes downcast, unable to say a word.

"We ran into some trouble this afternoon," Raad added. "We didn't know where to go, so after we drove around for a while, we thought of you."

"What sort of trouble?" Yawsip asked, his brow furrowed with concern. "What happened?"

"Some men started shooting at our car when we got back to Hanne and Fadi's apartment this afternoon," Raad explained.

"They were waiting for us, it seems."

Yawsip didn't know that Fadi was an interpreter for the Americans—Fadi never told anyone about it—but he instantly understood that they were in grave danger.

"You must stay with us tonight," Yawsip said firmly. "It is not safe for you to go back there. But you already know this of course," he added. Yawsip stroked his gray, well-trimmed beard. His friend's kids were in a dangerous spot.

Margueritte set the tray of tea down before them.

Fadi sighed in relief. "We figured you'd understand," he said. "I'm glad you were home."

"You'll be safe with us. Your wife's father was a dear friend of mine, God rest his soul."

"Thank you, Yawsip," Raad said, looking around the spacious room with its carved cherry wood furniture and elegant silk drapes. Yawsip had done well in business and had plenty of room for guests.

"My mother-in-law's home is too close to the apartment," Fadi explained. "We didn't want to lead anyone back there." He turned to Raad. "You're going to have to call Nora and tell her and Mariam not to open the door to anyone—absolutely no one! Do you understand? And call Saeed, too. He should stay there at the house with them tonight."

Raad nodded and headed to the kitchen to make the calls.

Fadi turned to Hanne. "Perhaps Margueritte can show you where you can lie down and rest for awhile, *azizta*," he said softly, squeezing her hand. "You look exhausted."

Margueritte nodded. "Come on, Hanne," she said, rising from her chair. "We'll go to my room where we can talk and then rest a bit."

Hanne stood up and followed Margueritte down a long corridor to the bedrooms. Fadi watched the two women go and waited until he heard a door close.

## A Martyr's Crown

"Yawsip," he said, "I can't tell you how much I appreciate this."

"Oh, please, it's nothing," Yawsip protested. "Hanne's father was like a brother to me." He leaned forward in his seat and looked Fadi in the eye. "I am so very sorry about your daughter. My family and I, we were not at Mar Addai that morning, but we heard about it from others. Such a terrible tragedy. I simply cannot understand how men can do such evil things."

Fadi looked down at his hands, afraid to speak, knowing his voice might break.

"Thank you," he finally said.

Yawsip shook his head. "These terrorists, they've got to be stopped. They're destroying our country. We are rid of Saddam but things here are worse than ever for Christians," he sighed. "Every day I hear of another family leaving. Soon there will be no Christians left in Iraq!"

"Things seemed better for a while after the elections," Raad said, "but there's still so much crime. And so many people out of work."

Fadi listened as the two men spoke, but his mind was really elsewhere. He knew time was not on his side. The sooner he could get back to the apartment, the sooner he could gather some of their things. Important papers. His laptop. A few items of clothing. That's if the men who were after him hadn't already broken in and taken everything. He and Hanne, he decided, were going to have to leave Iraq, and quickly.

He thought back to that last time he'd gone out with the Americans, just before the massacre at Mar Addai. The work he did for them was so much more than simply translating important documents or facilitating communication. They depended on him to be their eyes and ears—and often for their personal safety as well.

Back in November, Major Johnson asked him to accompany him to a former police station. A family was living in the vacant building, basically squatting there. The major needed to tell the family to move out, that he had people who could help them relocate.

No one came to the door at first, but Johnson kept knocking. Finally, the husband appeared and he didn't look too happy.

"You're going to have to leave," Major Johnson said. As Fadi translated Johnson's words, a restless crowd began to gather, murmuring, threatening. Fadi could sense the tension escalating in the throng. An elderly man approached and told him he thought something bad was about to happen.

"If we don't get out of here now, Johnson," Fadi told him, "things are going to get ugly. These people are mad enough to kill us, and I don't think we should stick around to find out."

They quickly turned and left. Fadi was sure they barely escaped with their lives that day.

He thought then of his friend, Ali. The last time they spoke, Ali was excited and happy because the paychecks he was earning as an interpreter were making things so much better for his family.

"My kids aren't hungry anymore," he told Fadi. "They don't cry themselves to sleep at night now. My wife, she worries about me, but she's thankful I have a job."

A few weeks later, the Humvee Ali was riding in hit a roadside bomb.

"Dead," Johnson told him. "Ali is dead." Dozens of translators had been killed or mutilated that way, blown to pieces.

His mind turned to the men who shot at their car that afternoon in the parking garage. Fadi heard that the insurgents took pictures of those they suspected of cooperating with the U.S. and posted the photos on the walls of local mosques, calling for their deaths. When they killed one, they drew a big red "X" over it. He wondered then if his own picture was on display somewhere.

He knew from the beginning that this interpreting work was dangerous, but now he realized that it wasn't just risky for him—

# A Martyr's Crown

Hanne was in danger, too.

"The neighbors have been asking why they never see you anymore," Hanne told him a couple days before the attack on Mar Addai. "I didn't know what I should say, but I told them you've been visiting your brother who is sick."

Perhaps they'd grown suspicious and followed him. It was only a matter of time until they devoured him—he was sure of it. One of his co-workers, Walid, told him what happened last year after a man threatened a group of interpreters who were waiting for a bus to the American base.

"We know where you're going and what you're doing, you traitors," the man snarled at them, "You better watch out!"

Two men in the group, deeply shaken, immediately went to the American embassy and asked for asylum. The next day, the bus that transported interpreters was demolished by a suicide bomber.

"Nothing left of them," Walid said, shaking his head, "just a burned-out bus and body parts." It was madness, a terrifying madness, this interpreting work for the Americans, though at the time he signed up, it didn't seem so. Now it was apparent that he'd have no choice but to leave Iraq.

Fadi leaned his head back and sank into the cushions of the overstuffed couch, weary. The pain in his side was returning. He wished then that he'd kept a few pills in his pocket for an emergency. He was beginning to sweat and he tried to calm himself, tried to block the pain. Raad and Yawsip were still talking politics.

As far as Fadi was concerned, all this talk was useless. He and his friends had grown up in the shadow of war and invasion, surrounded by destruction, danger and death. The tanks rolling through the streets. The buildings reduced to rubble. Soldiers and terrorists with machine guns. The roar of helicopters overhead. The stench of death in the air. He was sick of it all, sick of the fear and uncertainty—sick of the wasted lives and resources, the funerals.

America seemed to beckon to him. There in a new land, there was the promise of a better future, one far from the despair of war. Wasn't that what he wanted for Hanne, for them both? And what about their children? Surely they could try again to build a family, in a place where they wouldn't have to live in fear. Noor would always be their daughter in heaven, but perhaps God would bless them with new life again, a child they could hold in their arms once more. A child who would grow up in peace.

Watching Raad and Yawsip chat, he smiled and nodded politely at regular intervals, but in his mind, Fadi was slowly beginning to formulate a plan. The next morning he would have Raad drop Hanne and Nahida off at Mariam's house. He'd have to have trustworthy Iraqi security forces escort him back to the apartment to gather his and Hanne's things. He knew just the man to ask for help.

ש ש ש ש ש ש ש

A Martyr's Crown

# Chapter 21
Phoenix
Thursday, January 7, 2010

Sarah grabbed a coke from the fridge and stepped outside to call Father George. Sitting there on the patio swing in the cool air, she spied a bird's nest high in one of the graceful ash trees Javier planted when they first bought the house, years ago, in what now seemed like another life. In the springtime, the mourning doves built nests in the trees and Sarah liked to watch the mother birds swoop down to gather food for their babies who lay crying in the nest, awaiting their return. On this cold January day, the nest was empty, but doves still searched for food in the late afternoon sunshine.

Sarah thought of the people of Iraq, the cousins and parents and friends of those she'd seen at the candlelight vigil, and how they weren't able to enjoy the pleasure of a carefree afternoon, sitting in the sun, enjoying the beauty of nature. She had done a little research on the Internet and found images of Mosul, the city where the bloody attack on the church took place.

In some of the pictures she found, you could see the city had grown up beside the mighty Tigris River, a swath of blue against fields of green, the ancient source of water that allowed Iraqis to irrigate their fields. Other images showed armored tanks and helicopters, soldiers arresting insurgents, bombed out buildings. One heartbreaking photo showed a soldier carrying a little girl, injured and bleeding, through streets of rubble.

Out of the corner of her eye, Sarah glimpsed Reilly dashing across the lawn, headed straight toward a seemingly oblivious dove. In a fraction of a second, the tiny creature lifted her gray and white wings and ascended to the trees, sounding the note of alarm to the other birds. Sarah took another sip of her coke and wondered about the mother whose baby daughter was killed right in front of her at Mar Addai. *How is she coping? What's her story? Where is she?* Sarah could picture the poor baby's cherubic face and dark curls.

She found herself wondering about what kind of person, what kind of evil motivated an act so ruthless, so barbaric. For three nights after the vigil at Mar Ephrem, she'd had trouble sleeping, images of the murdered baby haunting her, tormenting her. She wanted to not only tell the world of the terrible injustice that had been done, she felt a force pulling her in, begging her to not look away, not avert her eyes, but to do something to help.

Tomorrow was the second anniversary of the day they'd lost Patrick. For two years now, she'd been struggling with her own grief, her own black hole of sorrow. But right in front of her was an entire people who had been persecuted for their faith, who'd lost countless loved ones in a bloody repression, generation upon generation. She remembered Father George's words: "No one seems to know we exist."

Sarah shook her head, wondering what had gotten into her. Didn't she have enough to do with three kids, a job and an unhappy husband threatening to leave? She took a last sip of her drink and dialed Father George.

"Ready for some good news, Father George?"

"Things are better with Javier?"

"Not yet. But that's not why I'm calling."

## A Martyr's Crown

"Oh. So what is the news?"

"Well, I've been getting some feedback on the story I wrote about your church."

" What do you mean? What is it, this feedback?"

"Letters. And email. Remember my friend Sholeh, the Muslim convert who gave you the donation? She wanted me to give you a call."

"She did? Why?"

"Well, her son is involved in a youth group at St. Clare Church here in Phoenix and they are looking for a service project. She was thinking that maybe there was something they could do for your community."

There was a slight pause on the other end of the line. Sarah sensed he was stalling for time, and then it occurred to her that he might be suspicious of an Iranian-born, former Muslim offering assistance.

"I would have to think about what kind of project we could have them do," Father George said cautiously. "This would take some planning."

"Sholeh is really a very devout Catholic," Sarah said, certain that Sholeh undoubtedly had a much stronger Catholic faith than she did. "She was very touched by your story and wants to help somehow. She feels a kinship with you, being from the Middle East. And I've heard good things about St. Clare's youth group."

"Well, it is true we could use some help around here," Father George said cautiously. God knew that was true. But who was this Iranian woman? "Maybe the two of you could attend a Mass out here at Mar Ephrem. We could talk afterward."

"I'll talk to Sholeh and see what she'd like to do," Sarah said, "but I know she'll want to come."

"Perhaps Monday night will work," Father George said. "I will celebrate the 6:30 p.m. Mass on that night."

"I have something else to tell you about, too," Sarah said.

"You discovered more Iranians to help us?" Father George quipped.

"Actually, it's an American soldier," Sarah said as she dropped her soda can in the recycle bin. "I got a letter from an Iraq war veteran who said he liked the article and wanted to help you, too."

"I think this soldier, he maybe called here and left a message."

"Exactly. He said he did and he understands that you might think it strange that a soldier would be contacting you."

"Well, it did make me wonder a little. I do not know why he would call here."

"I don't know this guy, Father George, but he wrote a nice letter," Sarah added helpfully. "His name is Peter Franklin and he said something about wanting to assist your community. Seems like that might be something you need," Sarah said kiddingly.

"Would he be a carpenter or a millionaire perhaps? Our roof is really leaking now, and the rain yesterday, it made things worse. Father Michael and I had to purchase more buckets. And we need to order new catechism books for the kids. This morning, I discovered there is something wrong with our church van. So yes, money or a carpenter would come in handy, that is for sure."

"Sounds like we'll have a lot to talk about."

"So you will come?"

"I'll talk to Sholeh about it at the game tonight. Put us down as a definite maybe."

"OK, Sarah. Let me know what you two decide. But tell me, how are things at home with Javier?"

"I've been doing some thinking, Father George. I've realized something."

"Oh? And what is this you realize?"

"I understand now that I've wasted a lot of time on bitterness. My birthday is coming up next month and I guess I'm thinking about getting older. I want to use whatever time I have left to show God that I love Him, that I'm sorry," Sarah's voice began to break

## A Martyr's Crown

with the raw emotion of the admission. "I'm not sure how, Father George, but I want to help you, and I don't mean just this project with Sholeh."

"God has touched your heart then. This is good news."

"I saw Him in you, Father George. Thank you for showing me His face."

"I am only His instrument, His humble servant, and I have many weaknesses. Come to our Mass, Sarah. You will find Him there, too. Bring your whole family."

"The Aramaic might be too much for them."

"This will not be a problem. I celebrate Mass in English at 11 a.m. on Sundays. Will I see you there?"

"I'll do my best, Father."

※ ※ ※ ※ ※ ※ ※

Sarah sat close to Javier during the basketball game that night, holding his hand. Little by little, she was trying to break down the massive wall of ice that stood between them.

At first, he had remained distant, refusing to budge. She started sending him brief text messages or emails during the day, just to remind him that she was thinking of him and trying to make amends. One night, she crept out to the garage and taped a note on the steering wheel of his car so he'd find it the next morning before work.

*Javier, you are the love of my life. I don't know what I'd do without you. Let's start over.*

On January 8, the two-year anniversary of the day they lost Patrick, the two of them met at the cemetery at lunch time. Sarah brought two balloons for them to release—green, Patrick's favorite color. They stood there, arm in arm, and staring down at his grave, feeling the weight of their grief, the expanse of the distance between them.

"Let's say an Our Father," Sarah whispered, so they did. Finishing, they let go of the balloons and stood, craning their necks and watching the two emerald green orbs float through the cloudless sky until they disappeared in the glare of the midday sun. Sarah leaned her head on Javier's shoulder. After a few moments of silence, she turned to Javier, wanting to say just the right words.

"Javier, I don't know how I would have survived these last two years without you by my side," Sarah said, looking straight into his eyes. "You've been a good husband to me and I know I hurt you. Will you forgive me, please?"

Javier put his arms around Sarah and held her close. "But you were right, Sarah. It *was* my fault. Patrick would still be here if I had gotten that airbag inspected. I'll never forgive myself for that."

"Don't think like that. You're not the one who got drunk and got behind the wheel. Patrick did that all on his own. You can't blame yourself for what happened. All I know is, I don't want to go through the rest of this life without you. I can't," Sarah said, her voice breaking.

"I've got to get back to work now," Javier said wearily. "We'll talk about it later."

Driving back to the office, Sarah wondered if he'd already made travel plans. Maybe he just needed a trip home to Puerto Rico, to see his mom and rest a little. He deserved that, didn't he? But she didn't like it. Not one bit.

שׁ שׁ שׁ שׁ שׁ שׁ שׁ

A Martyr's Crown

# Chapter 22
Mosul
Friday, January 8, 2010

Raad was going to drive Fadi to police headquarters in Mosul so they could get an escort back to the apartment. He'd already discreetly called Major Johnson, one of his American contacts, to explain that he'd been discovered and needed to leave the country.

"Make sure you ask for Lieutenant Hamdani," Johnson said. "He's trustworthy. Tell him you worked for me."

Johnson still felt terrible about Wisam, the interpreter who worked with his team before Fadi. The poor man had disappeared, never to be heard from again.

Every now and then, Wisam's wife would call. "Have you heard from him? Anything at all?"

He could hear children crying in the background.

"Sorry, ma'am. We haven't seen or heard from him in over a year."

Johnson wanted to make sure that didn't happen to Fadi, who had proved to be not only highly skilled, but fiercely loyal. Once the insurgents found out that an Iraqi was cooperating with the Americans, he or she was doomed.

"There's a lot of paperwork involved, Fadi," Johnson told him. "I heard that only 50 interpreters a year get one of those special visas you'll need. If you get one, Hanne does, too."

"What do I have to do to get the visa? Whatever it takes, I will find a way."

"Make absolutely sure you get your passports and birth certificates from the apartment," Major Johnson told him. "Oh, and your marriage certificate, too. I sure hope you have that stuff in a safe place."

Fadi thought about that. He knew there was a strong possibility that the insurgents had ransacked his apartment if they knew he lived somewhere in the building. Thank God he didn't leave their important papers out in the open. Right after he'd started working with the U.S. forces about a year and half ago, he'd decided one day to put his and Hanne's passports and birth certificates in a place they'd never be found if their apartment was burglarized.

He remembered Hanne's surprise when she found him kneeling in the back of their closet one afternoon.

"What on earth are you doing in there, Fadi?" she'd asked in surprise.

Fadi pulled out a crate of old textbooks. Beside him on the floor were the passports, birth certificates, a few other important papers and a thick wad of cash.

"We need a safe place to keep these things, *azizta* ," he told her. "Just in case."

"In case of what?" she asked, nervously running her fingers through her hair.

"You know how dangerous it is in Mosul now. So many break-ins, robberies, kidnappings. We can't afford to lose these things," he said as he placed the documents and cash in her hands.

"Where am I supposed to hide all this?"

"Well, I was thinking you could cut a hole in the lining of this old winter coat that was in here with all these books. We'll put our things inside, and then you can sew it back up. I doubt anyone will be interested in a shabby old coat underneath 'A Key to Ancient

## A Martyr's Crown

Languages, Fifth Edition.'"

Hanne laughed as she took the coat from him and examined the lining. "It's definitely not on my reading list. Alright, let me get my sewing basket."

Today he would dig out the old coat, rip open the seam and retrieve their stash. He started thinking about the other things they would need for their new life in America and what he could jam into a couple suitcases.

Fadi sipped his coffee and decided he would take Hanne aside after breakfast and explain everything. Hanne was smart, and he knew he would need to tell her exactly what he was planning before he left for the police station. She would no doubt be upset, even angry. But after their brush with the insurgents yesterday, he knew she would understand precisely how serious all this was and that they really had no other choice.

Hanne was helping Margueritte and her mother finish cleaning up the breakfast dishes when Fadi decided to make his move.

"Hanne, dear, we need to talk," he whispered in her ear.

Hanne nervously dried her hands on a towel and followed him to the living room. Yawsip and Raad were still sitting at the kitchen table, talking and recounting stories from years gone by.

"Raad and I are going back to the apartment with the police this morning, Hanne," he began. "There's no easy way to say this. We're in serious danger and we need to leave the country. We've got to get out of here, Hanne. I've already spoken to the Americans."

Hanne covered her mouth with her hand. "Oh, Fadi," she said softly. She sat down on the couch and covered her face with her hands. "I can't believe this is happening!"

Fadi sat down beside her on the couch and took her hand. How he loved this woman. He hated having to tear her from her family and all she'd ever known, but he just didn't see any other solution.

"I talked to the soldier I was working with and he told me who to ask for at the police station. They'll escort me to the apartment and Raad and I will gather our belongings." He put his arm around Hanne, knowing how hard this was for her.

"We have to tell my family. We can't just leave without telling them."

"Of course, *azizta,* of course. Yawsip will drop you off at your mom's house and then I'll meet you there. But not until I have our things and we're ready to go. Tomorrow we'll go to Baghdad to arrange everything."

"Baghdad?"

"We'll need to go to the American embassy there to do all the paperwork and pay the fee for the visas we'll need."

"There's a fee? After all you've done for them?"

"Remember that money we hid? That should cover it. And the Americans will help us once we get to the U.S."

"I suppose we could stay with my aunt in Baghdad while we get that all worked out," Hanne said, brushing away tears. "She's not too far from the embassy."

"That would be good. It might take a few days to get the papers in order. There are forms to be filled out, papers to sign. And they're going to interview us, too."

"But why do they need to interview us? How will I know what to say?"

"They want to make sure we're not troublemakers or terrorists, I suppose."

"What about all our things? Our furniture? Our clothes?"

"We're only going to take our essentials, Hanne. We can't take much on the plane and we certainly can't afford to ship it. We'll let Nahida and Nora take the rest. Who knows? Maybe they'll join us in America someday!"

Hanne rested her head on Fadi's shoulder, trying to absorb it all. They were leaving Iraq, leaving their loved ones, their home…it all seemed so sudden.

"Fadi, *aziza*, there's one thing I want to make sure you get from the apartment."

"I know—our wedding pictures. Right?"

"Well of course! But there's something else, too," Hanne said, closing her eyes. She swallowed hard. "Remember to bring Noor's pink blanket, the one *Yemmi* made."

"Of course. The blanket. I'll make sure to get it," Fadi said, making a mental note. "Look, Hanne, I know this is difficult. I wish there were another way. But we really don't have any other choice."

"I know. I don't want anything to happen to you. I just… yesterday was so scary…" Hanne's voice trailed off.

"Definitely. Thank God we got away," Fadi said, taking her face in his hands. "Leaving like this—it's not the way things should be, but it's just the way things are." Fadi rose from the couch and took her hand. "I'll see you at *Yemmi's* later."

Hanne forced herself to smile. She would try to be strong for her husband—she knew he was doing this for both of them. Fadi kissed her tenderly, then went to get Raad.

As they drove to the police station, Fadi slouched down in the seat and pulled his hat down over his eyes, thinking about all the things Major Johnson had told him he needed to get to the U.S.

"You're going to have to translate your marriage certificate and your birth certificates, too," Johnson told him, "Oh, and the passports. They won't accept anything unless it's in English. Think you can handle that?"

"You know I can. I just hope they didn't take my laptop. If they know where we live, they may have gotten into our apartment!"

"Yeah, but your relatives must have a computer you can use, don't they?"

"Of course. I'd just hate to lose that laptop,"

"As long as we don't lose you, Fadi. That's the main thing."

The Americans wouldn't consider his application unless he had all the required documentation. Fadi pulled an old envelope from the glove compartment of the car and began scribbling some notes, making a list of all the items they were going to need.

Johnson explained that the American government did everything according to the fiscal year, which began back in October. Fadi hoped to God there was still one of those 50 special visas available. There was no way he was staying in Iraq. If they had to, they'd go to Greece or Turkey for a while and file again in October.

When they arrived at police headquarters, Fadi asked to see Lieutenant Hamdani, the man Johnson recommended. A short, burly man, Hamdani ushered them into a small, windowless office to discuss details.

"Major Johnson called and told me you'd be coming in," Hamdani said briskly. "I have some officers who will escort you to the apartment and stand guard while you gather your things. I only ask that you do so as quickly as possible. These men are needed badly and I'm doing this as a favor to Johnson."

"I understand, Lieutenant," Fadi said. "My brother-in-law will help me. I'm thinking we'll be done in under an hour."

"Fine," Hamdani said gruffly. "I'll let my men know you'll be leaving here shortly. Johnson said something about a police certificate you needed."

"Right. I need something from you stating that I haven't been under investigation and that your men haven't arrested me."

"We already looked you up of course. There's no evidence of that sort of thing. I'll put something together for you."

"Thank you, Lieutenant."

Hamdani nodded. "Be ready to leave here in 15 minutes then. I'll send my men ahead of you to block off the entrance to the apartment building and secure the premises. You can wait here while I prepare the certificate."

Hamdani shut the door behind him. Raad turned to Fadi. "So

## A Martyr's Crown

this is it. You're really leaving us."

"We have no choice. You know that."

Raad shifted in his seat and frowned. He would miss Hanne, of course, but he'd also miss Fadi, who had become like a brother to them all. Fadi was right though—they were out of options.

Hamdani returned shortly with the certificate and handed it to Fadi. "A couple of my men will walk you to your car. They'll follow you back to the apartment now."

"Thank you, Lieutenant," Fadi said. "I appreciate your help with all this."

"Good luck," Hamdani told him. "You're going to need a lot of that these next few days."

As Raad drove them to the apartment, he kept checking the rearview mirror to make sure the police were still following them. The last thing he wanted to do was lose their bodyguards.

Fadi looked out the window, realizing this would be his last day in Mosul. He saw two scrawny looking boys walking along the street, their threadbare clothes worn and faded. The people of his city had suffered so much and he wondered if they would ever know peace. As much as he loved his homeland, Fadi was thankful they were leaving. He only wished they had Noor to take with them.

Noor. When they drove past Mar Addai, Fadi shuddered. The church was still closed. He would never step inside its walls again to confess, to pray. Perhaps that was for the best. The ordeal he'd endured was forever fresh in his mind, no matter how much he tried to bury it. The men who did this to them—how *could* they? They must have killed their consciences long ago, succumbed to the poison of hatred. To live in a country where one had to endure such cruelties was intolerable, Fadi thought to himself. Better to leave. Better to turn away from such horrors.

A scraggly stray dog, sniffing at the broken bottles and trash that littered the street corner caught his eye. As Raad came to a stop at the corner, the dog turned and wagged his tail, hoping for a treat.

"Sorry, boy," Fadi said, even though the windows were tightly shut.

When at last Raad pulled up to the apartment building, they could see that the police had already barricaded the entrance. Raad drove up to the barrier and rolled down his window. Fadi leaned forward.

"Fadi Yacoub?" the police officer inquired, nodding at the police escort vehicle behind them.

"That's me."

"I've got men patrolling the building. They haven't seen any troublemakers so far. I'll have a couple officers walk you to your apartment. You can park over there," he said, pointing to a nearby space. "We'll keep an eye on your vehicle."

The power to the area was out again—an irritating fact of life in Iraq—so the elevators weren't working. Fadi dreaded climbing the stairs to the second floor, knowing it would feel more like the fifth. But what else could he do? He had to get their belongings, especially the passports, or they wouldn't be allowed to leave the country.

The two police officers walked up the stairs to the apartment with Fadi and Raad, each keeping their hand on their holsters. Fadi, panting, paused every few steps to catch his breath. When at last they reached the second floor and came to number 204, Fadi slipped his key in the lock and pushed open the door. He stood back and gasped.

שׁשׁשׁשׁשׁשׁשׁ

### A Martyr's Crown

# Chapter 23
Phoenix
Saturday, January 9, 2010

Sarah was already at the kitchen table reading the newspaper when Javier came down. He looked dejected.

"Morning," Sarah said brightly as she turned the page. "Some eggs on the stove there if you want, honey."

"Thanks." Javier took a plate from the cabinet and put a couple of pieces of bread in the toaster. He sat down at the table across from Sarah and sighed. She slid the sports section his way.

"I called my mom," Javier said.

Sarah froze. "Oh?" she said, trying to sound casual.

"I told her I was coming to stay with her for a while."

Sarah's heart sank. So he was going to go through with it after all, going to go back to Puerto Rico.

"What did she say?"

"Actually, she told me not to come."

"She did? Why?"

"She was disappointed that I wasn't bringing you and the kids to visit, too. She said she was doing some traveling herself and that she was leaving soon to visit my brother in Florida. She said she'd rather come here, that it was easier for one person to travel than five."

"So she's coming here? When?" Sarah's heart skipped a beat.

"She said she wants to be here in May for Zach's graduation."

Sarah was stunned. She folded up the newspaper. The toaster popped and Javier got up to retrieve the strawberry jam from the fridge. When he turned around again, Sarah could see his face had changed. Softened. She stood up, took off her reading glasses and went to him. They stood like that for a moment, not knowing what to say.

"I'm glad you're not going to Puerto Rico," Sarah said softly.

"Are you sure about that?"

"Of course I am. You think I'm crazy enough to try and raise a houseful of teenage boys without you?"

"Oh, so you only want me around because of the kids?" Javier retorted.

"I didn't mean it like that," Sarah said hurriedly. "I don't want you to leave, Javier—not now. Not ever."

"You've been mad at me for a long time. And I've been mad at myself. Not an hour went by during the last two years that I didn't wish I had done things differently."

"I know. I'm sorry. I feel terrible about the things I've said, the way I've acted. I told you that. I said I was sorry, didn't I?" Sarah could feel tears of regret stinging her eyes.

"You blaming me—that really hurts. You know how much I loved Patrick, that I'd give anything to have him back here with us!"

"I know you would. So would I. It sounds stupid, but maybe I just needed someone to blame."

"And I was the most convenient target?"

"I guess so, yeah."

"So what's changed? What made you suddenly feel differently about it?" Javier looked doubtful and Sarah noticed the way he folded his arms across his chest as if to say, "Prove it."

"Listen, Javier, I was wrong, OK? I admit it. I'm seeing things differently now."

"Meaning what?"

"It's strange, but ever since I met Father George, I've had this desire to change my life, to return to God. I don't want to waste any more time on anger and bitterness. It's like I realize now that I have a choice."

"A choice about what? Patrick is gone. There's nothing we can do to change that."

"That's true. We can't change what happened. But we do have a choice to make about how to spend the rest of our lives. We can let this sorrow and anger destroy us and break up our marriage. Or, we can choose to honor Patrick's memory by spending the time we have left on earth doing something good."

"Such as?"

"Helping Father George and his people, the Chaldeans. There are so many needs there, Javier, so many people fleeing the violence and persecution in their homeland."

"I don't see what any of that has to do with Patrick. And honestly, I'm not sure I'll ever feel the same about us," Javier said as he turned away and went to sit at the table.

Sarah's heart was pumping faster as she scrambled to think of a way to turn the conversation in a more positive direction. She sat down across from him as he spread the jam on his toast.

"I think maybe it might help us if we could channel our energy into serving others. Actually, Father George invited us to come to his Mass tomorrow."

"But I thought you said their Masses were in Aramaic! We won't understand it."

"He said they have an English Mass. I say we should go. Besides, it would be a good experience for the kids. It might open their eyes to something new."

Benny came down the stairs just then, rubbing his eyes.

"What would be a good experience for us?"

"You're up early," Sarah said, surprised.

"I was hungry," Benny replied.

After breakfast, Sarah ventured outside and surveyed the carpet of yellow and brown leaves that covered the lawn. Grabbing a rake from the shed, she set to work under the clear, cold January sky.

"There's something about time spent working outdoors," Sarah's dad used to say. "It's as though you can feel the breath of God, His presence in creation."

Sarah supposed it was true. It had been a long time since she cared about seeking the presence of God, about finding Him in those ordinary moments of life that could at once become extraordinary when transformed by grace. She felt Him, His tenderness, in the gust of wind that blew the leaves from the trees and cooled her brow as she raked the leaves into a pile.

"I am but a speck in this vast universe, dear God. I've let You down so many times," Sarah said as she leaned against the trunk of the towering ash tree. "I'm nothing like Father George—but still You love me. I know that now." Tears sprang to her eyes then, tears of regret over the years wasted. "Use me, Lord. Do whatever You will with me. I'm done wandering. But please, save my marriage."

ש ש ש ש ש ש ש

Javier looked up from the college football game he was watching on television. "Going somewhere?"

"A walk. Want to join me? I'm just taking the path through the neighborhood," Sarah said as she filled a water bottle.

"I guess so. The game's a blow-out anyway. And I could definitely use the exercise." He stood up from the couch and went to find his old pair of Nikes.

Sarah gathered her hair in a pony tail and plucked her sunglasses from the counter. She couldn't remember the last time she and Javier

## A Martyr's Crown

had gone for a walk together. Perhaps their cold war was coming to an end after all. She only hoped it wasn't too late.

Maybe they'd have a chance to talk about a few things. Sarah was thinking of asking him to take a look at Father George's van. It was probably just a simple repair that was needed. She was sure that once she explained to Javier how many needs the Chaldeans had, he would want to do something. One thing was for sure: the man never turned down a request for help. She was thankful her mother-in-law told him not to come.

♛ ♛ ♛ ♛ ♛ ♛ ♛

# Chapter 24
Mosul
Saturday, January 9, 2010

"Unbelievable!" Fadi said as he looked around at the ransacked apartment. "Look at this place!"

"Thank God you weren't home," Raad said, examining the overturned furniture and broken fixtures.

They stood there in the doorway for a moment, surveying the damage. Whoever the intruders were, they'd destroyed the furniture, punched holes in the walls and scattered trash everywhere in their diabolical fury.

"They took the television."

"And my laptop."

Stepping over the debris, they threaded their way to the bedroom to pack. The dresser drawers had been yanked out, their contents dumped all over the floor.

"Makes it easier to pack, I suppose, seeing all the clothes at once," Fadi said ruefully as he stooped to pick up an armload. Beneath the pile he discovered pieces of the olivewood crucifix his parents had given him, the one that always hung on the wall over their bed, smashed to bits. They were glad Hanne was not there to see what had become of the place. Especially when they found the picture in the hallway.

## A Martyr's Crown

Someone had taken a can of red spray paint and made a big, ugly "X" over the framed portrait of their wedding day. *Kafir*, infidel, had been scrawled in huge letters on the wall over the picture. Fadi snorted. The nerve of these people. Behaving like wild animals and then accusing others of being beasts.

He saw the door to the closet standing open and the old textbooks strewn all over the floor. Holding his breath, he looked inside. Clothes had been pulled down and scattered. Fadi dug through the pile of books and came up with the old, tattered coat.

"Those geniuses may have taken my laptop, but at least they didn't find my secret stash," he told Raad. "I can always replace a computer, but this stuff, not so easily. See if you can find a knife or scissors in the kitchen to cut this open,"

Raad slipped on a puddle in the kitchen and stumbled on an overturned chair. He fell to the floor with a loud thud.

"Hey! What's going on back there?" one of the police officers called out.

"Oh, it's nothing, officers," Raad answered. "The floor was wet in here and I slipped. They left the freezer open and something must have melted."

Opening a drawer, he fished out a pair of scissors for Fadi.

Fadi could feel the papers and wad of cash through the lining of the coat and carefully cut along the seam. He sighed in relief as he pulled out their passports and marriage certificate. And the cash. He was definitely going to need the cash.

The two officers were still standing by the front door, keeping an eye out for trouble. Fadi could hear the chatter and squawking of their radios and knew he didn't have much time left.

"You almost done in there?" one of the men asked, rather testily.

"A few more minutes, please," Fadi replied. "There are a couple suitcases under the bed there, Raad," he said, pointing.

Raad got down on the floor, reached under the bed, and pulled out two worn suitcases, the ones that had belonged to Fadi's parents. He laid them on the bed and unzipped them, then followed Fadi around the apartment as he decided what to throw in.

Fadi grabbed some clothing from the floor and hurriedly piled it in the luggage. He went into the room where Noor's cradle stood—they'd left it just as it was before that terrible morning at Mar Addai—and picked up the delicate pink blanket Mariam had made for her. He stood there holding its exquisite softness for just a moment, thinking of her, of what they'd done to her and what they'd tried to do to him. Grimacing, he folded the blanket carefully and carried it over to the suitcase.

What else? What else could he quickly toss in the suitcase to make their journey and their new life more bearable? How did you pack up your life in less than an hour?

Fadi grabbed a plastic bag and deposited some toiletries and all of Hanne's cosmetics, some socks and underwear for both of them. He looked around for the jewelry box that was usually kept on top of the dresser.

"Can you think of anything else?" Raad asked, looking around at the disarray.

"I'm trying to find that cross Mariam gave her at Christmas. God only knows what they would have done with it."

"Ha! Sell it, of course. They're as greedy as any other criminal, no doubt."

Walking around to the other side of the bed, Fadi stumbled on the splintered jewelry box. They'd dumped the contents all over the floor. There was no cross to be found.

"You're right—it's gone. Let's get out of here."

Raad picked up both suitcases. "We're ready," he told the officers.

*I'll never step foot in here again,* Fadi thought to himself as they made their way down the stairs, but there wasn't time to waste getting sentimental. They needed to get out of the country, fast. He hoped to God it was still possible.

A Martyr's Crown

# Chapter 25
Phoenix
Sunday, January 10, 2010

"Are you serious? Thomas asked. "Do we have to?"

"Absolutely," Sarah said, giving Thomas her no-nonsense look.

"Why can't we just go to St. Clare's?" Zach moaned.

"Come on now. It's just one Sunday. Father George would like us to visit his church. The 11 o'clock Mass is in English. And they have food in the hall afterward. You like food, right?" The boys exchanged glances.

"Cool."

They sat up near the front, in the third pew. Sarah passed copies of the missal to the boys and Javier so they could follow along with the prayers of the Mass, which were different from the ones in the Roman-rite Mass.

"Jesus is telling us in today's Gospel how important it is for us to forgive, that being at peace with others should come *before* we worship," Father George said as he began his homily.

Sarah stole a glance at Javier. He was still awake, she noted. The poor man worked so hard that as soon as he sat down and got comfortable in a church or movie theater, he was prone to falling asleep. After two minutes of Father George's homily, he was still conscious, a tribute to either Father's preaching or Javier's second cup of coffee.

"I wonder how many of you teens out there have ever had an argument with your parents?" Father George said as he looked out over his parishioners. Some of the kids shifted in their seats or looked down at their feet.

Sarah thought of Patrick and some of the shouting matches they'd had over his drinking and smoking. How she regretted the harsh words, the slammed doors, the loud and angry voices. In her mind's eye, she could see Javier pounding his fist on the table, furiously, to no avail. The kid wouldn't listen.

What she wouldn't give to have one more night with Patrick, one more chance to tell him that she loved him, no matter what. That he was her son, no matter the heartache he'd caused. In spite of herself, she felt tears pooling in her eyes.

"How many of you parents have had arguments with your teens? Sworn and screamed at them? And you married couples out there: how many of you came here this morning and are not even speaking to each other?"

There was an uncomfortable silence throughout the church as Father George paused for effect, then spoke quietly:

"We do not deserve His mercy, yet He is always ready to offer us forgiveness anyway, always standing at the door, waiting for us to be reconciled with Him. And this is our model for family life. God is not calling us to be *perfect* families—He is calling us to be *holy* families."

Javier reached over and took Sarah's hand. She was blinking away tears now and couldn't take her eyes off Father George.

"My brothers and sisters, what would happen in our families, our communities today if people chose forgiveness instead of revenge?

"Forgiveness—it brings peace. Mercy is the great gift of God given to us, and He wants us to be merciful to others," Father George said. "Even when it seems impossible. Especially then."

## A Martyr's Crown

Sarah looked up at him. Father George was repeating what her father's journal said, that forgiveness brings peace. But how could Father George forgive what the terrorists did to him? *If he can forgive, then I can forgive.*

"Right now, let us all close our eyes and think of someone we need to forgive. Let us ask God to help us let go of this anger."

Father George thought of his captors, called to mind their faces. And in a moment of grace, he surrendered his burden once again, prayed to God for the strength to forgive what they had done to him in their fury.

Sarah closed her eyes and thought of Javier, big-hearted Javier, who'd known her since she was 19, back in college. Their marriage started out well, and they'd had the four boys in rapid succession.

Then, everything seemed to fall apart. They couldn't control Patrick, their firstborn. His wild teen years began driving a wedge between them and his death shattered their lives. It was true: until just a few days ago, Sarah blamed Javier for the accident. She knew now how unfair that was, how unreasonable. Javier loved Patrick; he was as devastated by the loss as she was. But instead of comforting him, she'd turned on him.

She regretted that now. She apologized to him the other day, but she could still feel the distance between them. Deep down, she knew she still hadn't let go of all the feelings completely. And Javier was still aloof, still hiding behind the wall that had grown up between them since Patrick's death. Father George's words made her realize how self-righteous and cruel she'd been to judge Javier. Sarah closed her eyes and prayed from the heart, feeling layers of pain melting away.

"Help me to let go of any leftover anger, Lord. And help me to remember how many times You have forgiven me," Sarah prayed.

On their way home after the Mass, Sarah decided to ask Javier about fixing Father George's van.

"Do you think you might have time next weekend to work on a

vehicle for someone?"

Javier raised his eyebrows. "Your mom's car needs work again? I just did the brakes last month. The car seemed fine."

"Not Mom. It's Father George. He told me their church van has been acting up. I was wondering if you might take a look at it. You know how it is: mechanics can take advantage of people who don't know about cars."

"Definitely. And I'm guessing Father George is not independently wealthy."

"Not exactly."

"Alright. Tell him I'll take a look at it. It might be something very simple."

"Good. I'll let him know. He'll be happy. Thank you, Javier."

He almost smiled.

*The old Javier is in there somewhere. He must still love me, even now,* Sarah thought to herself as she watched him. *I hope he's not still thinking about leaving us.* There had to be some way to rekindle their marriage.

"Do you ever feel like picking up your guitar and singing anymore?" Sarah asked, looking at how the sorrow of the last two years had etched lines around his eyes.

"Not really," Javier sighed. "I don't even have calluses on my fingertips anymore. It would be hard to start over again. And work—there's always work to do."

"But maybe it would do your heart good to take out the old Gibson. It used to make you so happy. I still remember the first time we met, and I saw that guitar strapped to your back," Sarah said. She could picture him with the humble guitar and the stack of books, the way he smiled at her when he asked if she needed help.

"You mean the day I fixed your car?"

"Remember how hot it was that day? It was the first day of the semester and the traffic was insane."

"I could tell just by looking that you didn't know what to do."

## A Martyr's Crown

"You're not impugning my mechanical abilities now, are you?" Sarah said with a laugh. They both knew that even Benny was better at putting things together than Sarah.

"What got me was that you were standing there with the hood propped up, looking at the engine, but I knew you didn't have a clue what to do next."

"It's a good thing you were walking home and stopped to help me or we might not even be here," Sarah said solemnly.

Javier remained silent, thinking about what she'd said. Life was like that—you never knew what was around the next corner.

"It's strange," Sarah said, looking out the window, admiring the mountains in the distance, "but there's just something about Father George and his community that's tugging on my heart and won't let go. It's like I'm being drawn in there, and I can't really explain it. Wasn't it nice going to Mass up there today?"

"You always did have a soft spot for outsiders."

"So you're finally admitting that it wasn't my column in *University Times* that captured your heart?

There it was, the sheepish grin. The one from before their lives changed.

Later that afternoon, they sat on the patio, watching the sunset.

"Javier, I was thinking about what Father George said today. And I'm sorry for...well, for blaming you the way I did, for the way I acted. That was cruel." Sarah took Javier's hand. "It wasn't your fault. I know you didn't mean for it to happen." Tears began to fill her eyes.

Javier squeezed her hand. "It's OK, Sarah. I probably would have reacted the same way. We were both angry and confused. The thing is, I miss him now more than ever," Javier said with a sigh. "What I wouldn't give to go back and do things differently."

"Same here," Sarah said. "I can't believe he's been gone two years. In some ways, it feels longer."

They sat there in silence for a while, watching as purple and pink clouds cloaked the setting sun. There were simply no words, even now, to express the depth of the loss they knew. Patrick's death had left a gaping hole in their hearts, one that would always be there.

"It's like my dad used to say, though, and I guess there's some wisdom in it. 'It's the card we've been dealt.' We can't keep looking back or we'll never be able to move forward," Sarah said, shaking her head. "Even as I say it, it seems impossible."

"You've been reading his journal every night, haven't you?"

Sarah nodded. "It's almost like I can hear his voice when I read those pages."

Javier took the last sip of his beer and set the bottle down on the table.

"I wonder what our kids will think of us when we're gone. Like, what will they treasure? What will they find of ours to remind them of us?"

They sat there in the twilight, considering the possibilities. What would the children cherish? An article Sarah had written in the paper? Javier's old tool box? They were in their late forties, probably past the midpoint of their earthly existence.

What were they doing with their lives to make a difference in the world? To teach their kids about what really mattered? Maybe they could move forward, in spite of their heartache, and do something good with whatever time they had left.

*What would it be?* Sarah wondered. Whatever it was, maybe she and Javier could do it together. And that's when she heard it, a faint whisper in her heart: *Father George will show you what you ought to do. Listen to him.*

שׁ שׁ שׁ שׁ שׁ שׁ

A Martyr's Crown

# Chapter 26
Mosul
Monday, January 11, 2010

Hanne and Fadi stayed up far into the night talking with Mariam and Hanne's brothers and sisters, trying to savor every moment, knowing their time together in Mosul was about to come to an end. They told stories about the old days, about the times their father took them to visit relatives in surrounding villages, about happier days, about holidays and birthdays and school days.

"Remember the final exam in high school?" Saeed said. Everyone groaned. Who could forget? The pressure was insane, the stakes all too high. Boys who didn't fare well would be forced to serve in Saddam's army, a fate not many willingly suffered. One of Saeed's classmates was so frightened that he took his own life the night before the test.

Since neither Raad nor Saeed did well on the exam, they both ended up serving two years in the military. Mariam prayed fervently every day for their safe return. Finally, when they came back unscathed, they took over the family restaurant. "Thank God for that," Raad said with a grin. "I never was one for books anyway—not like you, Hanne."

Mariam remembered the day they learned that Hanne would be allowed to study at the University of Mosul. Like her father, she had a love of languages and hoped to study English.

"Perhaps God placed this desire in your heart, Hanne, as a way to prepare you for life in America," Mariam said quietly, to which they all nodded their heads in agreement. "We're in the palm of His hand, of that I am convinced." Mariam said it in as confident a voice as she could muster, but inside, she was worried about her eldest daughter.

"She's going to be 12,000 kilometers away," Nora whispered to Nahida as they boiled the rice and browned the chicken. "How will we ever see her again? We've never been separated like this before!"

"I wish she could stay here with us," Nahida said. "She's not the one who worked for the Americans."

"You know she'd never do that, let Fadi go without her!"

"Of course not," Nahida retorted, "I'm just saying. It doesn't seem fair."

"Since when has anything ever been fair in our country?"

"Never."

"Exactly my point. So we'll just have to visit them. It's the only way."

"What are you talking about?" Hanne asked as she entered the kitchen. "What's the only way?"

"Oh, it's nothing," Nora said. "We're just arguing about the recipe here. Nahida never cooks the rice long enough."

Hanne looked at them doubtfully. She knew her sisters better than that.

"I wish I could stay here with you," Hanne said with a catch in her voice, "but it's impossible. Fadi says we have to leave."

"We're going to miss you so much!" Nahida cried, throwing her arms around Hanne.

"But we'll come visit you in America. Somehow we'll do it!" Nora said. "We'll find a way there. Won't we Nahida?"

"Of course we will. Nothing will stop us."

## A Martyr's Crown

None of them went to bed that night, not even Mariam, though she did doze from time to time in her favorite chair, the one by the window where she'd often prayed for Saeed and Raad's safe return all those years ago.

"It's not like you'll never see me again," Hanne said, swallowing the lump in her throat and trying her best to console her sisters. "I mean, I won't be able to come back here, it's true, but maybe we can meet somewhere else."

"Fadi says that sometimes people like us meet their families in another country, like Turkey or France. Hey—that's an idea! Maybe we could meet in Rome! Wouldn't that be great? We could see the pope! Visit the catacombs!"

Nahida and Nora nodded their heads, brushing away tears. The three girls leaned in to hug each other and instead bumped heads.

"A headache for my send-off—thanks a lot!" Hanne said with a laugh.

"*Yemmi* always said you had a hard head," Nahida said playfully.

"Promise me you'll come visit me in America someday."

"Of course," Nora said, trying to be brave. "I mean, you're not going to the moon. Lots of Chaldeans live in America."

"That's right," Hanne said. "And I'll call home as much as I can, too. We've got the Internet—we'll be able to see each other with the video cam."

"And there's always Facebook," Nahida said. "We can chat on there, too."

Just then there was a tap at the door. It was Fadi.

"*Azizta*, we've got a long drive ahead of us if we're going to get to Baghdad by this afternoon."

Hanne rose slowly from the bed and the three sisters made their way to the kitchen. Mariam was already preparing some fried eggs, bread and tea for a quick breakfast.

Raad and Saeed tried to keep the mood light at the table.

"Send us a picture of the Grand Canyon when you get there, Hanne," Saeed said between sips of tea. "And maybe you'll get to visit Disneyland, too. You won't be far from California."

Hanne and Fadi did their best to smile.

When breakfast was over, they all gathered in the living room to say their farewells. Raad had called a taxi and the driver was already waiting impatiently out front on the street.

"My beautiful, strong daughter," Mariam said as she embraced Hanne. "Promise me you'll be careful, that you'll call me from Aunt Talia's and let me know how you are as soon as you arrive."

"I promise, *Yemmi*," Hanne said, "You know I will."

"And call me when you get to America. I want to know that you're safe, and that you're with Fadi's family."

"I'll call, I will," Hanne said. "Oh, *Yemmi*!"

Raad and Saeed began carrying the luggage outside and loading it into the cab.

"I want you to take this with you," Mariam said, removing a black-beaded rosary bracelet from her frail wrist. "Your father gave it to me long ago. Whenever you pray this rosary," she said, looking intently into Hanne's eyes, "the Blessed Virgin Mary will pray for you and me and for all of us. We will be together again someday, *inshallah*—God willing."

"Thank you, *Yemmi*," Hanne said, sniffling, "I'll treasure it always. I'm going to miss you..." she said, holding her again, her voice trailing off.

Mariam nodded her head, unable to speak.

Nahida and Nora threw their arms around Hanne, wishing they had a little more time, that they could all go together to America, knowing that it was impossible. It really was goodbye.

Saeed and Raad kissed Hanne on both cheeks.

"Take good care of our sister," Saeed said to Fadi.

"I will—you know I will."

"Call us if you run into any trouble on the road to Baghdad,"

## A Martyr's Crown

Raad said.

"We'll be fine, *inshalla*."

Finally, the young couple got into the cab and drove away, turning and looking out the back window and waving all the way down the street until they turned the corner and vanished.

Hanne watched the streets go by through the window, memorizing the familiar sights and sounds of her neighborhood in Mosul. They passed Raad and Saeed's restaurant on the corner with its "Closed" sign in the window. Up the street stood the bakery—Hanne could almost smell the bread Mr. Petros baked fresh daily—with its cakes and pastries laid out in a glass display case near the window. And on the next corner, Hanne spied the dilapidated pharmacy, its paint faded and peeling. A skinny, stray cat with a litter of kittens was crouched in the shade near the front door, hoping some kind soul might take pity on her. "Poor thing," Hanne said under her breath as they passed by. There wasn't much kindness to be had in a land that showed scant mercy for its human inhabitants.

As they turned up the next street, Hanne glimpsed the bell tower of Mar Addai. The church had still not reopened since the attack. Hanne knew instinctively that it would eventually reopen. Chaldeans were not about to give up the place where they worshipped. They would rise and rebuild.

Leaning against Fadi's shoulder, Hanne let out a sigh. The cab driver, a smoker, was hunched over the steering wheel, watching out for potholes and debris in the roadway. Every now and then, they passed burned-out cars and rubble piled up along the side of the road. Abandoned, half-demolished homes, their windows smashed and roofs sagging, dotted the lonely landscape.

Hanne fingered the rosary bracelet Mariam had given her, already missing home. She wondered then how people without any faith ever made it through the storms of life. Knowing that there was life beyond this world, that there were joys and consolations in the world to come—that was what was carrying her through this steep and treacherous valley. Without faith, she would have given up all hope that day in Mar Addai. There would be no reason to go on breathing.

The car continued south on the road to Baghdad for what seemed like an eternity. Suddenly, the driver began to slow down and Hanne could feel her heart beating faster, her mouth growing dry. There was a check point up ahead in the road.

"Remember, don't look them in the eyes and don't say anything. Just look straight ahead," Fadi whispered, squeezing her hand.

They braced themselves, knowing they'd be questioned, fervently hoping the security forces would let them through so they could make it to the embassy.

The taxi driver came to a stop some 20 feet in front of a stern-looking man armed with a machine gun standing in the middle of the deteriorating roadway. Another man, dressed in well-worn combat fatigues and heavy black boots, strode toward the cab. Hanne and Fadi could scarcely breathe. Who were these men? Security forces or insurgents?

"Oh dear God," Fadi prayed under his breath, "Please, let us get through. We've got to get to the American embassy!"

שׁ שׁ שׁ שׁ שׁ שׁ

### A Martyr's Crown

# Chapter 27
Phoenix
Monday, January 11, 2010

"The liturgy is in Aramaic?" Sholeh asked when Sarah told her of Father George's invitation to attend evening Mass during the week so they could discuss the service project for the St. Clare youth group. "Well, that should be interesting. I mean, it's the language Jesus spoke. The only time I've ever heard it is in that movie 'The Passion of the Christ.'"

"Yeah, but this time there won't be any subtitles," Sarah quipped. "I heard a little of it when I went up there for the candlelight vigil. It's kind of soothing in a way."

"I wonder if it sounds anything like Farsi."

"No idea. But I do know one word in Aramaic. They say it a lot during their Mass. *Qadysha.*"

"*Qadysha.* What does that mean?"

"That's the word for 'holy.' I think I'd kind of like to learn some of their language."

"Why would you want to do that?"

"Well, when I went to Puerto Rico to meet Javier's family, they were very touched that I knew Spanish. If you really want to understand people, you have to speak their language. It opens up your world—it allows you to have more friends."

Back when Sarah and Javier were first getting to know each other, they were both still learning each other's language.

"Will you tell me if I make a mistake?" Javier asked her one day at the library. "I mean, I don't want to sound like an idiot. Will you correct my English if I say something stupid?"

"*Claro que sí*—of course. And feel free to correct my *español*. It's the only way we'll learn."

Somehow, the corrections didn't feel like criticism—they were offered in a spirit of charity. Well, mostly. Sometimes they couldn't help laughing at each other's mistakes.

"A little dog told me," Javier began to say one day as they were leaving the student union building. Sarah burst out laughing.

"What's so funny about that?"

"I think you mean a little *bird* told you," Sarah said.

"Fine. A little *bird* told me. I thought we weren't going to make fun of each other!"

"You make it so easy sometimes."

"Oh, you're going to pay for that, *muchacha*. Just you wait."

Thinking of those early days in their relationship reminded Sarah of something she'd read in her father's journal: "Criticism kills love. Nagging and finding fault will eventually crush it." Dad had written the words in his bold, neat handwriting back on May 18—his birthday—in 1972. *Mom and Dad seemed so happy together*, Sarah thought. *Was that little gem one of their secrets? Not criticizing?*

When Sarah told Javier that she and Sholeh were going up to Mar Ephrem that night, she wondered how he would react. Thankfully, he didn't look at her with those pitiful brown eyes that said, *Stay home! Don't leave me here with all these kids!*

"OK, enjoy," he said, switching off the television. "I just might play some guitar while you're gone."

Sarah raised her eyebrows in surprise. The old guitar had sat in the back of their closet, untouched for years, gathering dust. She felt her heart flutter, thinking of him fingering the strings, tuning the instrument. Perhaps the joy of music would help him find his way back to her again.

"Wow. That would be something. I hope you'll play it for me, too. I miss hearing you play—it's been too many years."

"We'll see."

When she walked out the door that night, Javier knew instinctively that something interesting was bound to come of her meeting with Father George. There was an element of that story she'd written about the Chaldeans that really touched her heart. Whatever it was, Javier mused, she seemed happier these days, as though the clouds were beginning to lift, like she'd found a new purpose in life. Perhaps this is what his mother meant when she told him to hang in there, to not give up, that better days were coming.

"You're not going to use a visit to me to run away from the pain, Javier," she told him the day he called. "I know. It's the second anniversary for Patrick. And it's been terrible, just awful for you and Sarah.

"But you'll never understand what marriage is, what real love is, *m'ijo,* until you've lived it in the valleys of life. 'Love bears all things, believes all things.' Remember? That was the reading at your wedding! We were all there. You think it was always easy for your *papá* and me?"

Javier smiled thinking about his mom. She didn't have more than a sixth-grade education and had never cracked open a book on parenting, but she'd done a spectacularly good job raising nine children using nothing but faith, love and common sense.

His parents had never lost a child, though, and he wondered if it was possible for a marriage to survive the kind of trauma that he and Sarah had experienced. He'd heard lots of people got divorced when tragedy struck.

It would be so much easier to walk away, to start over again, to not be reminded every day of all they'd lost. He could have his own apartment, a fresh start in life. Then again, his divorced friends told him the single life had its own set of struggles. He'd have to really think it over before coming to a decision about what he should do.

༒ ༒ ༒ ༒ ༒ ༒ ༒

Sarah and Sholeh took a seat off to the left, just behind a young mom wearing a stylish gray dress and black veil, accompanied by her three small children. *All boys, just like me*, Sarah noted with amusement. Taking little ones to church could be tricky. *But doing it alone, on a Tuesday night? Now that was simply courageous. Or ambitious,* Sarah couldn't decide which, but she definitely admired it.

A small chime sounded and everyone stood and began singing what must have been a very familiar hymn. They sang with gusto, from someplace deep inside. Sarah had no idea what they were singing about, but it sounded heartfelt.

Most of the Mass was chanted, and Sarah and Sholeh flipped through the missal, trying their best to follow along with the English translation. It wasn't easy: Aramaic was unlike any language they had ever heard before. None of the words sounded familiar, but when they heard "Catholiki" and "Halleluiah," they smiled, happy to have recognized two words. Every now and then, Father George would chant one of the prayers in English and they found their place in the missal again.

"So, this is Sholeh," Father George said after the Mass, extending his hand in greeting. "It is nice to meet you. Let us go to my office where we may talk."

Father George unlocked the door to the cramped space and motioned for them to sit down. "May I get you something to drink? Tea or juice perhaps?"

## A Martyr's Crown

"Um, juice sounds good," Sarah answered.

"Sounds good to me, too." Sholeh said.

"OK, give me a moment."

Father George, hobbled off to fetch the drinks, leaving them alone to talk.

"You didn't tell me about his leg," Sholeh whispered. "And that scar! What on earth happened to him?"

"I don't know any of the details, but he said he was kidnapped and tortured in Iraq by fanatics. His leg really bothers him sometimes. It's probably because he had to stand for so long during Mass, poor thing."

Sholeh's eyes widened. "God bless him. I feel honored to meet him. A priest, tortured for the faith."

Sarah nodded, glancing around the office. She noticed a big, thick, leather-bound book sitting right in the middle of Father George's cluttered desk. On the cover stamped in faded gold was a beautiful image of an intricate cross. *I wonder what that book is. Is it the Bible in Aramaic maybe?*

Father George returned with a tray of drinks for each of them and sat down.

"So, Sarah tells me your youth group is interested in doing service here at Mar Ephrem."

Sholeh set her glass down on the coffee table. "Well, we've got a big group of kids and we like to do different service projects around the Valley. It's a good way to teach them about reaching out to others."

Father George pressed his hands together, thinking about Sholeh's idea. "This is true. And there is benefit for them to do so, no?"

"Oh, but it's not for credit at school or anything like that, although every once in a while we do get a request to sign a paper from one of the schools," Sholeh said.

"No, what I mean is this service, it is a good way for them

to discover the joy that comes from helping others, from giving without expecting something in return. Young people, they do not hear such a message often."

"Exactly," Sholeh said. "We want them to see that there's more to life than just receiving. Most of our kids are from upper-middle-class families. They don't know too much about hardship."

"What kind of project do you think of doing?" Father George asked.

"Well, what are your needs? Sarah said your church hall might need some work."

"This is true. But this will take much money to do, and unfortunately, money is not something we have."

Sholeh smiled. "Let me talk to my pastor about that. Our parish has a grant program that might help with remodeling. Now, I can't promise anything, but I could put in a good word for you. Maybe Sarah can help you write a proposal to the committee."

"I could help you do that, Father," Sarah said leaning forward in her seat. "I mean, writing is what I do. It would be easy for me."

"This help, it will be wonderful. Perhaps if we get the grant funds, your youth group kids, they will help us with some of the work. You know, like ripping out tile or painting, this kind of work."

"That might keep them busy for a while. But how about something more long term? Like a partnership between the two parishes? You've got a youth group here, don't you?"

"Of course. We have many teenagers and we have some college students, too."

"Maybe the kids from both groups could work together to organize a series of soccer games or a Vacation Bible School program, something fun like that. You know—something that would help to build a relationship between the two parishes."

"This might work," Father George said. "But let us do this. I will discuss this idea with my parish council. You talk with your

## A Martyr's Crown

pastor and the other parents."

"You've got it, Father. I'll talk with Father Keller about it," Sholeh said.

"There's one more thing," Sarah added. "Javier is pretty good at fixing engines. He'd like to look at your church van to see if he can fix it for you. Can he come up here on Saturday?"

"Really? He will help us with this?"

"Of course he will. And knowing Javier, he'll want to come early in the morning. It might take him some time if it's anything major."

"You come too. We will have lunch together—and bring your boys. You are welcome to come too, Sholeh."

"Thanks, Father, but I've already got plans on Saturday," Sholeh replied. "It's Andrew's birthday," she added. "Isn't Zach coming over for that?"

"Oh that's right! I forgot. OK, well, I'll talk to Javier and the other boys and get back to you," Sarah said. "But before we go, can I ask you something?"

"Sure."

"What's that book on your desk? Is that your Bible?" Sarah pointed to the leather-bound tome.

Father George picked up the book and handed it to Sarah. She opened it up to the middle, but the words were a jumble of unrecognizable squiggles she assumed were Aramaic.

"This is 'The Book of Before and After,'" Father George explained, "the Divine Office for the Chaldean Rite."

Sarah vaguely remembered learning a little something about the Divine Office back at St. Dominic's High School.

"Oh, yeah, I have the prayer book for the Roman Rite," Sholeh said. "A friend of mine gave it to me a few years back."

"Some of the hymns and prayers in our book were composed by martyrs in the third and fourth centuries," Father George said as he watched Sarah examining the volume. "These are precious prayers, very dear to us."

Sarah turned the pages carefully. She could see that it was a well-used book, something Father George treasured.

He walked over to the massive bookcase and took something off the shelf.

"Here," he said, handing a book to Sarah. "Have this one. We have some copies in English."

Sarah took the book from his hands. "The Book of Before and After," it said on the cover in bold letters.

"What does the title mean exactly?" Sarah asked. *Something in her mind was tugging at her. It was odd; there was something about that title....what was it?*

"Oh, this means the prayers and hymns before and after the daily Psalms," Father George said.

"I see," Sarah said, paging through the book. "Wow. Thank you," she said looking up. "That's very nice of you."

"You are welcome," Father George said. "Thanks for helping our community. And for bringing Sholeh here."

Sarah and Sholeh nodded and rose to leave.

"I'll give you a call about Saturday," Sarah said.

"OK, sounds good," Father George said. Just then, his cell phone rang. He glanced at the screen. "I must take this call—it is my bishop," he said apologetically.

"No problem, Father," Sholeh said. "We'll see you later." The two women gathered their purses and headed for the door. Father George was already deep in conversation with his bishop.

"So, what did you think?" Sarah asked as they climbed into the car.

"Well, the Mass was beautiful," Sholeh began. "It's like my mind didn't understand the words, but my heart knew Jesus was there."

"Hmmm. That's a good way to put it," Sarah answered. "Are you sure you're not a journalist?"

## A Martyr's Crown

"No way," Sholeh said with a laugh. "That's your thing."

"What did you think of Father George?"

"He seems very kind. He's obviously loved by his people. And it's such a blessing that he gave you their book of prayer. I think you'll find that praying the Divine Office will make a difference in your life."

Sarah wasn't so sure.

"But it's just a book! I mean, I of all people love to read, but how can reading a book like that every day make such a difference? Doesn't it get old after a while?"

"Well, it's not really *reading* a book in that sense. You pray from that book three times a day for a while, and the next thing you know, you wouldn't dream of going through your day without it."

"So why did you decide to convert, anyway?"

"I felt God's presence once when I was a child, and I never forgot it," Sholeh said thoughtfully. "I always knew He was there, but it wasn't until I came to the United States that I found Him again.

"I wandered into a Catholic church one day, and the priest was consecrating the host. And in that moment, I felt God's presence again. I knew I had to become Catholic."

"How did your family take it?"

"Not too well. But once I understood that God was my Father who loved me, that He sent His Son to save me, I knew I had to be baptized. Life was never the same after that—in a good way."

Suddenly, it was as though a light illuminated Sarah's mind. Hadn't she thought to herself countless times since the accident that their family would always be seen through the lens of "before" Patrick's death and "after"?

Maybe there was a new way to look at their lives, a new chapter to be written. Sarah wondered what it could be. Whatever it was, it held out the promise of hope.

## Chapter 28
Highway to Baghdad
Monday, January 11, 2010

The cab driver rolled down his window as the man dressed in battle fatigues approached. He and the other men didn't look like Iraqi security forces. And they definitely weren't Americans.

"Your ID papers," the man demanded gruffly of the cab driver, after pulling a cigarette from his yellowed teeth.

Hanne and Fadi looked straight ahead, unblinking, not daring to breathe a word.

"And who are they?" he asked in a gravelly voice, pointing at the backseat. "Where are you taking them?"

"Uh, it's just a couple from Mosul. Say they're going to visit her aunt in Baghdad."

The man looked at the two of them searchingly.

"Your ID papers," he said to Fadi and Hanne.

Fadi retrieved their government ID cards and calmly presented them to the man. They watched as he examined the cards and then walked over to his comrades to confer. The man with the machine gun never moved from in front of the cab but continued to stare at them coldly. The other man, their interrogator, returned.

"Get out of the car."

"Why?" the cab driver asked, nervously.

"Did you hear me, old man? I said get out of the car—now!

## A Martyr's Crown

And you, in the backseat—you get out, too!"

The man with the machine gun was now standing at the rear of the vehicle, wordlessly pointing his weapon at them.

"Open the trunk."

Fadi's heart was thumping in his chest like a 100-pound weight. He'd heard how the insurgents kidnapped people and shoved them in the trunks of cars. Is this how their lives would end? Out here on the highway, trying to flee the country? He felt like he was moving in slow motion.

"You. Get those suitcases out of there and open them."

Hanne shuddered, wondering what these men might do to them. "*Marya Alaha*—Lord God," she prayed silently, "shield us from these evil men. Deliver us, O Lord!"

The cab driver pulled the suitcases from the trunk, then bent down and unzipped each.

The man began to rifle through their belongings. He stopped when he came upon a lumpy package wrapped in foil.

"And what's this?" he asked as he began to unwrap the bundle.

"Just some pastries and cheeses for our aunt," Fadi said.

The man grunted as he devoured a hunk of the cheese, then balled up the foil and tossed it aside. He checked Fadi's pockets, then went back to consult with the others. The man with the machine gun didn't move.

After a few minutes of heated discussion, the guard returned to the taxi and begrudgingly handed them their ID cards.

"Alright. Get out of here."

They stood there frozen, afraid to move.

"You heard what I said. Get out of here before I change my mind!"

They got into the cab and drove off.

"Thank God," Hanne whispered.

Beads of sweat stood out on Fadi's forehead. He knew some very dangerous men were looking for him and that his cover was blown. These guards at the check point had somehow failed to realize they were dealing with a "traitor," someone who helped the Americans. Fadi wasn't sure how they'd gotten through without trouble, but he was glad he'd given their intrepid taxi driver the detail about visiting an aunt. Hiding the cash and passports in a box of tissues had been a brilliant move.

*Now, if we could just make it to Baghdad and get to the embassy*, Fadi thought to himself.

Hanne was still gripping Fadi's arm, worried about what lay ahead.

"We'll be at your aunt's apartment by this afternoon, *azizta,"* Fadi said to her reassuringly. "How long till we get there?" he queried the taxi driver, who was eyeing them somewhat suspiciously in the rearview mirror.

"With stops like that, it's going to take a little longer," he said vaguely, clearly perturbed. "I don't know. A couple more hours, maybe three?" he shrugged. "I'm just the driver—I'm no fortuneteller."

Hanne looked out the window. There was nothing at all but desert for miles. She was glad *Yemmi* had insisted they take a jug of water with them for the long car ride. Her mouth felt dry and her lips were getting chapped.

The morning dragged on, but finally they could see the hazy skies and jagged outline of Baghdad in the distance. They'd already been through two more security checkpoints, much to the cab driver's chagrin.

Aunt Talia's apartment building was near the Green Zone, not far from the enormous new American embassy.

"I haven't seen her since I was 10 years old," she told Fadi.

"That's understandable. It's dangerous traveling to Baghdad."

"Thank God we made it."

As they approached the neighborhood where her aunt lived, Hanne took in the sights and sounds of the ancient city.

## A Martyr's Crown

Rebuilding was underway, but it would take years—generations, no doubt—to complete the work. Some things look as if they would never be rebuilt, Hanne thought as they drove past heaps of rubble and garbage. A woman in an all-encompassing black burqa that billowed in the wind, nothing but her eyes visible, stood on the sidewalk in front of a bombed-out building, looking distraught.

"I wonder if that was her house," Hanne said softly.

At last, they pulled up to the gray stone apartment complex. The cab driver popped the trunk but kept the engine running as Hanne and Fadi stepped onto the littered curb.

Aunt Talia, knowing that Fadi was still recovering from the gunshot wound he'd suffered, had sent her two sons, Daud and Basil, to wait on the street at the entrance to the apartment complex. She showed them a picture of what the young couple looked like so they could be on the lookout.

As soon as they spied Fadi's massive frame climbing out of the taxi, followed by the petite, ebony-haired Hanne, they stepped forward.

"*Shlama*--welcome!" they called out. "Here—let us get your luggage from the trunk." The two men hoisted the bulging suitcases and other belongings from the cab, depositing them on the sidewalk beside Hanne and Fadi, who were both exhausted but relieved to have finally reached Baghdad.

The four of them took the elevator up to the fifth floor. Fadi hoped they could have a quiet afternoon napping, then report to the American embassy first thing in the morning.

Aunt Talia had been watching the proceedings from her window and was waiting just inside the door of her tiny apartment.

"Oh, how wonderful it is to see you, my dears! Thank God you've made it here," she exclaimed, embracing them as they came through the door. "Now then, you must sit down. I'm sure you're famished after your long drive! We'll have to call your mother right away after dinner and let her know you've arrived safely."

After such an uncomfortable taxi cab ride, the last thing Hanne and Fadi wanted to do was sit. They were drawn instead to the window overlooking the city below.

"Look, Hanne," Fadi said. "That must be the American embassy."

Just a few blocks away, they could see the American flag snapping in the wind at the entrance to the vast building.

Fadi read somewhere that the complex was the size of Vatican City and cost over $700 million to build. Tomorrow, *inshalla,* they would enter its confines and plead their case for asylum. Surely the letters Fadi carried from Major Johnson and the police chief in Mosul would help secure their departure.

Aunt Talia was bustling about, setting platters of food on the dining room table for the afternoon meal. She'd prepared *maraka 'd benjani*—eggplant stew and other delicacies in honor of their visit. The aroma was tantalizing, and Fadi heard his stomach rumbling.

"Tell me how your mother is, Hanne," she said as they sat around the table savoring the meal. "I haven't seen my dear sister-in-law in many years, not since my cousin's wedding here in Baghdad so long ago. How is she? Oh, I'm sure these last few weeks have been very difficult indeed."

"My mother is doing alright," Hanne replied. "My sisters will take good care of her. She sent along a gift for you. I'll get it from my bag after lunch."

"Oh my goodness—a gift. She didn't have to! How lovely!" she exclaimed, her eyes sparkling.

Hanne remembered what *Yemmi* had said before they left Mosul early that morning: *You will no doubt find your auntie to be as vivacious as ever. There's always an air of excitement in her midst.* *Yemmi* recounted how they'd all begged her to leave Baghdad and come live with them just before the invasion in 2003, but she had

## A Martyr's Crown

stood fast.

"Baghdad has been my home for many years," she said stubbornly. "Nothing could make me leave this city."

After lunch, Hanne retrieved the colorful, floral scarf *Yemmi* had sent as a gift.

"Well now. This is just perfect!" Aunt Talia declared as she tied the scarf about her neck, hurrying to the large, framed mirror on the wall to examine her reflection. "It's just right! Oh thank you!" she cried, kissing Hanne on both cheeks. "Now let's call your mother. She's probably worried sick about you two."

Hanne dialed the number to Mariam's home and listened as it rang. It was Nora who answered the phone.

"Oh thank God you've arrived," she breathed into the phone. "We've all been thinking about you since you left. *Yemmi* is napping, but…"

"Oh no, I'm not—I'm right here! I heard the phone ringing!" Mariam exclaimed as she sailed into the room and took the phone from Nora. "Hello? Hanne? Is that you, dear?"

Hanne could hear the concern in her mother's voice, the worry. She steeled herself, willing the tears not to come.

"Yes, *Yemmi,* it's me," Hanne answered. "Fadi and I are here in Baghdad and we're safe. And Auntie loves the scarf you sent."

"Oh, good," Mariam answered, trying to sound cheerful. She could tell Hanne was doing her best, too. "I'm so glad you're there now. How was the journey?"

"Not so bad," Hanne said, smiling at Fadi. She didn't want to complain, not when it would only burden her mother with more cares. "We just had lunch and wanted to call and let you know we're alright."

"How's Fadi?"

"Fine, just a little tired," Hanne answered. "We're all settled in here and we'll be up early tomorrow morning for our appointment." She didn't want to say anything over the phone about their plans. One never knew who might be listening.

"Alright then, *azizta.* I'll be waiting to hear from you again when things are decided. Now put your auntie on the line, would you please?"

Hanne gave the phone to Aunt Talia. Fadi was already in the guest room, lying on the bed, exhausted from their long drive. Hanne curled up beside him. Down below on the street, she could hear the traffic, the lonely sounds of life in a busy city. Every now and then, she heard a car backfire and it made her jump.

Later that night, when the moon rose and the din of the streets had subsided, Hanne lay awake, thinking about what the future held for her and Fadi: life in a strange land, life in exile. It wasn't at all what she'd dreamed of when they'd made their wedding vows.

"The cross," Father Ameer used to say, "there's no way to follow the Lord unless you embrace it."

Losing Noor, leaving her family, leaving her country—the cross seemed heavy, and Hanne felt its weight crushing her. Fadi talked about the freedom and the opportunities they would have in America, but Hanne could only feel sorrow and dread.

If all went according to plan, the Americans would grant them asylum and they'd soon be joining their relatives in Arizona. Fadi's Aunt Samira told Mariam there was a Chaldean parish near where they lived, where Hanne and Fadi would make friends.

"There are new families arriving almost every week," Samira said, hoping to encourage her. "They'll make new friends here."

Nevertheless, Hanne thought to herself, would any of these other people understand what it was like to lose a child? It had only been five weeks since Noor's death and in spite of all the hubbub of activity leading up to their departure, Hanne was still numb with grief. She knew Fadi felt the same, even though he tried to pretend otherwise. She lay awake for hours, unable to sleep amid the strange surroundings, then finally drifted off toward morning.

## A Martyr's Crown

"Hanne, it's time to wake up," Fadi said just after sunrise.

"Already?" Hanne said wearily.

"We can't be late for this appointment."

Hanne dragged herself from the bed.

After breakfast, Daud drove them to the embassy gate. Fadi and Hanne stepped out of the car and presented their ID cards to the guard, as well as the letter from Major Johnson, and were allowed to enter.

Though they arrived first thing in the morning, the embassy was already humming with activity. A businesslike receptionist directed them to stand in a long line. Hanne counted 11 people ahead of them and she wondered why they were there. Were they trying to leave the country, too?

Eventually, they reached the front of the queue. The middle-aged consular officer, an exceptionally polite woman dressed in a navy blue suit and immaculate white blouse, listened patiently as Fadi explained the details of their situation.

"May I see your passports, please?" she asked them crisply.

Fadi, hands shaking, presented her with the passports as well as their marriage certificate and all the other documents Major Johnson told him were necessary. She looked them over carefully, jotting down a few notes on a yellow legal pad.

"Now then Mr. Yacoub, if you and your wife will kindly have a seat out in the waiting area, I'll have my supervisor take a look at your documentation," she told them. "In the meantime, here's some paperwork for you to begin filling out," she said, handing Fadi a stack of papers and a black ballpoint pen.

Fadi thanked the woman and took the sheaf of papers. He and Hanne sat on a dark brown couch and began filling out the bewildering array of paperwork. Finally, just before the lunch hour, they were called to one of the smaller offices in the back.

"All your documentation seems to be in good order, Mr. Yacoub," the consular officer, an older gentleman with glasses, told them. "We're going to send it all overnight to our office in Nebraska. What I need for you to do now is pay your $375 fee so we can set up your visa interview for later this week."

Fadi reached into his wallet and pulled out the wad of cash, the same one he'd hidden in the lining of the old coat in their now-abandoned apartment, and handed it to the officer.

"Let's have you come back on Friday for the interview. I'm not really supposed to say this, but your case looks pretty solid, so perhaps you should start thinking about travel arrangements," the officer told them.

"How soon will we know?" Fadi asked anxiously.

"Well, let's have you come in first thing Friday," the man answered. "I would say you could be on your way to the U.S. rather shortly, but there's no telling with these things. Major Johnson did write a strong letter of recommendation for you, and you served for over a year doing some very dangerous work for us. He also told us about what happened to your daughter," the man said, lowering his voice. "I'm so sorry for your loss," he said sympathetically.

"Thank you," Fadi said, staring down at the ground. He hadn't realized Major Johnson had made such an effort to help them. He had braced himself for a bit of a battle, thinking there would be more hurdles standing in the way of his and Hanne's departure. So far, everything was going smoothly.

They spent the next couple of days at the apartment waiting, unsure of what might happen next. Hanne insisted on helping with the cooking, and in the evenings, the three men played dominoes.

By Friday morning, they were all a little nervous. Basil drove them to the embassy for the 8:30 a.m. interview.

"You'll do fine," he told them breezily on the way over. "Don't worry about a thing!"

Fadi wasn't so sure.

Once inside the embassy, they sat in the waiting room, anxiously

## A Martyr's Crown

watching the clock. At exactly 8:30, an officer called their names. Fadi and Hanne followed him to the interview room and sat in the two sturdy chairs stationed in front of the man's desk. He pulled out a thick manila folder and opened it, setting aside some papers.

The officer, a tall, muscular man with auburn hair and glasses, appeared to be in his late 30s. Hanne wondered to herself how many people's fates he had held in his hands, how many souls had been brought before him, hoping for the chance to settle in America.

He began by asking some basic questions, taking notes as he went along. He seemed pleased that they had relatives they could connect with in the States.

"Tell me about the interpreting work you did with Major Johnson," he asked Fadi.

"I went out on patrol with him regularly," Fadi said looking at Hanne. "We knocked on doors, questioned people, that sort of thing."

"I see," the man said, looking up. "I imagine some of that was rather—how can I put this—intense."

"Yes, sir," Fadi said, his hands shaking. "I would rather not talk about it, really. Especially with my wife here."

The man nodded his head sympathetically. "That's entirely understandable. And you, Mrs. Yacoub. You studied English. Do you speak it as well as your husband?"

Hanne blushed. "Not really. I…well, I am not as fluent," she stammered, "but I can have a conversation."

"That's good," he said, flipping through the pages of his files. "That should be of considerable help to you."

They sat in the uncomfortable wooden chairs, trying to glean some knowledge of what the officer was doing as he looked through their files. Finally, after making a few notations, he closed up the folder and stood up from the desk. "Let me go check something," he said. "I'll be back in a few minutes."

Hanne and Fadi sat there, shifting in their seats, not sure what to think. It seemed as though the interview went well, but who could tell? Maybe they would have to go to Turkey or Greece and wait out the year.

"Turkey wouldn't be too bad," Fadi said to Hanne. "I have an old friend who spent a couple years there before he was allowed to go to the U.S."

After what seemed like a very long time, the man returned, sat down at the desk and smiled at them.

"Congratulations, you two. My supervisor said we're going to be issuing you each a Special Immigrant Visa. You'll be free to settle in the United States of America."

And with that, he rose from his desk and extended his hand to Fadi.

"Thank you, sir," Fadi said. "Is there anything else we must do?"

"Pack your suitcases, I guess," the officer said with a shrug.

"Oh, we are packed up and ready, aren't we?" Fadi said, smiling at Hanne.

"I wish you all the best in the States," the officer said as they turned to leave. "I think you'll find the Arizona desert to be not unlike Iraq. I have a grandmother who lives there. Sends me postcards with rattlesnakes and coyotes."

*This is it,* Hanne thought to herself. *There's no turning back now.* Until the moment when the officer handed them their paperwork, stamped "APPROVED," there was a glimmer of hope that perhaps through some miracle they could go into hiding, that they might be allowed to stay in their homeland, remain close to their family.

Fadi was lost in thought, eager to get back to the apartment and make their final arrangements. Hanne noted that he walked a little more quickly, as though the news of their departure gave him sudden energy.

# A Martyr's Crown

"Marvelous," Aunt Talia said when they told her their news. "Now call your mother," she said, turning to Hanne. "I'm sure she's been worried about you."

"We'll leave on Monday," Fadi declared. "We'll take a cab to Amman and leave from there."

"Still no flights from Baghdad, that's true," Aunt Talia said. "It's a long trip to Jordan, but I'm very happy for you two. We need to have a proper celebration for such an important occasion."

"Absolutely," Daud said. "This is great news. You're going to America! That's fabulous!"

Hanne knew she should try to be thankful. At least they had relatives in America, and a Chaldean parish where they would feel at home.

*But will anyone there understand me? How will I manage without my sisters? I'll never see my home again.* Hanne felt a little sick, thinking of what lay ahead. She'd never been on a plane before, had never been outside the borders of Iraq.

They spent the weekend preparing for the long journey, washing clothes and packing their few belongings. On Sunday, some of Aunt Talia's friends came by to wish them a safe trip. After everyone had gone home, the two women cleaned up the kitchen.

"And now, my dear, I have something special to give you and Fadi," she said as she hung the dish towel. From the top shelf of her bookcase, she removed a dusty decorative tin and carried it over to the coffee table to show them.

"Open it," she told Hanne.

Hanne removed the cover and looked inside, wondering what it could be.

"Oh my goodness, no," Hanne cried, "We can't take this!"

"Oh yes you can, *azizta*. I've had that money set aside for a long time now and I want you to have it. Your father always took care of me and now I am able to repay his kindness. Go on! You're going to need it when you get there!"

Hanne pulled the stack of *dinars* from the canister, and her eyes widened in amazement. "But this is a small fortune. You can't be serious!"

"I can and I am," she responded firmly, her hand on Hanne's arm. "As I said, I've been saving a little here and there over the years and well, I figure my niece and her husband are going to need all the help they can get trying to establish themselves in a new country. God has been good to me," she said. "It is a joy to do this for you."

At these words, Hanne embraced the old woman, overcome at such generosity from a relative that, truth be told, she didn't really know all that well. Fadi stood there, unsure what to say. He hadn't seen this coming, but he wasn't surprised. The Garmos were some of the most loving people he'd ever known.

"Someday, you will have to come visit us," Fadi said. "Our home is your home."

"My dear, let us wait until you have a home first," Aunt Talia quipped. "But yes, it would be lovely to visit you there in America, though I fear I'm too old for such a journey."

"Oh, please don't say that! What will I do if my family doesn't visit us? We will be among strangers there," Hanne said sadly. "We only know Fadi's aunt and uncle."

"Now, Hanne dear, don't worry. You will make friends there in America—I know it. I feel it in my bones."

"I hope you're right," Hanne said, trying to sound brave, "Thank you for letting us stay here with you. We'll miss you."

"Now, now, let's not have any sad talk. Tomorrow is your big day! What time are you leaving?"

"Right at 6 a.m.," Fadi said. "We've got a 13-hour drive to Amman and a plane to catch."

"Well then, you'd best be getting some rest. I'll be up first thing getting a good breakfast ready for you."

Early the next morning, Daud loaded Fadi and Hanne's bulging suitcases and bags into the trunk of the battered taxi that would ferry them to Amman Queen Alia International Airport.

The cab driver, a quiet, middle-aged man with well-worn jeans and a crooked smile, deposited the stump of his cigarette on the sidewalk, crushed it with his heel and wordlessly yanked the back door open.

Aunt Talia held Hanne in her arms as they both blinked back tears.

"God be with you," she whispered in Hanne's ear, "God bless you, my child. May you find much joy and peace in America."

"Thank you, Auntie," Hanne said as she clung to the elderly woman's neck, trying not to cry. "Keep us in your prayers. And remember, we want you to come visit us someday."

Hanne and Fadi climbed into the taxi. They were really leaving.

Aunt Talia stood there on the curb in front of her apartment building, waving and squinting in the bright morning sun until the cab disappeared.

"Keep them safe, O Lord," she said under her breath as she turned to head home, praying an Our Father, imploring heaven's aid. *"Baban deele beshmaya..."*

The ride to the airport, some 20 miles south of Amman proper, seemed endless. Like the road from Mosul to Baghdad, the route was riddled with potholes, stretching through miles of desert and punctuated by security checkpoints where soldiers with machine guns checked their papers. Hanne absentmindedly chewed her fingernails.

As the afternoon dragged on, Fadi and Hanne forced themselves to snack on the cheese, grapes and homemade bread Aunt Talia insisted they take with them for the trip to keep up their strength. They looked out the dirty windows of the cab in mutual silence, knowing it was the last time they would behold Iraq.

Mercifully, they'd made it to the airport with a little time to spare. They'd found their way to their seats once onboard the plane and noticed their fellow passengers were already settling in for the night. In short order, Fadi slid his tired feet under the seat in front of them and began to snore.

Hanne stared out the window as the 747 shot down the runway, engines roaring, gradually lifting them heavenward, away from their homeland, away from the place where they'd lost Noor. She felt as though her heart had been torn from her chest that day and annihilated. It seemed as though the sun would never rise again.

Yet rise it did. Her heart—how could it be so?—still beat within her. What did it mean to be alive now? Life and all its sweetness, as far as Hanne knew, ended that day inside the church.

Beneath the thunderous jet, the glittering city of Amman, Jordan grew smaller and smaller until it seemed to vanish entirely. Suddenly, impossibly, they were floating through a starless, midnight sky.

Hanne closed her eyes and leaned her head on Fadi's shoulder, trying in vain to block out the sound of a baby's piercing cries. The mother was seated just two rows behind them, and Hanne could hear her tender attempts to soothe the child, who seemed beyond consolation.

*A baby*. Was not a child the most precious gift God gave woman? Hanne felt the aching void in her arms, the longing. This was her Calvary. He, Love, would have to carry her now. She had lost the will to take the slightest step forward.

The sun had risen 43 times since December 6, but to Hanne, it felt as though it had permanently set, as though the world and all its color had been swallowed into blackness, into oblivion.

And that is where she sat now, holding back tears, listening to the insistent cries of some other woman's baby.

Were it not for the bout of colic or earache or whatever it was that tormented the poor child, Hanne would have been fast asleep. After the grueling cab ride from Baghdad to Amman, they were beyond weary. Hanne pulled the plastic wrap from the airline pillow and

## A Martyr's Crown

placed it behind her head.

The unhappy baby finally fell asleep, and Fadi, exhausted from the journey, mumbled something in his sleep.

Hanne looked at the elderly gentleman sitting beside them. He, too, had dozed off, his weathered, gnarled hands clasped and resting in his lap. Slipping the black-beaded rosary bracelet from her wrist, the one her mother had given her at their parting, Hanne closed her eyes and began to pray.

After what seemed like a long time, she fell into a heavy sleep, lulled by the rumbling jet engines and the rhythm of the Hail Marys. As the jet thundered onward, Hanne slept fitfully and saw it all unfolding in front of her again. Father Ameer raising the chalice, chanting the prayers. The candles flickering on the altar. The doors suddenly crashing open. The baby crying. Then, utter terror.

"Fadi! Help! Our baby!" Hanne gasped. "Our baby!" She was sitting on the edge of her seat now, shaking violently. She could hear the baby behind them crying again. Slowly it dawned on her; they were on a plane, not in the church back in Mosul.

The elderly man sitting next to Fadi got up and made his way toward the restroom. "What's the matter with her?" someone murmured. "What's happening?"

"My love," Fadi said, putting his arms around Hanne, "Shhh, Hanne. It's OK. Sit back now. It's alright. I'm right here, my darling."

A petite female flight attendant, clad in her trademark Royal Jordanian Airlines crimson suit, headed down the aisle toward them, worriedly biting her lower lip. Passengers occasionally became unruly on long flights like this and she hoped she could avoid having to alert the captain, or for that matter, police in Madrid.   Her supervisor would certainly not be pleased if there was a ruckus onboard the aircraft.

"Sir, I'm going to have to ask you and your wife to keep it

down," the flight attendant said briskly.

"I'm sorry," Fadi said, holding Hanne and looking up in anguish.

The woman's expression softened. "Is everything alright? Can I get you something? A little tea perhaps?"

"Tea would be fine," Fadi murmured. "Tea, Hanne. A cup of tea will help."

Hanne nodded her head slowly, wiping her eyes. She swallowed hard. The baby's cry had pierced her heart like a sword.

The flight attendant busied herself fetching two cups of tea, whispering to her co-worker that she had another one of those war-traumatized passengers on her hands. Other members of the cabin crew walked about the cabin, reassuring passengers.

"A nervous young lady—nothing more. Go back to sleep. We'll be in Madrid before you know it."

The mother of the fussy baby was pacing the narrow aisle now, holding the child against her shoulder as she patted his back, trying unsuccessfully to elicit a burp and straining to avoid all eye contact with fellow passengers.

"Here you are, sir," the flight attendant said, handing Fadi two cups of steaming tea. "Let me know if I can get anything else for you or your wife. There is a doctor onboard the plane if you think that might be necessary. Maybe he can give her something to calm her nerves."

"Oh, please, Fadi," Hanne begged, feeling the panic rise again, "Get me off this plane. I want to go home!"

Tears flooded Fadi's eyes now, too. "I can't Hanne. We can't go home, my love." He wiped his nose with his sleeve and looked up at the flight attendant, who watched with wide eyes, unable at her age to summon the wisdom to determine what to say or do next.

"Thank you," Fadi told her. "I think we'll be OK for now."

Fadi stirred a packet of sugar into his wife's tea.

"Drink, Hanne," he said gently. "It will soothe your nerves a

## A Martyr's Crown

bit."

Hanne took the cup, hands trembling. "I'm sorry, Fadi. I don't know what came over me."

"Shhh, Hanne," Fadi said, placing his hand on her cheek. "We're together. We'll be safe together."

Without taking a drink, Hanne set the tea down, her unsteady hand spilling several drops, which rolled to the left edge of the tray and stopped at the lip. She put her head against the seat and stared straight ahead at the rumpled hair of the person seated in front of them.

"Safe? How can I ever feel safe again?" She looked at Fadi with bewildered eyes. "There is only one thing I want. We can run to the ends of the earth and Noor will not be there."

The baby let out his loudest, most pitiful cry.

Hanne placed her hands over her face and wept. Fadi pulled her into his chest and held her head there.

"What have they done to my beloved?" he exhaled in a whisper too soft to hear. "What have they done?"

♕ ♕ ♕ ♕ ♕ ♕

# Chapter 29
Phoenix
Saturday, January 16, 2010

"I hope it's nothing too complicated," Sarah said to Javier as they pulled into Mar Ephrem's parking lot. "He said there's an auto parts store nearby if you need it."

"First I've got to figure out what's wrong with it," Javier said as he lifted his tool box from the trunk of their car.

Javier and Sarah walked over to the church hall where catechism school was in session. Father George was standing just outside the doors, saying goodbye to a group of parents.

"Hello there," he called out as they approached. "And this must be Javier."

"Nice to meet you, Father," Javier said, extending his hand.

"It is nice to meet you, too. I have heard a lot about you," Father George said. "I guess Sarah told you our church van is not working."

"She said you were having trouble with it. I've got my tools and I'd like to take a look at it and see if there's a way I can fix it for you here so you don't have to take it to a shop."

"This would be wonderful. Come, I will show you where it is parked."

Sarah and Javier followed Father George over to the rectory.

## A Martyr's Crown

The blue van stood in the shade of a giant mesquite tree.

"What is it doing? Does it start?" Javier asked Father George.

"It tries to start but it will not," Father George explained. "It seems that it is empty of gas, but that cannot be. I filled the tank."

"Well, that could mean a couple things," Javier said as Father George handed him the keys. "I'll do a few checks to try to figure out what's wrong with it. If I were going to bet, I'd say your fuel pump needs to be replaced."

"Now *that* would be ironic," Sarah said as she surveyed the van.

"Why is this ironic?" Father George asked glancing back and forth at Javier and Sarah quizzically.

"That's how we met," Sarah said. "My car stalled just off campus on the first day of classes back in college. Javier was walking by and asked if I needed help. I told him almost the same thing you just did, and *voila!* Here we are, 23 years later."

"So, this bad fuel pump—this is your trick to meet people then, Javier?" Father George teased.

"Well, not exactly," Javier laughed as he popped the hood. "The thing is, growing up in Puerto Rico, if something broke—especially a car—you had to figure out how to fix it. There was no way to replace it cheaply. So my dad and brothers and I, well, we got to be experts at fixing cars."

"Of course," Father George said. "It was this way in Iraq, too."

"Javier fixes my mom's car, too," Sarah said. "And my nieces' cars."

"This is a very generous thing," Father George observed.

"I'm happy to help, Father," Javier answered from under the hood.

"Shall we go to see the catechism school while Javier works on the van?"

"Sure," Sarah said. "I've never been much good with a wrench. Are you OK out here, Javier, if I go over to the hall?"

"Absolutely," Javier said, "I'll be right here until I figure this thing out."

"Sarah and I will go to the hall," Father George said. "Here: take my cell phone number. You can call me if you need something."

Javier punched the number into his phone and stuffed it back in his jeans.

"Javier, he seems like a good man, Sarah," Father George said as they walked toward the hall. Sarah was careful to walk at a slower pace, wincing as Father made his way with difficulty. "He is kind to spend his Saturday morning fixing our van. Now why you did not bring your sons?"

"Zach and Thomas are at Sholeh's house for her son's birthday party. And Benny is home with a bad cold."

"How are things with Javier?"

"A little better I guess, but unfortunately, I think he's still considering leaving," Sarah said, looking off in the distance, trying to steady her voice. "But I took your advice—I really have forgiven him. And I think your prayers are helping, too."

"Forgiveness brings peace."

"I'm realizing that now."

"Sometimes it takes a while when the hurt is very deep. It has for me. I am still working on this area."

Sarah nodded. She could scarcely imagine how Father George could begin to forgive all the wrong that had been done to him.

"So tell me—what happened with Javier?" Father George asked. "Here, let us sit down on this bench in the shade. I want to hear the rest of your story."

It was a little rickety, as though hundreds of parishioners had sat there over the years in the shade of the mesquite tree near the church hall.

"Well, like I said, we had a big argument a few weeks ago," Sarah admitted. "He said he was going to go back to Puerto Rico after Christmas to stay with his mom, that he couldn't take me blaming him anymore.

## A Martyr's Crown

"But when he called her, she said, 'No, don't come. I'm going to be traveling, visiting your brother in Florida and I'll visit your family myself in the spring when I come to Arizona.' She said she wanted to be here for Zach's graduation. I wonder if she sensed Javier was thinking of leaving me."

"Maybe," Father George observed. "Mothers can be wise about these things."

"She is. And something else: she prays—a lot. As in, the rosary every day, Mass every day. Javier's father died several years ago and we saw then just how strong her faith is."

"So he is not going back to Puerto Rico. This is good," Father George said.

"Yeah. But that doesn't mean he won't move out. He's still thinking about doing that, I know it! But what you said at Mass on Sunday—that helped me a lot. It made me face the fact that even though I expected God to overlook my faults and forgive my sins, I was hanging onto some anger against Javier. And that was wrong."

"This is good news," Father George said slowly, "but I sense you are still troubled in some way."

"The thing is, I want to forgive him. And I know I have to. But it's hard to forget, so I feel guilty about that."

"Have you asked God to help you?"

Sarah nodded her head.

"Well, feelings are feelings. It takes time for them to change. The fact that you have asked God to help you forgive is in itself an act of forgiveness, Sarah. So you must be patient—patient with yourself and patient with Javier."

"I guess I'm not a very patient person."

"This is a rare quality, but with God, you can do anything."

"My father told me that once, long ago," Sarah said softly.

"I still think about what those men did to me, Sarah. And I live with this feeling every day. But one day—not long ago, in fact—I decided that I wasn't going to let them destroy me, destroy what is left of my life."

"Were they ever caught, those men?"

"Caught? Certainly not. Someday they will face God and account for their actions, but for now, they are unpunished. There are even those who consider them heroes."

Sarah shuddered to think of what Father George had suffered.

"Why does God allow such terrible things to happen?"

"Ah, you are asking the hard question. The mystery of suffering. We cannot see the big picture, but we must trust God. 'Strong is His love for us.' That is from the Morning Prayer. Have you been using The Book of Before and After that I gave you?"

"I admit that it sat on my desk for a while. But a few days ago, I picked it up and started reading. I've been meaning to talk with you about it."

He looked at her thoughtfully. "What do you think of them, these prayers?"

"They're beautiful, but it was the title of the book that really got my attention."

"The title? Why?"

"Because I used to think of my life that way—in terms of before and after. As in, before we lost Patrick—and then after. It seemed like our family would always be seen through that lens—like everything after that moment in time was ruined and colored by tragedy, that we could never really be happy again.

"But I'm moving forward now, little by little. I still miss Patrick so very much…it's just that I do see some hope now. I do find a little joy in things now. I even find reasons to laugh sometimes."

"Why?" Father George asked her. "What changed?"

"Well, for one thing, my mom gave me my father's journal at Christmas. He died the year after Patrick did. I was very close to my dad, and losing him on top of losing Patrick…it was as

## A Martyr's Crown

though grief swallowed me. Reading my father's words gave me some insight into how it was my parents stayed married so long, and how it was that my dad was really a very happy person, in spite of many difficulties.

"But I have to say that part of my healing has been getting to know you and your people. Seeing the pain and the trauma the Chaldeans have been through—it got me to think of others and how I might help them."

"Thinking of how to help others—this is a good way to forget our own pain."

Father George's cell phone went off. "Excuse me, Sarah, but I must answer this."

"Hello, this is Father George. Who is this?"

"Father George, it's Javier. I've got some news for you. Your van needs a new fuel pump."

"You are making a joke?"

"Nope, not kidding at all," Javier answered. "I'm going to head over to the auto parts store and pick up one for you."

"I will come now and give you some money to pay for it," Father George said.

"It's nothing. Don't worry about it."

"Are you sure?"

"Definitely," Javier said. "My pleasure."

"This is so very kind of you, Javier. Thank you," Father George said, relieved he wouldn't need to spend the day at the car dealership, dreading the bill. "Now remember, you and Sarah, you will have lunch here with us in the rectory. We eat at one o'clock, OK?

"Sounds good, Father. I'll see you then."

Father George switched off his phone and turned to Sarah with a broad smile.

"Javier figured out what's wrong with your van?"

"The fuel pump. Can you believe it?"

Sarah laughed. "That's actually pretty funny. I'm glad he can fix it for you. It's an expensive job to have done at a shop."

"I am sure it is. And I appreciate the two of you helping us so much. Even after your articles, I think most people still do not really know who we are or what we are doing here in America."

"If I have my way, Father George," Sarah said with a determined look, "that's going to change."

That night, after she'd finished reading her father's journal, Sarah checked her email and was surprised to see something from Father George.

"*Hi, Sarah,*" the email began, "*Please tell Javier again that I said thank you for fixing the van. I hope you are having a nice evening together there at home. I wanted to tell you that we will welcome a new family to the church. It is a young couple that just left Iraq.*

"*I think you will want to meet these people, but I do not wish to say why in an email. Please call me when you have a moment.*"

Sarah was instantly curious. Who could this couple be? It was almost nine o'clock; maybe she should call him tomorrow. *Nope. I won't be able to sleep.*

He answered his cell phone on the first ring.

"Hi, Sarah," Father George said. "How is your night?"

"Doing fine here, Father," Sarah answered as she stood at the window, admiring the full moon and the stars outside. "I just read your email. So who are these people you want me to meet?"

"Remember when you came to the prayer vigil at our church after the massacre at Mar Addai?"

"Of course I do," Sarah said. "How could I ever forget?" Instantly she pictured the crowd of mourners dressed in black, carrying candles and pictures of their murdered loved ones.

"The woman whose baby died that day at the church—she and her husband will arrive here on Monday," Father George said carefully.

Sarah drew in her breath sharply, shocked at the news. She sat down at her desk. She'd been wondering about this mother. *Hanne. That was her name. And now she was coming here.*

"Are you still there, Sarah?"

"I'm here," she said haltingly. To think this poor woman was on her way to Phoenix! "This person—her name is Hanne, right?"

"Yes—I did not realize you knew her name. How did you remember?"

*How could I ever forget?* Sarah thought to herself.

"Oh, it's stayed with me all this time. I've often wondered whatever happened to her."

"Yes, her husband's aunt is a member of our community," Father George continued. "She called me last night and told me about them coming. I knew you would want to meet her. Hanne speaks English."

"Really? She does?" Sarah asked, surprised to hear it.

"Her husband—his name is Fadi—he is a language professor and he used to interpret for the U.S. military. They had to leave Iraq after some death threats. And Hanne studied English at the university. Actually, Sarah, I was thinking of what you told me last weekend. You know, about Patrick. I am hoping that maybe you and Hanne will become friends. Not many people understand what it is like to lose a child."

Sarah was speechless. "I....I don't know what to say. I guess I'm in shock."

"This is understandable," Father George said. "We will not rush anything. I just thought you would want to know."

"Well, I would like to meet her," Sarah said. "What do you suggest?"

"There will be a dinner here at the parish next Wednesday. It will be the last night of our *Bautha*. This is like a mini-Lent for Chaldeans. Anyway, we have a Mass and dinner on Wednesday, the last night. It is only a simple meal—nothing elaborate. But Hanne and Fadi will be there and I was thinking maybe you and Javier will want to come, too."

"I'll talk to him about it," Sarah said slowly. "But one thing's for sure: If at all possible, I'm going to be there."

A Martyr's Crown

# Chapter 30
Flight to New York
Monday, January 18, 2010

Hanne awoke to the sound of flight attendants rolling their metal carts up the aisle as they served breakfast. She'd slept soundly after their stop in Madrid, probably due to sheer exhaustion.

Beside her, Fadi opened his eyes.

"We'll be in New York in an hour," he said, looking at his watch.

After breakfast, they filled out the form they'd need to present at customs. Since they didn't have anything to declare, it was rather simple. They'd left their homeland with nothing but a couple suitcases and the cash from Aunt Talia.

When the plane finally began its gradual descent, Hanne and Fadi were mesmerized by the expansive New York skyline. They'd seen their share of American movies, of course, so it wasn't like they were stunned by the sight. Still, neither one of them had ever been on a plane before. Staring out the cabin window, they both silently wondered where the World Trade Center towers once stood and shuddered as they thought of the hatred that knocked them down. It was that same grotesque darkness that had driven them from Iraq.

"Ladies and gentlemen, on behalf of Royal Jordanian Airlines, we welcome you to New York's La Guardia Airport," a flight attendant announced brightly. "It's been a pleasure traveling with you today."

The jumbo jet touched down, and some of the passengers politely applauded. Hanne and Fadi were amused. Was it applause for the pilot's prowess? Or was it perhaps gratitude that they were now on American soil?

Hanne stood and removed their carry-on luggage from the overhead bin. They had stuffed as much as they could into the bags and there was no way she was going to let Fadi hurt himself trying to get them down. Thank God they had wheels.

There were two hours to wait before the flight to Phoenix, so they decided to stretch their legs and walk through the airport a bit. The place was packed with travelers from all over the world.

All their money was in Iraqi bills and coins, so they couldn't buy a cup of coffee or a newspaper, as they would have liked. "We'll exchange our *dinars* when we get to Phoenix, *azizta*," Fadi said. "And they'll give us coffee on the next airplane, I'm sure."

Hanne nodded silently. They walked through the airport, people watching. For the first time ever, they beheld a group of pious Jews, the men with beards and forelocks, dressed in dark pants, jackets and broad-brimmed hats. Two women from India, dressed in colorful saris, were sitting on a bench, eating popcorn.

"America," Fadi said. "People come here from all over the world, just like us, *azizta*."

At last they were onboard the airplane headed toward Phoenix. Fadi's aunt and uncle were going to meet them at the airport, along with someone from Catholic Charities' resettlement program. The Americans at the embassy told Fadi they would have a furnished apartment waiting for them, in a complex with other refugee families.

"Are the other families from Iraq?" Fadi asked.

"Some are," the consular officer told them, "but many are not.

## A Martyr's Crown

Refugees from all over the world settle in Phoenix. At least you have your relatives nearby."

It was true. Compared to many others who fled to America, she and Fadi had some big advantages. They both spoke English, though Fadi had considerable more practice than Hanne. They had relatives who would look after them and a church waiting to receive them.

It was a direct flight to Phoenix, and though they were ravenous, all they received was a cup of coffee and some pretzels. Both of them felt a little out of sorts. It seemed a lifetime since they'd said goodbye to their family in Mosul and they were both dreaming of a shower and a comfortable bed.

When at last they arrived in Phoenix and got off the plane, they saw there was a woman standing patiently at the gate, holding a small placard with their names on it.

"Mr. and Mrs. Yacoub?" she asked them tentatively as they approached.

"I am Fadi Yacoub and this is my wife, Hanne," Fadi answered. "Are you the person from the refugee program?"

"Yes, I am," she said with a smile. "Welcome to America. My name is Rose McDonald and I'm here to help you get settled. I understand you've got relatives here in the Phoenix area. Are they coming to the airport too?"

"Yes," Fadi answered. "They said they will meet us at the baggage claim. Do you know where this claim is?"

"Right this way," Rose told them. "Now, tell me, are you hungry? I bet you are. We've got to get you something to eat. But let's find your relatives first. How was the trip?"

"It was a long trip," Fadi said.

"How is it that you both speak English? Most of our refugees don't."

"I am language professor at university in Mosul," Fadi said, "My wife, she study English in college. I hope to find job at the university here in America."

"I see. So you both have a college education," Rose said. "That will be a help here in the states. Alright, that's the baggage claim area. Your luggage should be on carousel number…"

"You made it!" Aunt Samira and Uncle Matay cried as they rushed up and embraced Fadi and Hanne, kissing them on both cheeks. "We're so glad you are here!" Fadi's cousin Reema was there with her parents to welcome them, too.

"Hi there," Rose said, offering her hand to Samira and Matay, "I'm from Catholic Charities. I'm here to show Fadi and Hanne where their apartment is and help get them settled."

Samira and Matay, who didn't speak much English, turned to Reema for an explanation. Who was this American lady and how did she know Hanne and Fadi?

"She's here to help them get settled," Reema said.

Matay loaded their luggage into the trunk of his car so they could follow Rose to the apartment building where they'd be living. After about 15 minutes of freeway driving, they saw her exit and turn onto a busy street, then into a driveway.

"Canyon River Apartments," a banner proclaimed from the front lawn of the large complex. Hanne noticed there were children playing in the shade of a large pine tree. One of them, a boy with dark curly hair and a red T-shirt, was tossing a ball to the others.

Matay pulled into the spot next to Rose and they all got out and stood in the bright afternoon sun to talk.

"Now then," Rose said, "the manager very kindly arranged for you to have an apartment on the first floor so you wouldn't have to be climbing stairs. I explained to him that you're recovering from an injury."

Fadi winced remembering how much pain he suffered after taking the stairs to their apartment in Mosul the day he packed up their belongings. They followed Rose down the long corridor, making their way past a swimming pool surrounded by a tall iron

## A Martyr's Crown

fence, and stopping in front of the last door.

Rose slipped a key in the lock and pushed the door open.

Hanne and Fadi stepped inside and beheld a sparsely furnished, though tidy room.

"I made sure to have everything you'll need here," Rose said as she walked them through the two-room apartment. "There's a loaf of bread on the counter, some cans of soup and eggs and milk in the refrigerator."

"Thank you," Hanne said.

Looking around, Hanne saw there was a simple table with two chairs set up in the kitchen area and a faded green couch near the window. A sagging mattress in a metal frame stood in the corner.

She thought of their comfortable, well-appointed apartment in Mosul and swallowed hard. At least no one would be hunting them down, she thought to herself. At least the streets weren't filled with bombed-out buildings and danger and armed men.

"Here are two keys for the apartment and a key to unlock the gate to the swimming pool," Rose said as she handed key rings to them. "You might want to use it when the weather gets warmer."

Hanne and Fadi looked at each other and laughed nervously. Neither one of them knew how to swim.

"Now then," Rose continued, "Your first three months of rent are already paid. I'm also giving you a debit card you can use to buy groceries as part of our food stamps program. There's a grocery store two blocks from here.

"Usually what we do is to show our new residents around, help get them acclimated, point out the bus stop, that kind of thing," Rose said, "but since you speak English and you've got relatives nearby, I'm thinking you won't need much more from me for now." She handed them her business card. "If there's anything else I can do for you, please call. I'll be checking up on you next week sometime to see how you're managing."

Hanne nodded as she slowly turned the keys over in the palm

of her hand. A new home in a new country.   Standing there in the tiny, colorless apartment, Hanne felt a stab of homesickness. *What time was it in Mosul? What was her family doing there now? And how on earth was she going to survive here?*

A Martyr's Crown

# Chapter 31
Phoenix
Tuesday, January 19, 2010

Sarah was going over her notes for a meeting with Rick to discuss some of the stories she was working on for the paper. The possible collaboration between St. Clare's and Mar Ephrem was a good possibility, if she could convince him of it.

"Why should readers care?" was the first thing he always asked when she pitched a story idea.

Father Keller had been supportive when Sholeh and Sarah approached him about seeking a grant for the Chaldean Catholic Church in Arizona. He knew a little about the Church's Eastern Rite and listened sympathetically as Sarah described the challenges the Chaldeans were facing.

"We'll be sitting down soon with the committee, so make sure you fill out that paperwork if you're serious about getting a grant," he told them.

"Hey, Sarah," Diane said from the doorway. "How's it going?"

"Pretty good, I guess," Sarah said. "Where are you off to?"

"Funny you should ask," Diane said slyly as she handed Sarah a sheet of paper. "I'm on my way to Rick's office." Sarah took the page and began reading.

"Seriously?" Sarah asked, looking up at her friend.

Diane nodded her head. "Want to grab a cup of coffee afterward so we can talk?"

"Definitely. You've got to give me all the details." Although she'd heard Diane might be moving on, it was hard to believe. They'd known each other since college.

Sarah hated goodbyes. It wasn't like she and Diane were best friends or anything, but still, she was sad to see her friend had accepted a job in Detroit of all places. It wasn't exactly next door. She doubted they would ever see each other again once Diane moved away.

What was it about saying goodbye to someone that made Sarah want to run away? She remembered how she felt when her older brothers and sisters left for college: abandoned, set adrift. She was glad the seven Murphy siblings still lived in the Phoenix area.

Diane returned a few moments later and the two women grabbed their sweaters and headed for the stairs.

"How'd it go?" Sarah asked as they walked toward the coffee shop.

"He said he was sorry to lose me but that he understood I had a great opportunity in Detroit."

"So—managing editor. How'd you land that one?" Sarah asked.

"Well, I've been thinking for a while that I needed to move on," Diane said as they stood in line waiting to place their order. "I don't have any family here and I'm not dating anybody. And I've always wanted to be editor."

"Really? I thought you liked reporting."

"I do, but I'm ready for a change. By the way, I've been meaning to tell you how much I liked the story you did about the Chaldean Church and the refugees. Didn't you say something about there being an even larger community in Michigan?"

"Yeah, I think Father George said there's something like seven Chaldean parishes in Michigan," Sarah said. "He said that some of the Chaldeans in Arizona settled in Michigan first before coming here. Who knows? Maybe you'll find yourself assigning a story to

## A Martyr's Crown

a reporter about it."

"Maybe," Diane laughed. "One thing's for sure though. I'm going to miss working with you at the *Sun-Times*."

"I'll miss you, too," Sarah admitted. "Who's going to be getting coffee with me now when I need a dose of caffeine?"

"Oh, you'll do fine without me," Diane said. "Maybe you'll grow to love the coffee Mary makes in the break room."

They both laughed, knowing that was impossible. The sludge their otherwise dependable office manager concocted was awful.

"Maybe you'll be an editor someday too," Diane said. "Have you ever thought about working for another publication maybe?"

"It's different when you have to balance work with family," Sarah said. "It's been a good thing having part-time work while the kids are growing up. I don't think I'm ready to be gone full-time yet with Benny being so young. We still have his high school years ahead of us."

They sat down on a bench in the sunshine to enjoy their coffee. A woman flanked by two young children and holding an infant walked past, probably on her way to the downtown library for story time. The little boy, wearing a Superman cap, was complaining, loudly, that he was hungry.

"Boys and food," Sarah said with a grin. "Can I relate or what?"

"Yeah, you've got your hands full taking care of all those boys," Diane agreed. "You must have a lot of patience. But do you ever wonder what life would be like without them? I mean, what if you were like me and never had kids?"

As soon as she realized what she'd said, Diane immediately regretted the words. Her mind spun thinking back to the day they'd all found out about Patrick.

"I'm so sorry," she said quickly, mortified. "That was such a dumb thing to say after all you've been through. I don't know what I was thinking."

"No, it's OK," Sarah said softly. "I think about Patrick every day and it's probably always going to be like that. But it's getting a little less horrible, day by day."

Diane looked at her friend in amazement. Sarah, who wasn't particularly ambitious, didn't wear designer clothes or travel to exotic destinations, was content with life, even after the tragedy she'd endured. She and what's-his-name had been married for years and had three other sons. She'd probably stay right there in suburbia with her part-time reporter job and YMCA membership.

And that's when Diane wondered if maybe, just maybe, Sarah had something on her.

The series of live-in boyfriends she'd had through the years left her with a feeling of emptiness inside that no promotion, no possession could ever fill. What was Sarah's secret? How was it that she was happy with such a mediocre, boring little life?

Sarah looked at her cell phone: 10:20 a.m. and nearly time to meet with Rick.

"I've got to get going," she said, rising from the bench. "Rick and I are meeting in a bit to talk about some stories I'm working on."

"OK, well I've still got two weeks here, Sarah," Diane said as she stood. "Maybe we can have lunch sometime before I leave."

"Sounds good, Diane. Just let me know when."

As they turned to walk in the building, Diane had the unsettling feeling that she'd just been outclassed by a woman in a worn-out pair of pumps and rather ordinary looking clothes.

A Martyr's Crown

# Chapter 32
Phoenix
Wednesday, January 19, 2010

Hanne and Fadi were slowly beginning to acquaint themselves with their new surroundings in Phoenix. The apartment wasn't luxurious by any standards, but it was decent. More importantly, it was located in a busy neighborhood, within walking distance of a grocery store and a bank.

Yesterday, they walked to the bank and presented the handful of cash from Aunt Talia. The teller was surprised when she saw the strange looking bills. She'd seen Euros before and even Israeli shekels, but never Iraqi *dinars.*

"We don't see these too often," she said as she examined the bills Fadi presented to her. "Let's have you sit down with a banker and set up an account."

The banker, a tall, thin man with salt-and-pepper hair, led them over to his desk and offered them each an upholstered chair. After they'd finished answering all his questions, he told them he would be exchanging their Iraqi currency for American dollars, but that the transaction would take a couple of days.

"With today's exchange rate, you've got about $1,500 here," the banker said as he consulted his computer. "That's more than most refugees start with when they get here."

"My aunt, she was very generous with us," Hanne said as she

closed her eyes, summoning the image of Aunt Talia in her mind's eye. "She knows we will need money."

The banker nodded his head. "That was very kind of her. But even so, that money will only last for so long. I hope you can find jobs around here. It's not easy these days."

Rose presented them each with a bus pass before she left on Monday night, telling them to try to get to know the city a little. Uncle Matay gave them a few American dollars.

"This is for now," he said, handing him the folded-up bills. "You could take the bus to my store and work there when you're feeling better."

Fadi appreciated the offer, but since both he and Hanne had college degrees and spoke English, he hoped they might find something that paid a little better.

"I know we don't have jobs yet, Fadi, but can we buy a computer?" Hanne pleaded. "Please, *aziza*? So we can talk with our family back home? We have the money from my aunt."

"Of course we will, Hanne, in a couple days, once the funds are available. You heard what they said at the bank. But there's no harm in looking today."

They waited on the corner for the bus. Traffic whizzed by in both directions and Hanne marveled at how new the cars looked, how clean the streets were. An old woman sitting patiently, waiting for the bus, looked at them curiously, wondering what language they spoke. It certainly wasn't Spanish.

"No soldiers on the street. I like that," Hanne said looking up and down the street.

"And no blown-up buildings."

When the bus finally lumbered to a stop in front of the bank, the two of them climbed aboard for the short ride to the mall.

They looked around the gigantic electronics store and were dazzled by the brightly lit display of computers, cell phones, stereos and other electronic goods. They'd never seen a store like it

## A Martyr's Crown

in Mosul.

"Look at all the laptops, Fadi," Hanne said, pointing at the array of technology. "So many different kinds."

A salesman quickly approached.

"May I help you folks find something?"

"We are just looking," Fadi said.

They walked around the store for a while, hand in hand. Fadi made mental notes about which computer might be best.

"Want to see some of the other stores while we're here?" Fadi asked Hanne. "We don't have to get back on the bus yet."

"I suppose," Hanne said, not sure she wanted to walk much farther. Maybe it would do them good though—Fadi needed the exercise.

They walked through clothing stores and even a kitchen store with all kinds of gadgets and appliances for cooking. The refugee agency had arranged for the essentials for their apartment but nothing more. They had a couple of plates and cups, a frying pan and some mismatched silverware, but that was about it.

Hanne eyed a beautiful set of dishes and couldn't help but think of the lovely set of blue-and-white china, a wedding gift that she'd had to leave behind in Iraq. *At least Nahida and Nora will make use of them.*

They walked on silently for a while, window shopping, lost in their thoughts. After about an hour, Hanne realized they had seen everything the mall had to offer. Fadi said they should have an ice cream cone before getting back on the bus.

"Ice cream? In January, Fadi?"

"Why not?" Fadi said. "It's not like it's snowing outside. It might cheer us up."

There were more than 20 flavors to choose from, many they'd never even heard of before. Hanne and Fadi took their time deciding on just the right one as the server, a bored-looking teenage boy who wordlessly brushed the hair from his eyes, awaited their decision.

"I can't remember the last time I had ice cream," Hanne said to Fadi as they sat at one of the metal tables in the food court, indulging in the treat.

"So what do you think of America so far, *azizta*?"

"Everyone has been very kind to us," Hanne admitted, wiping her mouth with a napkin. The dark chocolate ice cream she'd chosen was melting fast. "But I miss my family. I am trying not to think of them, but the more I try, the more I can't escape the feeling that we're so alone here. It feels like we've been gone a long time already."

"Once we get the computer, you'll be able to chat with them on Facebook every day if you want," Fadi assured her. "I promise."

Hanne nodded thoughtfully. It wasn't the same, but it would definitely help.

"And on Sunday, my uncle will pick us up so we can go to the Chaldean Church," Fadi added. "That will be a taste of home."

"We won't know anyone except your relatives."

"We'll get to know the others, Hanne," Fadi reassured her as he finished off his ice cream cone. "My uncle said there are two priests and they have a lot of activities there for the people, like fish barbecues during Lent and a Bible study. And *Bautha* is coming up, remember? I bet they will do something special for that."

Hanne thought for a moment of how her family back in Mosul observed the mini-Lent, a three-day period of fasting and prayer, or the "Supplication of Nineveh" as it was called in English. It would be different to keep the tradition here, in a new land. How would they do it, here on their own?

"I know what you're thinking, Hanne," Fadi said. "You're thinking it will be hard to feel part of the community here among strangers. But I'm sure if we get involved at Mar Ephrem, we'll meet others who have had to learn to get used to this new land, too."

## A Martyr's Crown

"I guess," Hanne said. "But still. I miss my family, even more than I thought I would. I miss our apartment and our things and our life there together. The thought that we can never, ever go back home…it's just hard to accept. Aren't you homesick? You don't have to pretend for me."

"Do I miss Iraq?" Fadi said aloud, looking up at the ceiling. "I miss our loved ones, yes, but I don't miss fearing for our lives. I don't miss living in the midst of all that violence and craziness. I don't miss the stress and the danger of the work I was doing for the Americans. No one's going to be trying to kill us here. We're going to make a good life for ourselves in America, Hanne, trust me."

"I hope you're right, *aziza*," Hanne said as she swallowed the last of her ice cream.

וְוְוְוְוְוְוְ

Sarah went over her list of stories with Rick, saving the one about Mar Ephrem for last.

"Are you still planning on interviewing that psychologist about New Year's resolutions and living up to them?"

"I did that one yesterday," Sarah replied. "He had some good pointers, that's for sure."

"Most people have already broken their resolutions and it's only January," Rick said with a snort. "What's he think about that I wonder?"

"Actually, he said it's much easier to fall into a bad habit than it is to establish a good one," Sarah said thoughtfully. "'It takes time to develop good patterns of behavior,'—that's what he said."

"Time. Just what everybody wishes they had more of these days."

"Everybody has the same 24 hours each day. That's what he told me."

"I suppose. Whatever. What else you got for me?"

"Remember the story I wrote about Mar Ephrem Chaldean Church?"

"The one with the people from Iraq?" Rick asked. "Wasn't that the church that had the party for the refugee children at Christmas?"

"That's the one," Sarah said, glad Rick remembered. "Looks like there's another very newsworthy story on the horizon."

"And what would that be?" Rick looked doubtful.

"Well, there's this former Muslim lady from Iran who converted to Catholicism. Obviously, she doesn't want her name getting out—you know, the apostasy laws and all that back in her homeland," Sarah explained. "Anyway, she read my article and took an interest in the Chaldeans since they come from the Middle East, too.

"She came up with this idea to have the youth group at St. Clare's do a service project at Mar Ephrem. The teens are going to have a series of Saturday afternoons with sports activities for the refugee kids. You know—soccer, basketball—that kind of thing. They'll have snacks afterwards and trophies. A lot of these refugee kids have never participated in organized sports before. Some of them are living with horrible memories of war."

"Kind of a religion story with a sports theme, I guess," Rick mused. "That's different. People love inspirational sports stories."

"There's more though," Sarah continued. "This Iranian lady also talked with the pastor of St. Clare's about a grant for some structural improvements at Mar Ephrem. St. Clare's has a grant program where they give 10 percent of their weekly collection to needy Catholic parishes and organizations in the area. They've helped out some of the inner city schools with remodeling, that sort of thing.

"Right now the St. Clare's grants committee is reviewing all the applications they've received so far, including one from Mar Ephrem. They're going to make their decision next week sometime. If Mar Ephrem is chosen—and I have a hunch they will be—they're going to have some remodeling done on their hall. The place is practically falling down around them."

"So we've got an upper-middle class parish teaming up with a parish of immigrants and refugees. And a Muslim convert to Catholicism in the middle of it all," Rick said. "I'd say that's pretty unique. I mean, the Iraqis and Iranians fought each other for years. But here they are in Phoenix, working together."

"Exactly," Sarah said. "I knew you'd like it."

"What makes you think St. Clare's is going to give them that grant money? There must be a lot of people who have their eyes on financial help right now. Lot of folks out of jobs."

"Well, when she spoke to the pastor, Father Keller, he knew exactly who the Chaldeans were. He told her to look up something written by John Paul II. Apparently JP2 encouraged more unity between East and West.

"As it turns out, Father Keller is very devoted to the late pope. So he's probably thinking that giving this grant money is fulfilling what John Paul II wanted. Even without all that, it's still a great story about a community coming together to help others."

"Alright then, let me know how it all turns out," Rick said. "If anything, you can always do a photo spread of the kids playing sports and just a short piece on how they organized the program."

"Sure thing, Rick. I'll keep you posted."

Sarah hoped the committee at St. Clare's would find it in their hearts to help Father George and his people. Arriving back at her cube, she texted Sholeh.

"I just got the OK for a story. Do you think Mar Ephrem will get the grant?"

Sholeh considered Sarah's text. A $10,000 grant would do some good, but as far as she was concerned, it wasn't nearly enough.

*I wonder. Perhaps there is another way*, Sholeh thought to herself as she evaluated her options. *I'll have to think this over carefully.*

"There's something I want to show you after dinner," Javier said when the boys began clearing the plates from the table that night.

Sarah cocked her head. "A surprise?"

Javier smiled. "Just a little something I've been working on." He winked at Benny. "Why don't you go out on the patio and wait for me. I'll be there in a minute."

Sarah stepped outside, wondering what Javier was up to. She sat down in the wicker rocking chair and looked up at the moon and the stars. Somewhere off in the distance, she could hear the sound of laughter. A neighbor was grilling steaks and the tantalizing aroma filled the night air.

She looked up when she heard Javier pull open the French doors leading to the patio. In his hands he held the Gibson guitar, the same one he'd strummed all those years ago when they had first fallen in love. Sarah's jaw dropped.

"Your guitar! I haven't heard you play it in years."

"Unbeknownst to you, I've been practicing while you've been holed up in the den at night, typing away," Javier said as he pulled up a chair. "Recognize this one?"

As soon as she heard the first notes, Sarah remembered the day Javier asked her to marry him. It was a gorgeous spring day, and they'd gone to a park just off campus.

*"Will you walk beside me forever, through the valleys and through the years, through our blessings and through our tears...."*

He set the guitar aside when the final note rang out, then took her hand into his own and kissed it tenderly. "Would you still marry me, now, even after all we've been through?"

Sarah fell into his arms then.

"A million times, yes. Please, Javier—promise you'll never leave me."

"How could I even think of it? I'd be crazy to leave you," he said as he held her close, held her the way he hadn't in two long years.

Sarah leaned her head on his shoulder, felt the strength in his arms. This was the man who had stolen her heart all those years ago. The wall between them had finally crumbled.

A Martyr's Crown

# Chapter 33
Phoenix
Wednesday, January 26, 2010

Father George, like most Chaldeans, was fasting. It was the third day of *Bautha* and no food—nothing except water—would pass his lips until much later in the day when he and the others would enjoy a simple meal of rice, *tahin* and *mepokhta*. He did his best to ignore the hunger pangs gnawing at his belly and focused instead on the task before him: figuring out how they were going to make the rent this month. Surely it would be by the grace of God.

"If I pay the insurance, there won't be enough for the rent," he realized as he added up the bills. "What am I going to do?"

So many of his parishioners, he thought as he went over the parish checkbook, were people who truly struggled for the basic necessities of life. Even if they were highly educated in Iraq, until they spoke English, they often had to work at menial jobs here in the States. He knew none of them was about to show up with the rent for Mar Ephrem.

Just last week a woman, a widow with two young daughters, came to him because the electric company was threatening to turn off the power to her home.

"*Aboona*, I don't know where else to turn," she said. "My husband didn't leave us with much, and without electricity, I can't cook for my girls."

He took $50 from his wallet and handed it to her, apologizing that it wasn't more.

Father George looked out his window at the dilapidated hall where the children studied catechism and where the parish would celebrate the end of *Bautha* after tonight's Mass. The sight of the building's sagging roof and peeling paint depressed him. Some of the neighbors had complained to the city that the church was an eyesore and he was worried that he might have legal trouble on top of everything else. The previous pastor allowed a remodeling project at the church but no one ever bothered to get permits. It was a sloppy job that left the place in even worse condition. He tried not to think about it.

There was one bright spot on the horizon and he chose to focus on that: Sarah had done a wonderful job writing up a grant proposal for St. Clare Parish. He hoped that God would answer his prayer to fix up the hall, make it at least decent, so the roof didn't leak every time it rained. There was no way they had enough money to do it on their own.

When Sholeh called and told him what her pastor said about John Paul II, it occurred to him that he'd finally encountered a Roman rite priest who was aware of the late pope's desire to see more collaboration between East and West.

"He told me to read something by John Paul II called '*Orientale Lumen.*' He said I could find it on the Internet. Have you ever heard of it?"

"Heard of it? Of course—this is his apostolic letter on the Eastern Church. Yes. You should read it."

He'd been a little suspicious of Sholeh at first, but he realized now that she was sincere about wanting to help the Chaldeans. Of course, back home in Iraq, whenever a Muslim said he or she wanted to convert, there was reason to worry.

"Be on guard in those situations," an older priest advised him once. "Sometimes these people, they just want to cause trouble

## A Martyr's Crown

from within. The ones who say they want to convert, you must question them closely to discover their intentions."

In Sholeh's case, his fears were now laid to rest. Her Catholic faith appeared to be deeply held. She was close to her pastor and attended daily Mass, two excellent indicators.

He wondered what would happen when Sarah met Hanne. After hearing her tell the story of the way they'd lost Patrick, he knew she was in need of healing. At least she'd finally realized it was wrong to blame her husband about what happened. He'd seen more than one marriage crumble after the death of a child.

ש ש ש ש ש ש ש

Javier and Sarah decided to attend the Mass and dinner at Mar Ephrem together that night after work. Father George said that Hanne and her husband would be there, too.

"Make sure you boys finish your homework," Sarah said to Zach and Thomas as she ladled chicken soup into bowls for the boys. Benny was already at the dining room table, working on a science assignment. "Don't you have a math test tomorrow, Thomas?"

"I'm on it, Mom, don't worry," Thomas said, stifling a yawn. "Dad's been helping me with it, remember?"

"OK, well, I hope I see good results when your progress report comes in a couple weeks." She felt for the kid. Math was never her favorite subject either.

"So am I going to understand anything in this Mass?" Javier asked her as they drove to Mar Ephrem. "I mean, Aramaic? I didn't know people were still speaking it."

"Yep. They do, and you're about to get an earful, my dear," Sarah said as they headed north to the church. "But they also do some of the Mass in English. We'll be able to follow along in the missal. The main parts of the Mass are the same really. Readings, intentions, Communion. I think you'll like it."

"We'll see," Javier said. "How do you feel about meeting this woman Hanne?"

"I don't know—it's strange. I mean, I've often wondered since that prayer vigil whatever happened to her. I can't imagine how she's coping. It's just hard to believe she's here now. I guess maybe I'm a little nervous."

"No one should ever have to bury a child," Javier said softly.

"No one should," Sarah said letting out a deep sigh. "But they do. And I don't think we'll ever know the reason for it."

They drove on in silence for a while, both of them thinking of Patrick. How he'd driven them mad with his drinking and wild ways. Yet at the same time, he'd touched their hearts with his spontaneous displays of generosity and compassion. It was Patrick who inevitably defended the kids at school who were being bullied, Patrick who picked wildflowers for Sarah on Mother's Day.

"Remember when he spent his entire allowance on a birthday gift for Benny?" Javier said.

"He bought him that set of Legos he'd been wishing for."

They arrived at Mar Ephrem and found the church nearly full. Javier and Sarah genuflected and then sat down beside an elderly couple in one of the last pews. The woman had long, tightly braided gray hair peeking out from under her veil. Sarah handed Javier one of the missals so he could follow along with the prayers.

"But this looks like Arabic!" Javier whispered.

"It is," Sarah whispered back. "Here, turn to the English section."

Just then, Father George emerged from the sacristy with the deacons and altar servers, all dressed in white robes. The congregation rose and began singing a hymn neither Sarah nor Javier had ever heard before.

The Mass wasn't as long as Javier worried it would be. He was

## A Martyr's Crown

relieved when Father George read the Gospel in English and also gave part of his homily in English. Sarah noticed Javier never dozed off even once.

"Amazing," she said under her breath.

When the Mass ended, they joined the crowd of people walking over to the hall for the dinner. Father George said it was a simple meal that would mark the end of *Bautha*. Sarah looked around, wondering where Hanne and Fadi were.

Women from the parish had spent hours preparing the meal and were busy uncovering large pans of rice and the *tahin* and *mepokhta*.

"Smells great," Javier said to Sarah as he eyed the buffet tables laden with platters of exotic-looking food.

"Looks good to me," Sarah said as they stood there in the long line. *I can't believe I made it the whole day with just a couple small pieces of bread!* She didn't tell Javier that she had been fasting that day and she wasn't entirely sure why she'd done it. She'd never deliberately deprived herself of food before and found out that although it was difficult, it really wasn't as hard as she once imagined.

"It's the way we show God we are sorry for our sins," Father George told her when she asked about what the purpose of fasting was. "People like to say that they love God, but fasting shows Him we mean it, that we don't let our selfish desires control us. It's a prayer of the whole body that reminds us of our dependence on God."

The strange and unexpected thing was that she felt closer now to understanding a little of what the poor endure. Who hadn't seen the pictures of children with their bloated bellies and pitiful eyes?

Volunteers were dishing out food to the people immediately in front of them now and Sarah picked up a couple plates from the stack on the end of the table. She handed one to Javier, who was busy talking to the man in line behind them. And in that instant, she decided that she and Javier ought to give some money to Father George for the refugees he was trying to help.

As her friendship with Father George grew, Sarah could feel her heart slowly opening, warming, as though springtime was gradually awakening it from a deep sleep. She was beginning to move away from what she now realized was loneliness and depression to the understanding that there was a whole unseen world out there, a new way to look at God and at others.

*As much as I have suffered in my life, here is an entire civilization of people who have endured so much more. And yet no one seems to know or care.*

Just as Javier was approaching the front of the line, Father George came up behind them. Sarah noticed his limp wasn't as bad today as when she'd last seen him. Every time she thought of what they did to him, how they'd tortured and nearly killed him, she felt a surge of admiration for his deep faith and courage. The scar on his face—it was a thing of terrible beauty, an outward sign of his love for God. Yet how many people saw past that? She wanted to tell the world, "Look! Look at this man who loved without counting the cost. This is the face of Christ, of unbounded love."

"Sarah, Javier, it is good to see you here," Father George said warmly.

"Thanks for inviting us, Father. How's the van running for you?" Javier asked as one of the ladies placed a dollop of rice on his plate.

"There are no issues since you fixed it."

"Glad to help, Father. Anytime you need help with it, you just let me know."

"After you have a chance to eat, I will introduce you two to Hanne and Fadi. They want to meet you, too," Father George said to Sarah.

Before Sarah had a chance to respond, someone in line behind them called out to Father George. It seemed that everyone there

## A Martyr's Crown

wanted his attention. Sarah's heart beat a little faster as she thought of meeting Hanne—maybe she really was a little nervous after all.

They carried their food over to one of the long, rectangular tables where a man and woman with two teenagers were already eating. The husband motioned for them to sit down and join them.

"Welcome, my friends," he said to them, wiping his hands on a napkin. "My name is Sam, and this is my wife, May, and our two kids."

"Nice to meet you. I'm Javier and this is my wife, Sarah."

"Ah, you are Americans," the man said with a smile. "How did you find out about us?"

"It's a long story," Sarah said, "but basically, I'm a journalist. I wrote an article about your church after the attack on Mar Addai in Mosul. I came out here for the prayer vigil."

The man's smile disappeared.

"His cousin died in that attack," the man's wife said quietly.

"I'm so sorry to hear that," Sarah said sympathetically. "What did you say your name is? May?"

"Yes. We were here that night for the vigil but my husband was so upset. We didn't see you."

"They killed so many people in that attack, even one of our priests," Sam said. "I left Iraq in 1980, but I still have a lot of family there."

"Why did you come to America?"

"I came here to study medicine and learn English," Sam said. "I went back a few times, but was able to get permission to stay here."

"So you're a doctor?" Sarah asked.

"Right. I take care of the priests here and a lot of the parishioners."

People were finishing their meals and starting to leave. Sarah saw Father George out of the corner of her eye. He was sitting at a table and talking with a young couple.

The woman, who looked to be in her late-20s, had long, dark hair and smooth, olive skin. The man, tall and regal-looking, seemed older—maybe by ten years, Sarah thought. Could this be Hanne and her husband?

Just then Father George looked up and motioned for her to come over. Javier was still talking with Sam about the situation in Iraq. Sarah took a sip of water, stood up and walked across the room to the other table.

"Sarah," Father George said, "This is Hanne and her husband Fadi."

For a moment, no one knew what to say. Then Hanne slowly rose from the table. The two women embraced. Sarah felt tears welling up in her eyes. *So this is Hanne. I can't believe she's here!*

"Father George, he told us of you," Hanne said in heavily accented English as she stood back and beheld Sarah. *So this was the journalist Father George was telling them about, the one who lost her son. God bless her.*

Sarah was speechless. It didn't seem possible that they were standing face to face in a church hall in Phoenix.

"You're really here with us," Sarah breathed. "I've been thinking about you since that day..." her voice trailed off. She'd hoped to say something brilliant upon meeting Hanne, but instead found that her voice was so thick with emotion she could barely speak.

"December 6," Hanne said softly. "This was the day."

"December 6," Sarah repeated, squeezing Hanne's hand. "I'm so sorry for what you've been through...your story—I couldn't stop thinking about what happened to you that day. Honestly, I couldn't sleep for several nights after talking with your aunt. I wondered how you were doing."

"Sarah, this is Fadi, Hanne's husband," Father George said as the language professor stood up. *He's so much taller than his wife—at least six feet tall,* Sarah thought to herself.

## A Martyr's Crown

Sarah reached out to shake Fadi's hand. "It's good to finally meet you," she said. "When did you two get here?"

"We came eight days ago," Fadi replied, his English not as heavily accented as Hanne's. "We still try to get accustomed."

"It takes a while," Sarah said. "My husband came here from Puerto Rico to go to college back in the 1980s. It was a huge change for him, but he adapted eventually."

"Here at the church we have a taste of home," Fadi said. "It helps."

Just then, Javier approached. "You must be Hanne and Fadi," he said shaking their hands. "My wife was very moved by your story. We're so sorry for all that you've been through."

"Thank you," Fadi said simply.

"I was thinking," Sarah said, looking over at Javier to gauge his reaction, "we should have Hanne and Fadi over for dinner. You, too, Father George. And Father Michael."

"Definitely," Javier said. "We'd like that very much. How about next week? Saturday barbecue maybe?"

Fadi and Hanne looked doubtful.

"We do not have a car. I am not certain there is a bus on Saturday night," Fadi said.

"Father Michael and I will drive you there," Father George said.

"That sounds perfect," Sarah said. "We'll have a chance to get to know each other better."

Later on that evening, Sarah checked her email. There was something from Father George.

*Sarah, thanks so much for inviting us to your home for dinner. I have a feeling you and Hanne will become good friends. You two need each other.*

*Remember when you told me that you wanted to spend the rest of your life doing something good for others? Listening to Hanne and helping her—this will be a great act of mercy. I think God has prepared your heart for this mission.*

*I want to ask you something:*

*Would you be interested in teaching an English class at Mar Ephrem? Many of our new families, they struggle to learn the English. I think that with time, Hanne and Fadi, they will help you with this project. What do you think? You maybe could teach this class once a week?*

"What would you think if I started teaching English as a second language over at Mar Ephrem once a week?" Sarah asked Javier. "Father George asked me if I'd be interested."

"I think you'd be very good at that. Go for it."

Sarah remembered what Father George told her back at the beginning, about how serving brings joy. The thought of working alongside the Chaldeans, helping them learn English, would be one way she could reach out to others.

"Your dad was big on volunteering, wasn't he?"

"That's true. I remembered that when I was reading his journal."

"Have you read the whole thing yet?"

"No. I'm trying to savor it. I realized something as I was reading it last night though. Love really does endure beyond the grave. I have this sense that he's praying for me, that he's still with me."

"Your father was a great man. I'm sure if he were still on this earth, he'd be right there with you at Mar Ephrem, teaching English."

ܨ ܨ ܨ ܨ ܨ ܨ ܨ

# Chapter 34
Phoenix
Tuesday, February 1, 2010

Sarah was perched in front of her computer, crafting the final paragraph of a story about a nurse from a local church who ventured out into the streets and under bridges to take care of the homeless. There was so much bad news to tell in a newspaper—the shootings, accidents and political mud-slinging—that stories of hope and love were too few, at least in her estimation. The religion beat was an oasis of sorts.

Just as she hit "send," she heard a text message come in. She glanced at her cell phone; it was from Father George.

"Happy news! We got the grant!" the message said.

"That's fantastic," Sarah said out loud. "Wow!" She quickly texted back "Congrats, so happy for you," knowing that Father George had to be ecstatic over the award.

"What's so fantastic?" Diane asked, popping into Sarah's cubicle.

"Oh, it's that Chaldean church I wrote about," Sarah said as she set her cell phone down. "They were just awarded a grant to do some remodeling of their hall. They really need help to get that place fixed up."

"Who'd they get the money from?" Diane asked. "Couldn't have been easy in this economy."

"From another parish in town—St. Clare's. They've got a grant program for needy parishes and organizations around town."

"Nice," Diane said. "I thought you were going to say it was some big corporation. Now let me guess; something tells me you helped them write a convincing grant proposal, didn't you?"

"Well, maybe I had a little something to do with it," Sarah said somewhat sheepishly. "I mean, it's the least I can do, right?"

Diane thought about that for a minute as she looked at her co-worker. Sarah looked genuinely happy, as though *she* were the one receiving all that money. She was glowing, almost like she'd fallen in love. But wasn't she still married to that Puerto Rican guy? Come to think of it, Sarah hadn't looked so good in years. What was her secret?

ܚ ܚ ܚ ܚ ܚ ܚ ܚ

Sarah checked in with Rick before leaving for home. She wanted to tell him that she was going to be able to write a story about St. Clare's teaming up with Mar Ephrem.

*He's going to love this story* she thought as she approached the boss's office.

"Hey, Rick," she said as she poked her head in the doorway.

"Sarah! How are you?" Rick asked as he looked up from his computer monitor and leaned back in his chair.

"I'm on my way home, but I just wanted to let you know that St. Clare's awarded the grant to the Chaldean Church. They're going to be fixing up their hall for them."

"Nice! So I guess you'll be doing that story then, won't you?"

"Yep. We'll get some great before and after photos, I'm sure."

"Extreme Church Makeover, episode one," Rick laughed.

"You want me to take some video for the website?"

"Actually, that's not a bad idea," Rick said, tilting his head to

## A Martyr's Crown

the right, the way he did when pondering something. "When are they going to start working on it?"

"I'm not sure. They only just learned they won the grant today. But I'll find out and let you know."

Sarah decided to call Father George on her long drive home from work. The freeway was going to be jammed at this hour and she was sure he'd want to talk about his happy news.

"That grant is an answer to prayers, Sarah," Father George said when he picked up. "Our roof, it would not endure another storm."

"Won't it be nice to get that fixed? So now, what happens next? Are you going over to St. Clare's to talk with them?"

"Actually, no. Father Keller and the grant committee are going to come here on Saturday afternoon. They will look at the hall and decide what needs to be done. He said that one of the men on the committee is a contractor and could do the work for less money."

"That's fantastic, Father George. I'm really happy they chose Mar Ephrem."

"I am happy, too. And I deeply appreciate you writing the grant proposal. I think that made a big difference."

"Will you still be able to come to our house on Saturday night for dinner?"

"Of course. Father Michael and I will pick up Hanne and Fadi after the 5 p.m. Mass."

"Perfect. So we'll see you around seven then?"

"Yes. We will be there at seven o'clock. I think you will like talking with Hanne and Fadi some more."

"I'm looking forward to it. I had no idea Hanne was so young."

"She is, but I think you might have more in common with her and Fadi than you realize."

"What makes you say that?"

"Well, remember, Hanne majored in English and Fadi was a

language professor at the University of Mosul. They both have a gift for words, the way you do."

"I guess that's something I inherited from my dad," Sarah said. "My brothers and sisters and I—we all worked at the bookstore my father started back in the 1950s. My parents really instilled a love of reading in us. We used to beg for a later bedtime just so we could read a little longer!"

"And your boys—they are like this, too?"

"Benny is—he's always got a book in his hands. The other boys like to read, but not as much. And Patrick, well, he wasn't too fond of it at all," Sarah said wistfully. It was hard to think of that. How she'd tried to get him to read more when he was little! She wished now she could take back all the nagging, all the bribing.

"So, Patrick was more like Javier maybe?"

"Not really. Javier enjoys reading, too. The thing with Patrick was, he struggled with dyslexia, and that made reading a real chore for him. One day a teacher told me, 'You're just going to have to accept him the way he is, the way he was made. Lots of dyslexic people grow up to be very successful,' she told me. And once that sank in, it was so much easier."

"Sometimes parents tell me that their children teach them lessons they did not learn in school," Father George said.

"It's so true," Sarah said. "Being a parent opens your eyes to realities you couldn't see before. I remember when Patrick was about six months old. I called my mom and I thanked her for all she and my dad did for us when we were kids. You don't realize until you're a parent what it is your own parents did for you. It's like you just can't see it."

"It must have been terrible for them too, when Patrick died," Father George said, knowing Sarah's mother and father must have been brokenhearted. He could tell Sarah was ready to open up some more about Patrick and that, he knew, was a good sign. It did the human heart no good to keep sorrow bottled up. Burdens were meant to be shared.

"They were devastated, just like us. In fact, I think it was doubly hard, because they had to watch their daughter and son-in-law deal with it," Sarah said with a catch in her voice. "I've often thought to myself that his passing took such a toll on my father's heart that it shortened his life."

"These things are mysteries, Sarah," Father George said gently. "You have had much sorrow, worse than many people could imagine. This is why I think you will be able to understand Hanne and Fadi's pain."

"Sometimes it doesn't feel like it," Sarah said. "It's the way the grief sneaks up on you in unexpected ways. Like the other day at the pharmacy. There I was, picking up a prescription, and I saw this young man who looked so much like Patrick!

"I mean, he had the same color hair, the same build, even some of the same mannerisms. I caught myself staring at him for a minute, wishing it really were Patrick. But of course, he wasn't.

"Sorry," Sarah said. "I don't mean to bring you down with my grief. How did we start talking about this anyway? Goodness." Sarah looked at the green highway road signs that named the freeway exits; she was still more than 10 miles from home.

"Do not apologize for saying how you feel, Sarah. Your real friends will always want to listen," Father George said.

"Well, thank you for being a real friend to me," Sarah said, and she meant it. She hadn't spoken in depth about her grief over Patrick until Father George came into her life. "The thing is, I really want to help your community. I mean, there's so much that people here can do for you."

"I am glad you want to help," Father George said gently. "But remember: there are many things we Chaldeans can give you, too. We do not wish to be pitied, Sarah. We want to be equals."

"I'm sorry, Father George," Sarah said, a little embarrassed. "I hope I didn't offend you."

"I am not offended, Sarah, this is not what I meant," Father George said matter-of-factly. "I just want to be clear: We do not want people to feel sorry for us—we want to be partners, with respect for both cultures."

"You're right, of course. I guess I wasn't thinking of it that way," Sarah said. "I've only known you a little while, but you've already taught me a lot."

"You are quick learner."

"No, I mean it," Sarah said. "Like fasting. I never thought about it much before. You reminded me of something the nuns at my grade school used to say."

"They talked about fasting?"

"Not in so many words. But they used to use the phrase 'self-control' a lot. And now that I think about it, that's kind of counter-cultural."

"American culture tends toward overindulgence."

"And yet with all that self-indulgence, we've got a very high suicide rate. All that indulging doesn't seem to bring people happiness!"

"This is because the only thing that really brings us joy is true love," Father George said, "and love means giving, serving, being willing to suffer."

"Not so popular these days."

"Sanctity seldom is."

"There's something else, too, Father. You know that prayer book you gave me?"

"*The Book of Before and After?*"

"Well, I remember how you said that some of the prayers and hymns were written by the early martyrs. So I started thinking about that, about how much courage and love they must have had to give their lives for Jesus. Then I thought about your friend, the priest who was murdered in that church in Mosul, and all the other people who died there that day." Sarah's voice began to shake and

## A Martyr's Crown

she swallowed hard. She didn't even know these people, and yet their deaths had given her life a whole new meaning, awakened faith in her.

"Sarah?"

"I'm still here," she answered, unable to disguise the rising emotion in her voice. "It's just...I realized how selfish and immature I've been. I don't have faith like that. I'm so weak! I haven't suffered anything for my faith! I'm not like you!" Sarah took the next exit and pulled over onto a small side street.

"Martyrdom is a gift, but it is not a gift that everyone receives," Father George said. "Do not be too hard on yourself, Sarah. Your heart is good. But think about this: Maybe God is calling you to a closer walk with Him."

Sarah turned the engine off and unbuckled her seatbelt. Father George could tell she had stopped driving; he took a sip of tea and settled in for what he felt would be a bit of a counseling session.

"After I started saying the prayers in that book every day, I began to have this longing in my heart to really talk to God, to tell Him how I feel and give Him my whole life. So I did that, and well, it really helped."

"This is good," Father George said. "You are growing in faith."

"My dad must be praying for me," Sarah said as she thought about how things had changed. "He had such a deep faith in God."

"Keep on it with that prayer book, Sarah," Father George said. "Those prayers will help. And just give God everything—your past, your present, your future. Give Him all your hopes and dreams. And give Him all your failures, too. Surrender it all to Him, Sarah. He is your Heavenly Father!"

Sarah sat there for a minute, trying to absorb what Father George was telling her. God as a Heavenly Father. Now that was something she could relate to.

"You didn't know my dad, Father George, but he was a saint," Sarah said simply. "My dad was so wise and so loving—I mean, it never was difficult to think of God as a father. Dad was the most patient person I've ever known. But the thing is, I know I've disappointed God. I'm a failure! Oh, I don't know why I'm telling you all this, really. I'm sorry."

But Father George knew exactly why these words were tumbling out. Sarah was a soul in need of healing.

"It's OK, Sarah," Father George said gently, "This is what priests do. We listen. We counsel. And we try to speak the words of healing that Christ would speak to you."

"Thank you for listening to me."

"Why do you think God is disappointed in you? Why do you say you're a failure?"

"Because of Patrick. He gave me Patrick and I was a terrible mother to him. I yelled at him, I lost my patience with him so many times…I never could control that child. Never! It's like I told you: we tried everything, we prayed, we went to counseling, but nothing worked. And now he's gone. Oh my God, what did I do…" Sarah's voice trailed off.

"You did your best, Sarah," Father George said. "God knows that. Sometimes these things are out of our hands." Father George paused, hoping the words would sink in and begin to heal this brokenhearted woman.

"Thank you, Father."

"I am always ready to listen, Sarah. And you know what? I am more convinced than ever that you and Hanne need to connect."

"Did you tell them about Patrick?"

"I told them that you lost your son about two years ago, but I did not give them any details."

"I wouldn't want to give them too many details, either. They're still in shock, I'm sure," Sarah said quickly.

"Exactly. Just let it unfold. I have no doubt God is bringing you together for a good reason."

A Martyr's Crown

# Chapter 35
Phoenix
Saturday, February 5, 2010

Father Keller and the grant committee from St. Clare stood there in the dilapidated church hall at St. Ephrem as Father George explained the needs of the community.

"Every Saturday, we have about 100 children from the parish who attend catechism classes here," Father George was saying. "Many of them are refugees. We provide them with a healthy snack and some fun activities, too.

"We also use the hall for feast day celebrations and community events. As you can see," Father George continued, "the place needs some serious remodeling."

"So where will you start?" Father Keller asked. "The grant is for $10,000. That would probably buy a new roof and a few small repairs around here."

"We definitely need a new roof," Father George said. "See all the water damage to the ceiling? And there's some plumbing work that needs to be done, too."

Sholeh looked around at the decrepit, windowless church hall with its popcorn ceilings and fluorescent lighting. She was glad that St. Clare Parish had decided to award the grant to Mar Ephrem, but she knew much more help was needed. *Wouldn't it be great if we could just bulldoze this place and build something really beautiful instead? Something new?*

One of the men from the grant committee, a contractor, said he knew a guy that would probably be willing to install a new roof at cost. Another lady mentioned that her husband was a plumber and could take a look at the aging fixtures in the restrooms.

The committee stepped into the commercial kitchen next, the place where the ladies of Mar Ephrem prepared banquets for feast days and receptions.

The first thing Sholeh noticed was the peeling, bright orange linoleum with matching orange counter tops. *Must have seemed really chic back around 1970 but now it's....awful—really awful.*

Father George led them into the restrooms next. As far as Sholeh could tell, they looked as though they hadn't been updated since the 1940s. The grant St. Clare Parish awarded was a start, but Sholeh could see the community needed much more help than simply a new roof.

Later, after they returned to St. Clare, Father Keller pulled her aside. In his estimation, Sholeh was an intelligent woman with a deep and vibrant faith. He knew from the parish tithing records that she was also extremely generous.

"So what did you think of Mar Ephrem?" he asked Sholeh casually as they stood outside the parish chapel under the palm trees.

"I'm glad we chose them for the grant," Sholeh said, "but it's not nearly enough for what needs to be done up there."

"What do you have in mind?"

"Let me think about it, Father," Sholeh said. "I'll let you know what I come up with."

# A Martyr's Crown

Hanne made a list of ingredients needed for the *cake 'd tumra,* the special date cake she was making to bring to the dinner at Sarah's house that night. It was a traditional Iraqi recipe, something her mother had taught her long ago in their sunlit kitchen in Mosul.

When she and Fadi walked to the grocery store that morning, Hanne was perplexed by the assortment of prepared cake mixes displayed on the shelves.

"Look at this, Fadi," Hanne said, handing him a box of the stuff, "all you do is add water and an egg and you get a cake!"

Fadi looked doubtful. "This cannot be a cake like yours, *azizta*," he said, looking at the box, puzzled. "Cake from a box?"

Hanne placed the mix back on the shelf, mildly pleased by the compliment. Fadi appreciated her gift for cooking. Before that horrible day at Mar Addai, he'd gained almost 10 kilos from her cooking. *We're both a lot thinner these days*, she thought to herself sadly.

The walk to the store was only a couple blocks from their apartment, but the exercise was good for both of them, especially Fadi. He still couldn't lift anything heavy, though he was feeling a bit stronger.

Fadi paid the cashier for their purchases and Hanne quickly gathered up the three bags of groceries.

"At least let me carry something, Hanne," Fadi protested. "Here—I'll take the bag with the eggs and dates." Hanne didn't realize how useless, how undignified he felt that his wife was lugging their groceries about, at least until the wound in his side healed.

Fadi wasn't sure, but he thought that maybe an injury like the one he'd sustained took a lot longer to heal when there was a broken heart involved as well. He didn't like to think of himself as an invalid or a victim. He resolved in that moment to try to push himself physically a little more, take longer walks, try to eat better.

Back at the apartment, Hanne busied herself in the kitchen.

Father George and Father Michael would be there at 6:30 p.m. to pick them up. She was tired, more than usual, and had to convince herself to get moving.

"Hanne, *azizta*, when you're done baking, let's call home," Fadi said. "We haven't talked to our families in a few days."

Fadi settled down in front of their brand-new laptop computer. Aunt Samira and Uncle Matay had accompanied them to the electronics store on Wednesday and the first thing he'd done was to install a program so they could call Mosul from the apartment.

Fadi logged on to check his email and then visited the website for Arizona State University. Once he was stronger and received permission to work in the U.S., he wanted to join the Arabic Studies Department at the university. He knew that as a language studies professor, he could teach Arabic and perhaps even an Aramaic language course.

After Hanne carefully slid the cake into the oven, she set the timer and pulled a chair up beside Fadi so they could call *Yemmi*. It was after 9 p.m. in Iraq now and Hanne felt sure her mom and sisters were home. Raad and Saeed were no doubt still at the restaurant.

Nahida must have been standing right by the phone.

"*Shlama*, Hanne!" Nahida cried, "It's you!"

"It's good to hear your voice," Hanne said weakly. *How could Nahida sound so impossibly close when she was thousands of kilometers away? Oh, how she missed her family and her home!*

"We were just talking about you two, Hanne," Nahida said. "How are you doing there in Arizona?"

"We're doing alright so far. It's…well, we're missing you!" Hanne said, trying to sound brave.

"Remember what we said now," Nahida said kindly, "We're going to find a way to come visit you somehow. You have to think of that, Hanne!"

"How's *Yemmi*?"

## A Martyr's Crown

"Here, I'll put her on the phone so you can ask her yourself," Nahida said as cheerfully as she could, "She's right here." Nahida covered the receiver of the phone so Hanne wouldn't hear what she was about to say to Mariam.

"Don't mention the news," Nahida whispered. "It will only upset her, poor thing. She'll learn of it soon enough."

Mariam nodded and picked up the receiver.

"Hanne, my darling daughter, how are you?" Mariam exclaimed. "It's great to hear from you. How are you getting on there?"

"We're doing fine, *Yemmi*, truly," Hanne said, wanting to reassure her mom. "Don't worry about us."

"You sound tired. Are you sure you're feeling OK? And how is Fadi doing?" Mariam asked, trying not to sound worried.

"Actually, he's doing better. And I'm fine, just a little sleepy, I guess. But tonight we are going to another family's home for dinner. I'm bringing the cake you taught me to prepare when I was a little girl."

"Good manners, just as I raised you, bringing something to share," Mariam said, sounding pleased. "Is this one of the families from church?"

"Not exactly, but we met them there. It's an American family. The wife is a journalist who wrote a story about the Chaldean Church in Arizona. The priest here introduced us to them."

"A journalist. Well," Mariam said, her heart racing. The last thing she wanted was for Hanne to be frightened and upset about what happened last night in Mosul. A reporter interested in Chaldeans might know of it. Mariam hoped the woman would graciously avoid the topic.

Hanne and Fadi chatted with Mariam for a while, and then Nora and finally Nahida again. All the while, a delightful aroma began to fill the apartment. After they said their goodbyes, promising to call again soon, Hanne pulled the dense, flavorful cake from the oven and set it on a rack to cool. In just a few hours, they'd be with the two priests at the Castillos's house.

"How are your sisters doing?" Fadi asked, eyeing the cake.

"They sound good, but it's almost like there's something they're not telling me."

"Why on earth would you suspect that? You three tell each other everything!"

"That's true. But still. They sounded…nervous. Worried," Hanne said pensively, "as though they didn't want me to know something."

"I'm sure it's nothing, *azizta*. You'll feel better when we get the little camera installed on the computer so you can see their faces."

"Maybe," Hanne said as she put away dishes.

ש ש ש ש ש ש ש

Sarah was busy in the kitchen with the last-minute preparations for the dinner party. She wanted her guests to feel at home, that they could relax and enjoy themselves. The boys had been a big help that afternoon mowing the lawn and cleaning up the yard. Sarah had even taken the time to plant a few more flowers in large ceramic pots on the patio. She looked out the kitchen window and smiled: there stood Javier over the grill, turning the chicken. Benny was at his side, helping.

*Two months ago, I would have been completely overwhelmed to try and pull off something like this. A dinner party with two priests and grieving parents?*
When the doorbell rang a few minutes later, Sarah dried her hands on a dish towel and headed for the entryway. There on the doorstep stood Hanne and Fadi beside Father George and Father Michael.

"So glad you could make it," Sarah said as they came through the door. Hanne presented a plate to Sarah.

## A Martyr's Crown

"I made a cake, something from home," she explained shyly.

"Oh my goodness!" Sarah said, touched at the gesture. "That was very kind of you. I can't wait to try it. Here, let's go set it in the kitchen."

"Where is your husband?" Fadi asked.

"He's out back with Benny, our youngest, cooking the meat. Why don't we go out there and join them? I've got a cooler on the patio with some drinks."

They stepped through the French doors that led to the patio into the backyard. The grass was a beautifully manicured carpet of dark green. Four large trees, their graceful limbs interlocking, stood in a row along the back wall. Containers of pink, purple and white petunias adorned the patio and a curved, flagstone path connected with a fire pit and grill.

"Hey there," Javier called, "You came at the perfect time. I'm just getting ready to take this chicken off."

Sarah motioned to the black wrought-iron table where they would enjoy dinner. "I thought we'd sit outside tonight since it's so nice." She'd already lighted candles and set them at the center of the table.

When the meal ended, the boys went out front to play basketball while the adults sat and talked. Hanne, seated next to Sarah, listened as Fadi explained his hope that he might someday work at the university in town.

"It's a great school," Javier told Fadi. "Huge campus, lots of opportunities. Maybe we can walk around there when you're feeling better."

"That reminds me, Father George," Sarah said suddenly. "I got a call from a doctor who runs a free medical clinic in town. I interviewed her for a story about it, but she called because she read the article about Mar Ephrem."

"She takes care of people for free?" Father George asked. "We have some parishioners who will want to know about that."

"Well, that's why she called. She said she was intrigued by the article about your church. Apparently her husband's parents were from Baghdad."

"Really? What is her name?"

"Emily Shallal. Her husband died a few years ago and she decided to open this clinic. I'll send you her number. She said for you to call her so you could talk."

"I'll do it. Now, what have you heard about the soccer match between St. Clare's and Mar Ephrem?"

"Soccer? The churches have a soccer team here?" Fadi asked. "Who will be the coach for this team?"

"Actually," Father George said, "an Iraq War vet who read Sarah's article about us in the *Sun-Times* said he will be the coach for our team. They will meet at the park near Mar Ephrem on Friday afternoon."

Sarah turned to Hanne, thinking that she looked more than a little wistful. *It's so soon for her. I could barely function at this point. I don't know how she's making it!*

"So, how are you doing? Do you feel like you're beginning to get used to things here in America?" Sarah asked Hanne gently.

"We are alright maybe," Hanne said simply. "We must adjust to the life here. It is different from our life in Iraq."

"Have you spoken with your family much since you got here?"

"Today we called my mother and my sisters," Hanne said. "They hope to visit us one day."

"That would be nice. I know it's hard for Javier sometimes. He grew up in Puerto Rico, and he doesn't get to visit there very often."

Hanne nodded politely, not sure what to say. She understood most of what Sarah said, but she was a little tired and that made it harder to concentrate.

"Why don't we go inside and have some tea? It's getting a little chilly out here for me," Sarah said. The men were still deep in

# A Martyr's Crown

conversation.

Hanne followed Sarah into the house. She'd seen something that caught her eye when they first walked in. A table off in the corner somewhere.

"We can sit in the living room while the water boils," Sarah suggested, leading the way. The two women sat on the brown leather sofa in front of the window that looked out on the street. Hanne could see the boys dribbling the basketball and taking shots at the hoop mounted over the garage.

"It is a nice family you have," Hanne said. As she turned back toward Sarah, she saw the delicately carved, dark wood table with the tall white candle standing in the middle. Just behind it was a large, framed photograph of a young man, whom Hanne guessed was the son Sarah had lost. Smaller photographs and mementos were arranged around the candle.

"That's Patrick," Sarah said, following Hanne's gaze, "his senior portrait. It was taken just six months before we lost him."

"I am so sorry this happen to you," Hanne said. "He was a handsome young man, your son, God bless him."

Sarah stood up from the couch and walked over to the table. Hanne rose and followed her. "We wanted to set aside a special place for him here," she said as she picked up the portrait and passed it to Hanne, who looked at it intently. Patrick had his father's dark, curly hair and his mother's green eyes, an unusual, pleasing combination.

"And these are some of the trophies he won playing basketball. And this...this was his cell phone," Sarah said as she opened it. "And here's his school ID." Hanne looked at all the precious mementos Sarah had so carefully arranged.

"Zach and Thomas wear his clothes, but Benny is still too small. We still have his bed, just as it was. Sometimes Zach sleeps in it when he's really missing him."

Hanne listened carefully. "To honor your son this way—it is so good. This helps you?"

"It does," Sarah said. "People sometimes think you just need to 'get over' a loss like this, but you don't—not ever. I promise you this though: it eventually does get a little less painful over time."

"That does not seem possible."

"Of course not," Sarah said. "You're still at the beginning—you're still in shock, I would imagine."

Hanne had tears in her eyes. "I tell myself, no cry here. Not by you."

Sarah put her arms around Hanne. "You are my sister in Christ. You can cry on me any time you want. I mean it. I know what it means to feel like your heart's been torn from you, like you'd rather not go on living. I know it well."

Hanne could hardly believe that this woman she hardly knew would speak so openly, but she knew it was from the heart. And it was true—there was a kinship between them, borne of their pain.

"Maybe we can make a little memorial like this in your apartment," Sarah said as she offered Hanne a tissue. "Tell me about your baby. I don't know anything about her, not even her name."

The whistle of the tea kettle summoned them to the kitchen. Sarah poured two cups of herbal tea and gave one to Hanne. After they sat for a moment in silence sipping their drinks, Hanne began, slowly, to tell the story.

"Her name was Noor and she was an angel, the sweetest child you could think of. I lost one baby the year before she was born. Noor was our miracle, a piece of heaven.

"The day it happened…it was the day we were going to have her baptized," Hanne said. Her chin began to tremble. Sarah clasped the young woman's hand. *This poor, dear girl. To have her baby taken from her so violently!*

Sarah reached for the box of tissues and gave a couple to Hanne.

## A Martyr's Crown

"Thank you," she said, drying her tears and blowing her nose. "I am broken person. I cry all the day. The sad heart—it does not go away from me. I cannot sleep and yet I am so tired."

Sarah nodded sympathetically. "I'm amazed at you, Hanne, I really am. You've been through so much. And here you are, in a new country, trying to make new friends. You're in much better shape than I was at this point. I mean that. I could barely get out of bed most days at first."

"My sisters, they never leave me. And my brothers and mother, they help, too. I miss them so much," Hanne said, brushing away fresh tears.

"That's understandable. It's good you get to call home. Do you use Facebook at all?"

"Facebook. Yes. To see the pictures of my family and my friends. I have many pictures of Noor on my page. You want to see these?"

"Of course I would. Let's go into the den where my computer is. You can show me in there."

Sarah flipped on the light in the den, revealing her neatly arranged work space, and pulled up an extra chair in front of the computer.

"This is where you write?"

"Partly," Sarah said. "I do have to go into the office downtown about three times a week. But I do a lot from home."

Hanne noticed the leather bound volume and The Book of Before and After sitting beside the computer monitor.

"How you get Chaldean book of prayer?"

"Father George gave it to me a while back. I've been using it lately."

"I do not see it in English before," Hanne said as she paged through the book. "I sometimes go to *Ramsha*—evening prayer—at our church in Mosul."

"We don't have that at our parish here, but they do have

Morning Prayer before Mass each day," Sarah said. "My friend Sholeh said she goes after she drops her kids off at school."

"I just say the other prayers at home," Sholeh told her. "It's helped a lot, especially since the divorce. It keeps my mind on God throughout the day."

"These prayers are precious to me," Hanne said. "I did not realize someone translates them into English."

"Your faith must have helped you get through all the pain of these last months."

"Without God, it is impossible," Hanne said as she closed the book carefully. "But still. Sometimes it is hard to pray."

"He is there, even when we cannot find the words to pray," Sarah said. "Would you let me be your American sister? I mean it. I want to walk through this with you—I really do." Sarah was looking at Hanne, pleading with her eyes. "These last two years—well, I didn't have the strong faith that you do. But I found God again. I saw Him in Father George and in the story of the Chaldeans. And I see Him in you."

"I do not know how you see Him in me," Hanne said, shaking her head, dismissing the idea outright. "Some days, I wish I die, too. I say, 'God, why you let this happen to me? Why?'"

Sarah listened as Hanne poured out her feelings. She knew each one of them—had felt them herself, in fact.

"Hanne, when I heard what happened to you—to your beautiful baby—it affected me deeply. I decided right then that I only have one life to live and I don't want to waste it. I don't know why He allows such suffering, but I do know this: He's with us in the midst of it."

Hanne fell into Sarah's arms, sobbing. "You believe this?"

"With all my heart. I know that God is holding us, even as our hearts break. Oh, Hanne. I can't tell you how much it means to me to finally meet you, to have you in my home. If it weren't for you—well, let's just put it this way: my life was falling apart fast."

## A Martyr's Crown

"This does not seem possible."

"It's been a long process, believe me. Now I want to see those pictures you've got of Noor."

Hanne pulled up her Facebook page and clicked on the photo gallery. Up came the pictures of Noor—dozens of them. Dressed in a tiny, lavender colored dress, in Fadi's arms. Fast asleep in her crib. Wrapped up in a towel after her bath.

"What a beautiful child," Sarah said softly, putting her arm around Hanne.

"Thank you. Yes, she very beautiful," Hanne said sadly.
She was scrolling through pictures now and stopped on one that showed an elderly woman cradling newborn Noor.

"That is my mother," Hanne said. "We call her *Yemmi*. Noor was her first—how you say—grandchild?"

"Yes, her first grandchild."

Hanne clicked through the photos. "I am the first daughter in my family. These are my sisters, Nahida and Nora. And these are my brothers, Raad and Saeed." There were close-ups of each of them holding the baby, all bundled up in a delicate pink blanket, each of them smiling as though it was the happiest day of their life. "My mom, she make that blanket when I have Noor inside. She say, 'It is a girl.' She was right."

"Do you still have the blanket?"

"Oh yes. It is one of the things we bring with us." Hanne pursed her lips. "We must leave many things in Iraq, but we have her blanket."

"Maybe we could set up a corner for Noor in your apartment, kind of like I have here for Patrick," Sarah ventured. "We could print out some of your pictures and frame them, too. If you want, I could help you. It would do us both good I think."

"You will do this for me?" Hanne asked. "This is so kind. You are busy journalist lady."

Sarah looked at Hanne. *What was she, late-twenties maybe? So young. Too young to be going through this, to be away from her family.*

"I would love to do it for you. We could do it next week."

"Do you not have your work?"

"The nice thing about part-time jobs is that you've got room in your schedule to do other things. Remember, I do a lot of writing from home, so my job is flexible."

Hanne nodded. "It will have to be something simple. Fadi and I, we do not work now."

"Why don't you let me worry about that," Sarah said. "It would do my heart good to help you with this. Just send me the photos you'd like to get printed. I'm free on Wednesday."

ש ש ש ש ש ש ש

A Martyr's Crown

# Chapter 36
Phoenix
Sunday, February 6, 2010

Father George watched as the members of his congregation streamed into the church for Sunday Mass. Orphans, widows, burn victims, the war-traumatized and war-weary immigrants—his people had suffered through the hardships of their homeland and found their way here to America, to this humble church in the desert.

He was father to all of them, these people with their broken hearts and dreams. He felt as though he was fighting an uphill battle for their souls. Between their poverty and their marital woes, their war memories and their employment struggles, his parishioners were in dire need of encouragement, but more than that, they needed grace—they needed God.

*And now I have to tell them about Bishop Abbo.* His heart sank, envisioning the congregation's reaction.

Bishop Abbo was a holy man, a fearless apostle who refused to be frightened by the death threats and the rising violence in their homeland. When he ordained him and Father Ameer back in 1999, he repeated the words of Pope John Paul II, "Be not afraid."

"Don't be afraid," he told them, "to preach the Gospel, to challenge our people to live their faith more deeply, to embrace their cross." He'd always been a loving father to the priests he ordained, encouraging them, calling them to holiness, admonishing them when necessary.

The people of Mosul were praying for their bishop now, praying feverishly that he would be released, that his captors would be found. It was just after dark when jihadists shot his bodyguard and pushed him into their car. By now 36 hours had elapsed.

*Where had they taken him? Why wasn't there a ransom being demanded?* No one had any answers, but Father George knew he would have to break the news to his people about this latest outrage.

"My dear brothers and sisters in Christ," Father George began, "Some of you may have already heard the news about Bishop Abbo of Mosul." He could hear them begin to murmur to each other, saw them raising their eyebrows.

Hanne, her eyes wide with fear, looked at Fadi. *What news? What was Father George talking about?*

"There is no easy way to tell you. Bishop Abbo was kidnapped Friday night and his bodyguard was killed. We don't know much more than that, unfortunately. Now, he made it very clear in the last few years that if he were ever kidnapped, he did not want the Church to pay a ransom for him. 'I'm not afraid to give my life for Christ,' he told us.

"As far as I know, there has been no demand for ransom. No one has heard from him and no one has been able to find him. He's an older man and he's not in the best of health. Without his medications—well, all we can do is pray."

The congregation was stunned. Hanne clutched Fadi's arm. She felt a little sick to her stomach and closed her eyes, trying in vain to remain calm.

When Mass was over, Father George stood outside with Father Michael, talking to parishioners and doing his best to encourage them.

"Horrible," many of them said. "We'll pray for him, Father."

## A Martyr's Crown

Later that afternoon, back at the rectory, Father George logged onto his email. Not surprisingly, there was something from Sarah. He knew she monitored the news services and had probably heard something by now.

*Dear Father George*, the email began, *I'm sure you already know about the bishop kidnapped in Mosul. Do you know him? What can you tell me about him and about the situation? I heard just a brief reference to it on the news this morning. I've never heard of a bishop being kidnapped before! If you get a chance later, please call so we can talk."*

Father George dialed Sarah's number.

"Thanks for calling me back so quickly, Father. What scary news about the bishop!"

"It's terrible, Sarah. I am afraid for his life."

"So you do know him then?"

"Bishop Abbo ordained me, and he ordained Father Ameer, too, the priest who was going to baptize Hanne's baby. In fact, he said the funeral Mass for all the victims of the attack."

Sarah sat down at her computer and began to take notes.

"What's the latest? Is there any more information available? Who else should I talk to?"

"There is no other information now, but as I told my people this morning, Bishop Abbo has diabetes. Without his medication, he will not survive. And God only knows what they may have done to him by now."

Sarah could feel her heart thumping, the wheels in her mind spinning. It was a story that would shock most Catholics in the U.S., who had never known their shepherd's vocation to be such that the very exercise of it jeopardized his life. Here was a bishop living in the midst of violence and persecution, presiding over the diaspora of his people. As far as Sarah knew, no U.S. bishop had ever been kidnapped, had ever met with such violence.

"I will be sure to keep Bishop Abbo in my prayers," Sarah told

Father George. "I know you must be very worried about him. Let me know if you hear anything else."

Sarah put the phone down and instantly thought of Hanne. What must she be thinking? After the trauma she'd been through, the knowledge that Bishop Abbo was now being held against his will had to be incredibly painful.

Sarah checked her email. Sure enough, Hanne sent her the files of the pictures she wanted for Noor's memorial.

"Maybe you know this, Sarah, but they kidnapped our bishop," she wrote. "Please, Sarah. Pray for this man of God."

שׁ שׁ שׁ שׁ שׁ שׁ שׁ

Hanne and Sarah were at a thrift shop checking out the furniture when they saw it: a beautifully carved, table that was just the right size for Noor's memorial.

"It costs many dollars. Is too much," Hanne said. "We cannot."

"Don't you worry about that," Sarah told her reassuringly. "My sisters helped me set up Patrick's memorial. It's my turn to help now. It's like I told you, Hanne. You're my sister in Christ now."

Hanne was overwhelmed by this woman's kindness. There was no way Fadi was going to let her spend $75 on a table, not when they were counting their pennies. So far, he hadn't received a response to the resume he'd sent to the university.

Back at the apartment, the two women took to setting up the memorial. Sarah carefully removed the tissue paper from the porcelain frames and candleholder they'd chosen at a local department store.

Hanne emerged from the bedroom with a small box of Noor's things. She looked a little pale, at least to Sarah. Taking a seat at the table, she began showing Sarah the few items they'd been able to take when they fled the country. It wasn't much really.

## A Martyr's Crown

There was the handmade pink blanket, of course, but there were a few other mementos as well.

"I find these things in my purse after the day," Hanne said as she handed Sarah a tiny pair of lacy socks and a pacifier. "I keep these in my bag. And this," she said, handing Sarah Noor's birth certificate.

"Also this toy. Fadi found in baby bed the day we leave. Is all we have of her, our Noor." Hanne, trembling, held out the teddy bear to Sarah.

After they'd arranged everything, Sarah and Hanne stood back to take in the scene. Sarah put her arm around Hanne's narrow shoulders, thankful they were able to share the moment. That's when it suddenly hit her: Hanne would never be able to visit the place where Noor was buried.

"You know, I'm really amazed at what a strong young woman you are," Sarah said softly.

"I am not so strong," Hanne said with a catch in her voice, "but I know I will see her again—I *know* I will."

"Of course you will," Sarah said. "That's true. I'm afraid I didn't have the same reaction when Patrick died."

"Our people," Hanne said, "we must live all these years with—how you say it—this persecution. Many people, they hate Christians. Bishop Abbo told us, we are church of martyrs, and Noor, she is one of the youngest ever."

Sarah hadn't really thought of it before, but she supposed it was true. Little Noor was killed because she was there in the church that day to be baptized.

"She wears the martyr crown, just like our priest, and maybe now even our bishop."

"Have you heard anything about Bishop Abbo yet?"

"No. And Fadi says that these people who do this, they have no mercy," Hanne said shaking her head. "No mercy at all. They hate and kill. They hate Christians, say we must leave Iraq or die."

When she got home later that afternoon, Sarah logged onto her computer and saw there was an email from Father George. The subject line simply said "news."

"They found Bishop Abbo's body today, Sarah. Here is a link to an article about it. Please pray for the repose of his soul and for our people."

Sarah clicked on the link. Police had found the body of Bishop Stefan Abbo in a shallow grave on a narrow road outside Mosul early that morning.

ש ש ש ש ש ש ש

**A Martyr's Crown**

# Chapter 37
Phoenix
Thursday, February 10, 2010

Sholeh re-read Sarah's email about the murder of Bishop Abbo. Coming from Iran as she did, she had no doubt what had befallen the martyred bishop. In her homeland, it was not all that uncommon for Christians to be kidnapped or killed. Government officials would usually blame the deaths on an "accident."

Sholeh shook her head. In the years since she'd converted, she'd longed for a way to help the Christians of the Middle East who were suffering such tremendous persecution. Until Sarah's story about the Chaldeans, she didn't know much about Catholics in the Middle East. She'd entered the Church at a Roman Rite parish in Chicago in her 20s.

Logging onto her investment portfolio, Sholeh appraised where she stood. Over the years, she'd invested wisely in land and buildings and done quite nicely. Even with the real estate market struggling, she still had rent coming in from properties around the United States. She'd also inherited a substantial sum of money after her parents died. When Andrew was born, they established a college fund for him. The younger two kids each had college funds, too.

What about these Chaldeans though? Who was helping them? Sholeh tapped her pen on the desk, pondering. So many worthwhile causes to consider—she seemed to be on every charity's mailing list.

Though she'd always been generous with her parish, Sholeh thought about the Chaldeans and she felt a kinship with them. She thought back to a recent visit to Iran, when a Muslim fanatic found out she'd converted. By the grace of God, she'd managed to escape before he turned her into the authorities. But what about these Iraqi immigrants? They seemed to have no one on their side.

And in that moment, she made a decision. Humming a little tune, she picked up the phone and called Sarah.

"Are you sure about this?" Sarah asked, stunned at the proposal.

"Absolutely. Why don't you give Father George a call so we can set up a meeting?"

׆ ׆ ׆ ׆ ׆ ׆ ׆

Fadi saw that she'd fallen asleep shortly after dinner again, completely exhausted. Perhaps it was the long walks they were taking in the afternoon as they explored the neighborhood near the apartment complex. He unfolded the pale blue quilt and carefully covered her, then shut off the lights.

*They were in a clearing, standing in the midst of lush green grass. Hanne looked up, and there stood Father Ameer, holding Noor in his arms. She could feel an ocean of love, an overwhelming peace flowing from both their hearts. Then she heard a voice, gentle as the wind:*

*"Come share in your Master's joy."*

*He was more radiant than she could have ever imagined. He stretched out His arms to embrace them and she saw the deep scars on His hands, the ones wrought by the nails. She felt the depth of His love and knew utter peace.*

*He turned with a smile and held her gaze for a moment, His*

## A Martyr's Crown

*eyes filled with tenderness. It was as though in that look of love, He absorbed her deepest pain.*

*He turned then and placed a tiny, ruby-encrusted crown atop Noor's curls and a brilliant crown of gold on Father Ameer's head.*

۞ ۞ ۞ ۞ ۞ ۞ ۞

Hanne woke up early that morning and as soon as she opened her eyes, she knew it was true.

That unmistakable feeling—the nausea—caused her to jump from the bed and rush to the bathroom. She knelt in front of the toilet, heaving.

Fadi could hear her, and immediately, he knew, too. She'd been so sleepy lately. And queasy. The usual symptoms, just like before.

"Hanne, *azizta*," Fadi said from the doorway, "Is this what I think it is?"

She sat there on the floor, trembling, face buried in her hands. Fadi was at her side in an instant. He took Hanne in his arms and kissed the top of her head. Such a beautiful woman, his wife, his beloved.

"I think so, *aziza*," Hanne said, exhausted but smiling weakly. "A baby."

"New life, Hanne!" Fadi cried. "This is wonderful! New life! What more could a man ask for? Let's call your mom!"

"In a little while, Fadi. I'm going to lie down, I think."

"Oh, of course, of course, my love," Fadi said. "Do you need anything? Some crackers maybe? A cup of tea? I could walk to the grocery store."

"Not now…later maybe."

The next thing he knew, she was asleep again. She was giving him another child, the greatest blessing he could imagine.

That afternoon, they called Mariam.

"Are you sure?"

"Yes, *Yemmi*. I took one of those home tests," Hanne said. "It's positive, definitely."

"Well, it's going to be wonderful to hold your child in my arms," Mariam said.

Hanne wondered if maybe her mother was showing signs of dementia. They were 12,000 kilometers away with no hope of ever returning to Mosul.

"Hanne, are you there?"

"Yes, *Yemmi*. I'm here."

"Hanne, we're coming to America. I don't know how, I don't know when, but we're coming! Nahida, Nora, your brothers and I—we can't take it here anymore. Christians are receiving death threats every day. We're getting out of here, and soon."

Hanne gasped. "Here? You're coming here, here to America? But how?"

"Your sister Nahida has it all figured out. She's been on the Internet and talking with friends. Here, I'll put her on the line." Mariam passed the phone to Nahida.

"We can't stand it here without you and Fadi," Nahida confessed. "And after what they did to Bishop Abbo, well, we've had enough. If we have to go through Greece or Turkey or Syria first, we will. But eventually we'll wind up with you there in America, *inshallah*."

Hanne felt as though her heart would burst from joy. How could it be that in the midst of so much sorrow, that joy had broken through, and so unexpectedly? It was love: God's love, Fadi's love, her family's love. And now Sarah, her new sister in Christ.

Hanne placed both hands on her belly and smiled. New life within her, the fruit of love.

♕♕♕♕♕♕♕

## A Martyr's Crown

Father George sat in his office, looking at the letter from the architect from St. Clare's, wondering what he could do with such a hopeless situation.

"I regret to inform you that upon inspection, the entire building is in such poor shape that it ought to be condemned," the architect wrote. "In good conscience, I must warn you that the church hall is unsafe. Whoever did the remodeling on it 10 years ago removed a load-bearing wall. There is imminent danger of collapse. You must not, under any circumstances, occupy the building. It is my ethical obligation to inform the city of my findings. Obviously I will have to inform Father Keller as well. The parish cannot grant funds for a building that's about to be condemned."

Father George folded up the letter and set it aside. Surely God had a plan, but right now, things looked pretty bleak.

He wondered then what Sarah and Sholeh were up to, why they'd insisted they had to meet as soon as possible. When Sarah called earlier that morning, she'd been evasive with him. Something about wanting to discuss the future of the Chaldeans in Arizona. He supposed they had questions about Bishop Abbo. They probably didn't realize that his own bishop, the one he served, resided in California. The bishop of Mosul was the one who ordained him, but he'd been transferred here to this diocese in the southwestern United States five years ago.

At 2 p.m. sharp, Sarah and Sholeh rang the doorbell at Mar Ephrem's office beside the church.

"Hello, ladies. It is nice to see you," Father George said as they stepped into the brightly lit room. "I have already made a pot of tea for us."

"We were so very sorry to hear about Bishop Abbo," Sarah began. "This must be a difficult time for your community here. Did many of them know him?"

"Yes, some did. We have a lot of people from Baghdad, too, who did not, but they are all affected by Bishop Abbo's death. We will have a special Mass in his honor tomorrow."

"Father, let me explain why we've come here today," Sholeh began. "When I heard about what happened to Bishop Abbo, I thought about the many Christians in my homeland and throughout the Middle East who have died for the faith. As much as our persecutors have tried to destroy us, the Church survives."

"This is true," Father George said. "Our enemies have all the political and military power—they have entire armies and governments on their side—but they have never been able to eliminate us."

"God's been good to me here in the United States," Sholeh continued, taking a deep breath, "so I've been thinking; as someone who was raised as a Muslim in a country that fought your homeland, I want to do something to show solidarity with you."

Sholeh took a single, typewritten sheet from the manila file folder on her lap. "I've written up a proposal for you, one that I hope you'll agree to." She handed the paper to Father George.

As he read, a smile slowly spread across his face.

"You would do this for us?"

"I'm just God's instrument," Sholeh said. "He's put this in my heart and given me the means to accomplish it."

Father George handed the letter from the architect to Sholeh.

"Frankly, I'm not surprised. I own a lot of different properties and am used to inspecting buildings. I had a feeling that day we toured your hall that it would need to be razed. I knew the grant from St. Clare's would never be enough to accomplish all that needed to be done here. That's why Fr. Keller has agreed to go ahead with the grant to help with the new construction costs."

Sholeh's proposal was to demolish the hall entirely. She would provide the lion's share of the funds to build a brand new facility, one with a large meeting room, individual classrooms, a stage, a commercial kitchen and modern bathrooms. From parties to meetings to catechism classes, the new hall would meet the

## A Martyr's Crown

parish's needs. St. Clare's would kick in their original grant of $10,000.

"I just have a few requests in exchange," Sholeh said. "I'd like you to name the new facility 'Bishop Stefan Abbo Hall.'"

"Of course," Father George said. "This is a wonderful idea."

"I'd also like you to have a rose garden planted in front of the hall. My proposal is to have a bronze plaque with a picture of Father Ameer and Noor Yacoub and then a couple benches where people could sit and reflect, and hopefully, pray."

Sarah was beaming by now, looking back and forth at Father George and Sholeh and enjoying the exchange between the two.

"You are very generous to offer to do this for us, Sholeh," Father George said. "I think I am, how do you say it? In shock? You are not even Chaldean!"

"No, but I'm Catholic," Sholeh said with a laugh. "We've got to have more unity between us. I'd say 99 percent of Roman Catholics have no idea who the Chaldeans are. Unless they've read Sarah's articles, of course."

Sarah smiled. There was no way she and Javier could donate the money it would take to tear down the hall at Mar Ephrem and build a new one in its place.

But she could tell the world, tell everyone she knew about this new understanding, this new chapter. Here in America, away from the bombings, away from the kidnappings and the relentless persecution, Chaldeans would build a culture of life, a vibrant Church where their children and grandchildren could learn the faith.

They would build it together, stone by stone.

Joyce Coronel

# Epilogue

In November of 2010, while writing for *The Catholic Sun Newspaper* in Phoenix, Arizona, I stumbled on a story that would change my life forever. In some ways, Sarah's story is my story. I actually did meet a woman whose cousin had her baby torn from her arms by terrorists inside a Catholic church in Iraq. They held her down and shot her beautiful baby, a boy, whose face I shall never forget. Evil like that really does exist.

The good news is, there's a Love even stronger than death that reaches beyond the grave. I witnessed that love in my dear parents and I continue to experience it, most notably in my husband, who has stood by my side throughout 27 years of marriage. This book would not have been possible without his unwavering support.

While the events chronicled in "A Martyr's Crown" are fictionalized, they are based on what I've learned through the dozens of interviews I've conducted with Chaldean immigrants over the last two years in the course of writing articles for *The Catholic Sun Newspaper.* I will be forever grateful to those who poured out their hearts to me, sharing the tremendous suffering and hardships they endured in their homeland. More than half of Iraq's Christian population has fled the country in recent years, an immense tragedy when you consider that these are the descendents of those evangelized by St. Thomas the Apostle. A priest from the region told me he fears that "soon there will be no more Christians in the Middle East."

## A Martyr's Crown

One event chronicled in "A Martyr's Crown" is in fact largely based on an actual occurrence. In 2008, the archbishop of Mosul, Archbishop Paulos Rahho, was kidnapped and died while in the custody of his assailants. As with Bishop Abbo in "A Martyr's Crown," Archbishop Rahho was not in the best of health and required medication which he naturally did not receive during his ordeal. His body was discovered some time later. There was disagreement over whether he died from natural causes, a beating or from gunshot wounds.

The character known as Father George is a composite of several Chaldean priests I have come to know since 2010, two of whom were in fact tortured for the faith. It is my great honor and privilege to have met these men of great courage. Their deep faith, lived so vibrantly, ought to inspire each of us to want to live a more authentically Catholic life.

Blessed John Paul once remarked that the Church needs to breathe with both lungs, East and West. Now more than ever, the world needs the unified voice of the Catholic Church, East and West: Yes to life. Yes to Love. And a resounding no to hatred and the culture of death.

> JOYCE CORONEL
> PHOENIX, ARIZONA
> FEBRUARY 8, 2013

Joyce Coronel is a longtime columnist and correspondent for The Catholic Sun Newspaper in Phoenix. She and her husband are the parents of five sons, each a unique and unrepeatable gift of God. Though active in her Roman Catholic parish, Joyce has been adopted into the Chaldean family and considers herself deeply blessed to serve as a catechist at Holy Cross Chaldean Catholic Mission, preparing children to receive their First Holy Communion.

www.ingramcontent.com/pod-product-compliance
Lightning Source LLC
Chambersburg PA
CBHW020847090426
42736CB00008B/264